Flying the B-26
Marauder Over Europe

This book was
funded by the
Violet Lawing Trust

ALSO BY CARL H. MOORE
AND FROM MCFARLAND

The Federal Reserve System: A History of the First 75 Years (1990; paperback 2011)

Money: Its Origin, Development and Modern Use (1987; paperback 2011)

Flying the B-26 Marauder Over Europe

Memoir of a World War II Navigator

Carl H. Moore

SECOND EDITION

McFarland & Company, Inc., Publishers
Jefferson, North Carolina, and London

LIBRARY OF CONGRESS CATALOGUING-IN-PUBLICATION DATA

Moore, Carl H.
Flying the B-26 Marauder over Europe : memoir of a World War II navigator / Carl H. Moore. —2nd ed.
p. cm.
Includes index.

ISBN 978-0-7864-7357-1
softcover : acid free paper ♾

1. World War, 1939–1945—Aerial operations, American.
2. World War, 1939–1945—Personal narratives, American.
3. Moore, Carl H. 4. Marauder (Bomber)—History.
5. United States. Air Force—Biography. 6. Air pilots, Military—United States—Biography. I. Title.

D790.M576 2013 940.54'4973092—dc23 [B] 2013015815

BRITISH LIBRARY CATALOGUING DATA ARE AVAILABLE

On the cover: The crew of the Martin B-26 nicknamed *Tom's Tantalizer* (author front row, right)

Manufactured in the United States of America

McFarland & Company, Inc., Publishers
Box 611, Jefferson, North Carolina 28640
www.mcfarlandpub.com

To Popsey,
my wife, my partner, my lover, my friend
for more than 65 years.

Table of Contents

Preface and Acknowledgments

The call "bail out" and the ugly sound of the bell used to signal "abandon ship" are probably the most dreaded sounds to a crewman of any aircraft.

I never heard those sounds except in dry run drills. Fortunate? Yes, very. The sturdy Marauder, in which I spent over 800 hours, never failed our crew to the extent we had to abandon it. We came back from missions with holes in the wings, holes in the cockpit, severed hydraulic lines, and other souvenirs of the German 88mms, but none that stopped this great airplane from bringing us home.

This book is the story of my affair with the much maligned and criticized Martin B-26, labeled by the British (who named all of their planes) the Marauder. It is not a history of the aircraft. Nor is it a story of its role in World War II, although some of each is a part of my experience. It is a story of a young man of 24 who wanted no part of any war or preparation for war, but one who, once caught up in the military draft, sought to make the most of the experience.

I first published this story in book form in 1980. Since that time, most of our crew has passed on. In 2013, only George, our bombardier, and I remain. The plane itself, too, has almost passed from history. To my knowledge only six remain, and only one of those is in flying condition. In revising this text, I again searched through notes, records and memories. It has been interesting and at times frustrating.

I entered the Army before the war as a draftee, doing the basic one year service that was required of all my age at the time. Before the year ended, Pearl Harbor was attacked and my world, like that of many of my generation, changed.

Trained as a company supply clerk at old Fort Lee, Virginia, and winding up a chauffeur at Camp Livingston, Louisiana, I didn't feel challenged. Why not learn to fly? I had never been in an airplane, but it would be different and more exciting than filling out forms in the Quartermaster Corps.

Since the Marauder came to be such an integral part of my war experience, I have coordinated its development with my journey from reluctant civilian to enthusiastic navigator and back to a more knowledgeable and experienced civilian.

My story obviously is intertwined with that of other members of *Tom's Tantalizer*'s crew. When I was writing the original book in 1980, their suggestions, comments, corrections and encouragement were a vital key to that portion of my life. George Eldridge's fantastic memory, Dorr Tippens' enthusiasm and vivid recall, Tom Johnson's encouragement and John Graves' careful review of facts and reading of the original manuscript were invaluable in recording events of those unforgettable years of World War II. Major General Robert M. Stillman (Retired) also read the original copy and made helpful suggestions. In addition, his colorful personal account of the second disastrous mission to Ijmuiden provided the story of the turning point in the Marauder's use in Europe. Many personal friends gave encouragement and suggestions. I especially appreciated my late wife (known as Popsy in this text) reading the entire manuscript of the first edition for continuity and interest. Keeping tabs on my grammar and sentence structure was my daughter, Susan.

Much of the typing was done by Darteshia Adams. My son, Henry, practically memorized the 1980 version of my story, and without his continued interest it is questionable that this manuscript would have ever made it to a printing press. Also, Peggy Rothenberger, Henry's paralegal, spent countless hours formatting the text and photographs, putting this book in its final form.

The public relations department of Martin Marietta Aerospace provided valuable information and photographs, and some of the material in this book has been published previously by Challenge Publications, Inc. The Air Force Museum and the 1361st Audiovisual Squadron, Arlington, Virginia, provided several photographs and helpful information about the Marauder. Peyton Magruder, designer of the Marauder, was an inexhaustible storehouse of information and stories. His review of Chapter 1 was especially helpful, as was his contribution of photographs.

Part I : The Memoir

Chapter 1

Development of the Marauder

"Hold your altitude, Major! There's a flight crossing below you! Okay, it's clear now. Drop as fast as you like."

Coming off a hot target with burst after burst of anti-aircraft fire blackening the sky and bouncing us around, Major Bill Hale, leading the 344th Bomb Group, pointed our lead Marauder down and away from the city of Dunkerque. He wanted more speed—and quickly—to get out of range of those German 88s. The 185 mph on the bomb run was pushed to well over 200 as Major Hale dropped the nose and added power. Black clouds of flak followed us as we swept out over the Straits of Dover and regrouped for the 20 minute flight back to England. Our target had been gun positions in the city (a short two-hour mission but one we would not soon forget). Lucky me,

Black clouds of flak zero in on this flight of Marauders from the 456th Squadron, 323rd Bomb Group. Plane on the left received heaviest damage. Bombardier was killed and one gunner seriously injured. Each black cloud represents one 88mm shell exploding, sending shrapnel in all directions (courtesy U.S. Air Force).

I had gone on a mission to another Dunkerque position the day before with our own crew headed by Captain Tom Johnson, and served as lead navigator on both missions.

Shaken but still in one piece, the crew checked to see what damage had been done. Radio Operator–Gunner Staff Sergeant Dorr Tippens was wounded but came forward to send his report. Numerous holes were evident in wings and fuselage. Both of those good ol' Pratt and Whitney R-2800 engines continued to purr smoothly, for which we were grateful. As we returned to our base and lowered wheels for landing one tire appeared to be flat, but as we touched down it held. However, the left brake failed, and Major Hale swung the plane to a safe stop off the right side of the runway. The second plane landing behind us had no right brake and the pilot brought it to a halt on the left side of the runway opposite our plane. The third plane landing had *no* brakes and stumbled to a stop off the end of the runway. It must have been fate or luck or the Almighty watching over us, because we could have had three Marauders piled up in one heap. Reversible pitch props were only a dream in 1944.

Successful execution of missions like this was the culmination of years of designing and building the aircraft and training of crews. In the case of the Marauder, it all began more than five years before this mission was flown. In 1939 most Americans considered the bragging of Adolf Hitler and the sweep of his Panzer divisions over Central Europe none of their concern. At this time I was completing my senior year at Michigan State College and was more interested in getting a ticket to the senior prom than with events in Europe.

War Clouds Gather

Not so with other men more closely associated with world events. The "peace in our time" proclaimed by British Prime Minister Neville Chamberlain was fast falling apart. U.S. military leaders were well aware of our probable involvement and our woeful lack of preparedness. Already we were sending material to Britain.

The Boeing Company was well along in production of its B-17 heavy bomber and Consolidated had the B-24 near final plans. Our small fleet of P-39 and P-40 fighters and outdated B-10 and B-18 bombers was far from adequate to defend even our own shores. Helping another nation such as England or France would be impossible.

With these facts in mind, many plans for defense were accelerated. One that would have an impact on my life occurred on January 25, 1939, when

Our crew beside 573, better known to us as K9-3. Back row, left to right: T/Sgt. Michael Ondra, crew chief; S/Sgt. Charles W. Calkins, turret gunner; S/Sgt. Joseph Castoro, tail gunner; T/Sgt. Dorr E. Tippens, radio operator and waist gunner; and S/Sgt. Marini, asst. crew chief. Front row, left to right: Major Tom Johnson, pilot; First Lt. George W. Eldridge, bombardier; First Lt. Carl H. Moore, navigator. Note the absence of the fixed nose gun. None of our Marauders had the fixed gun in the nose. They did have the package of four mounted, two on either side of the fuselage, which were controlled by the pilot. The single nose gun was flexible and fired by the bombardier.

the Army requested designs for a medium bomber. It was to have a speed of 250–350 mph, a range of 3,000 miles, a service ceiling of 20,000 to 30,000 feet, maximum bomb load capacity, and an armament of four .30-caliber machine guns. This "type specification" was sent to about 40 firms, including the Glenn L. Martin Company of Baltimore, Maryland.

On March 11, 1939, the Material Division at Wright Field issued Circular 39-640 asking for the new bomber and a procedure calling for production directly from plans with no prototype for testing, thus abandoning its long-standing policy of "fly before buy." Events in Europe were not encouraging. Hitler continued to build up his forces of elite troops, tanks, and vastly improved aircraft such as the Messerschmitt 109, Heinkel 111, and the screaming Stuka dive bomber. Time was running out for the U.S. to prepare.

Martin Company Wins Contract

On July 5, 1939, the Army opened bids on the proposed new medium bomber. Five companies had submitted bids, and when the Board of Officers completed its evaluation, the Glenn L. Martin Company's Model 179 scored highest by more than 100 points. North American was second. On July 17, 1939, the Army ordered 201 of Martin's Model 179 and 184 of the Model NA62 (later designated B-25) from North American. Ordering planes from two companies would serve to spread the risk of production failures and also was necessary because Martin had limited production capacity.

Once the order was given to the Glenn L. Martin Company, their chief designer, Peyton M. Magruder, went to work completing the design and specifications. His experience with the B-10 bomber and a degree in aero engineering gave him an insight into the problems that were involved in moving into new areas without benefit of a prototype. This plane had to fly the first time it rolled down the runway.

Special Design Problems

Several unique design requirements were almost unheard of at this time in the development of aircraft. First, the speed of over 300 mph for a bomber was almost unbelievable. Second, the requirement that the plane carry two 2,000-pound bombs was far beyond the capacity of anything yet built of this size. Several other specifications gave Magruder and his crew new challenges. For no obvious reason, except for ease of taxiing, the wing tip had to be visible from the pilot's seat. A significant omission from the specifications was that no stalling speed was specified — a fact that Magruder used to his advantage.

Which Engine to Use?

Selection of the power plant became a major decision. Considering the speed of 350 mph needed, and the heavy bomb load, it had to be a powerful engine. Not many were available at the time. The Wright R-2600 was considered but discarded as being too small. Of the 17 specific bids submitted on Model 179, Magruder preferred number 14. This would have given a speed in excess of 400 mph and take-off power of 2,200 horsepower. However, the unavailability of the Wright 3350 engine forced Magruder to go to the Pratt and Whitney R-2800 single stage engine with turbocharger, giving a high speed of 325 mph and take-off power of 2,000 horsepower. Even so, to achieve

This is a wind tunnel model of the Marauder used during early designing. Note the twin tail. At the time, the common conception was that a twin tail gave better control, but it was abandoned in favor of a single tail so that the tail gunner would have a better view of his field of fire (courtesy Peyton M. Magruder, Jr.).

the desired speed the lines of the plane had to be clean and the shape of the fuselage lean and windswept.

Utilizing butt seams for the skin rather than the lap joint then in general use achieved the smooth, low air-resistant cover of the fuselage. The long, sleek body gave the plane a "cigar shape," but one that looked more like a rocket than the conventional shape of aircraft. The tricycle landing gear which was specified also gave the plane the impression of being "ready to go." The original design of twin tails was abandoned to give the tail gunner a better view. With no stall speed specified, Magruder settled on 97 mph with full flaps: unheard of in 1939! A stall speed higher than 70 mph in those days was considered suicidal. The choice of 97 mph was partly psychological. It didn't sound nearly as fast as "100 mph," but the actual difference was not significant in performance.

Who Can Make These New Gadgets?

Problems of design were second only to the problems of finding people who would make the parts to fit Magruder's new requirements and ideas. He argued, pleaded, and cajoled firms into trying the impossible. One human interest story comes from the effort to stretch large sheets of aluminum to the desired shape. It had never been done, but Magruder's crew set about to build the necessary hydraulic presses to give them the skin for the plane. When the first sheets were put to the test, they bulged and then cracked. In desperation, the engineers and experts tried and tried again. Watching the whole process was an old-time mechanic, who with appropriate nonchalance and confidence said, "Put a little grease on 'er." With tongue in cheek, the engineers tried his suggestion and one more problem was solved.

Completing the design and obtaining production of parts went on day and night. One obstacle after another was hurdled and it looked like the plane would soon be ready for production. But one major problem remained unresolved. Wright Field had sent Magruder a wire asking if an electric turret could replace the hydraulic one, as hydraulic turrets had many problems including fluid leaks and sensitivity to cold weather. What to do? No one had ever built an electric turret before. This problem was finally overcome when General Electric came up with a suitable motor. But then Magruder was told that it would take nine months to produce the motors!

Off to Schenectedy, New York (General Electric Headquarters), went Magruder, furious. By chance his seatmate on the flight was Charles E. Wilson, then head of General Electric. Unaware of the identity of the man beside him, Magruder unloaded his problem and his anger on Wilson. Upon arriving at Schenectady, Wilson offered Magruder a ride to the plant and the problem of the electric motors was soon resolved.

What would toy trains and Marauders have in common? You'd be surprised. It doesn't sound logical but there is a connection. Faced with the problem of how to store adequate ammunition for the tail turret guns, Magruder searched for a way to store ammunition near the bomb bay where there was plenty of room and still have it feed automatically to the guns in the tail turret. The "experts" said the guns would not pull the chain of ammunition that far.

"They would if I had the right kind of track for it to move on," thought Magruder. "Now who makes small tracks that might move .50-caliber ammunition?"

Without hesitation, Magruder presented the problem to Lionel, the toy train manufacturer. He soon had an agreement with them to furnish the miles of track needed for thousands of Marauders and later for other combat planes. Now the tail gunner would have over 400 rounds of ammunition for each of his guns.

Other Design Firsts

A bomb bay bigger than the B-17? In a twin engine bomber? That's what Magruder and his crew put in the Marauder. Magruder personally went to Wright Field and measured the bomb bay of the B-17 and returned to Baltimore and made room in Model 179 for one just as big. However, the original specifications called for the Marauder to carry thirty 100-pound bombs, and there were only twenty bomb stations in the main bomb bay. So Magruder and his crew added a rear bomb bay that would carry the other ten. By loading the main bay with four 1,100-pound bombs and putting four 600-pound bombs in the rear bay, the plane could carry a bomb load of 6,800 pounds, compared with 4,000 pounds for the B-17. As more weight was added to the plane, including armor plate, guns, radios and so forth, it was necessary to eliminate the rear bomb bay. But the mighty Marauder still could carry about 5,000 pounds of bombs, depending upon the size used.

Electrical releases for the bombs? It won't work. "Why not?" asked Magruder, and he proceeded to design a system that would work, thus eliminating the need for some 30 rods from the bomb bay to the bombardier's station, an arrangement that would have been a real mess in this tidy aircraft.

Now how about better fuel tanks? In combat one hit could put a hole in the existing tanks and cause not only a loss of fuel but a serious fire hazard. No rubber self-sealing tanks had ever been used in military aircraft, but Magruder wrote these into the specifications for the Marauder and they soon became standard equipment for all military planes.

The design and construction crew for the Marauder, under the leadership of Peyton Magruder, refused to take no for an answer to any proposed improvement that they knew would make a more effective fighting machine. Their understanding of what was needed and what would work was far ahead of their time. Their ingenuity and persistence in solving unsolvable problems under the pressure of time and lack of opportunity for testing are a tribute to their profession and made a major contribution to the war effort.

Marauder Production Under Way

Production of the Model 179 got under way, and on November 25, 1940, the first plane rolled off the assembly line. On November 29, 1940, test pilot and Chief Engineer William K Ebel (with Ed Fenimore as co-pilot and Al Melelwsky, flight engineer) took No. 40-1361—the first Marauder—down the runway and into the air.

Number 40-1631 takes to the air, the first Marauder ever built. Test pilot and Chief Engineer William K. Ebel is at the controls with Copilot Ed Fenimore and Flight Engineer Al Melewsky along to help. *Old Grandpappy*, as 1631 was affectionately named, served as a trainer for several years (courtesy Peyton M. Magruder, Jr.).

How did it do? Terrific! The Army immediately ordered a speed up in service testing of the aircraft. France had fallen and an even greater sense of urgency was apparent in the minds of those who were aware of our dangerous lack of preparation. Martin pushed production at its Baltimore, Maryland, plant, and in March 1941 a new plant was ordered to be built at Omaha, Nebraska, to provide additional production. Before production was halted in 1945, a total of 5,787 Martin Marauders had been built. This included 550 converted to unarmed AT-23, used for towing targets and reconnaissance, and 521 built for the British.

Early Problems

By December 1941, production was moving smoothly and 53 planes were sent to Australia immediately after the attack on Pearl Harbor. The experienced crews did the impossible with those red hot bombers. They performed beautifully. But trouble was brewing on the home front. Experienced pilots were in combat zones. Training time for new pilots was shortened. There was not time for seasoning. Get them in the air and fly those machines coming off the assembly lines of Martin, Lockheed, Consolidated, Boeing and a dozen other manufacturers.

Marauder 40-1631 with wheels up, doors closed and showing off its clean lines and graceful proportions (courtesy Peyton M. Magruder, Jr.).

The Marauder was a great plane. It was sturdy, fast, responsive, and a marvelous fighting machine. But it wasn't a PT-1 or an AT-6 or even a twin Beechcraft. It didn't forgive mistakes and the young pilots coming out of flight school had little experience with 130 mph landing speeds and single engine operation of multiengine aircraft. Mechanics were in short supply and unfamiliar with the plane. The number of training accidents ballooned. Wrecked planes and crew fatalities threw fear into men assigned to the Marauder. "A plane a day in Tampa Bay" was not an idle phrase as McDill Air Base at Tampa, Florida, lost plane after plane. Takeoff at the base was usually over Tampa Bay and loss of power as the Marauder struggled for altitude was generally disastrous.

By the fall of 1942 an investigation was ordered to find out what was wrong and to develop a solution. After a brief inquiry, the investigating board ordered all B-26s grounded. But these planes were desperately needed, and soon. The Martin Company and the Army soon learned the major causes of the problems ... inexperience and lack of proper training of both ground and flight crews. And the Army kept adding weight — more than 5,000 pounds.

A crash program was begun at all training bases. Mechanics and engineers from the Martin Company worked side by side with ground crews, teaching them proper maintenance of the Pratt and Whitney engines so they wouldn't quit on takeoff. Trained pilots flew with instructors and demonstrated that

Martin Company crew putting the finishing touches on a new Marauder (courtesy Lockheed Martin).

Checking out a new Marauder at the Baltimore plant of the Glenn Martin Company (courtesy Lockheed Martin).

the Marauder would fly on one engine. The single engine procedure wasn't complicated but had to be done properly and promptly.

When an engine quit, airspeed quickly dropped to near stalling speed (150 mph or less), which was why number one step was full power on the good engine — and *right now.* Then you could worry about feathering the prop on the dead engine to reduce drag and trimming the ship for straight and level flight. Restarting the engine in flight was simple. Unfeather the prop and let it windmill, turn on the ignition, open the throttle, and away she would go.

There were other mechanical problems. Largely because a subcontractor used an inferior material to save a few pennies, the diaphragm on the carburetor deteriorated and caused the engine to cut out. Takeoff crashes increased. This was corrected using a nylon diaphragm with a rubber cover. The electrically controlled props were erratic, causing pitch to vary and resulting in loss of power. This was corrected. Eventually, the wingspan was increased by six feet to compensate for added weight. The rudder was enlarged to give better control on one engine.

The change in armament was nothing short of dramatic. Originally the Marauder was designed with twin .50-caliber machine guns in the dorsal turret, one hand-held .30-caliber gun in the tail, a hand-held .30 in the nose,

Marauders on the line at the Baltimore plant of the Martin Company (courtesy Lockheed Martin).

and one fixed .30 in the nose controlled by the pilot. The plane in which I flew in 1943 had the following:

- Four .50-caliber fixed forward firing guns attached to the fuselage and fired by the pilot.
- Twin .50s in the tail.
- Twin .50s in the dorsal turret.
- One .50-caliber in each of the waist windows, behind the bomb bays.
- One .50-caliber hand-held in the nose controlled by the bombardier.

That's a lot of firepower. No wonder enemy fighters treated those bombers with respect! But it did add thousands of pounds of weight.

Many men were involved in keeping the Marauder in the stable of U.S. bombers. Engineers, mechanics, and determined pilots refused to give up. Lt. Colonel Millard Lewis, already an experienced flyer in 1941, probably did as much as any one man to keep the Marauder in business. He saw this fast, sturdy plane as a valuable weapon in combat. He argued, pleaded, and risked his life to obtain the needed improvements and modifications. His contribution to the training of pilots who were assigned to the Marauder may have been the turning point in the history of this great ship.

Chapter 2

Pearl Harbor: Marauders in the Pacific — Cadet Training

December 7, 1941! We couldn't believe it was true. I was in our darkroom developing pictures at the Station Compliment, Camp Livingston, Louisiana, when a friend came by and said Pearl Harbor had been attacked.

"Impossible."

"Did we drive them off?"

Little by little as more information was broadcast, it dawned on us that the little armament available had been dealt a severe if not fatal blow. Within hours we were no longer singing "Goodbye dear, I'll be back in a year," but beginning to look seriously at this game of war and what our role might be in it. I well remember the statement by a salty regular Army cavalry major as he strode into a training class at Camp Livingston the morning of December 8, 1941. Dressed in riding britches, polished brown boots and carrying a swagger stick, he flung his prepared speech across the stage and said, "Men, we are at war! And to win a war you kill more of the enemy than he kills of your troops!" With that he wished us well, said he was volunteering to go to the Philippines *now* and strode out of the room.

Marauders Do the Impossible in the Pacific

As mentioned earlier, that same morning of December 8, 53 Marauders of the 22nd Bombardment Group left Langley Field, Virginia, for Australia. According to the Aussies, they arrived just in time to save their thinly defended continent from the Japanese. These hot bombers flew in all kinds of weather and against Japanese fighters. At one time they flew 600 miles to a refueling stop, then another 600 miles to hit Japanese air fields, shipping and other targets. Mechanics made parts, cannibalized wrecked planes and worked day and night to keep the "flying cigars" in the air. Pilots did the impossible with the versatile Marauder. They outran the Japanese Zeros on the deck and their firepower made them an unhealthy target for the Zeros at higher altitudes. These men of the 22nd Bombardment Group didn't know the word quit. It was reported that in a six-month period not one Marauder was lost nor a crew member wounded. The *New York Times* reported that 90 Zeros were destroyed with the loss of only six Marauders. After eighteen months of fighting with no replacements and almost no spare parts, 30 of the original 53 Marauders were still flying and fighting. Most of the time they flew without fighter escort.

Marauders were involved in action at Moresby, Timor, Buna, Gona, Lae, Guadalcanal and wherever else the Japanese were found. Carrying torpedoes under their bellies, they hit Japanese carriers at Midway and Kiska, turning back a major threat. Other fantastic performances by these devils of the air in the South Pacific include flying for four hours on one engine from Lae to Moresby (shooting down four Zeros on the way); taking off at night with more than 38, 000 pounds gross weight from a rough dirt field; and fighting for over a week with a bed sheet for a patch over a flak hole.

From Chauffeur to Cadet

Meanwhile back at Camp Livingston, Louisiana, as a private first class, I was fighting the war by driving the camp commander's car — a relatively safe but not very interesting or exciting job. Since this looked like a long war, I decided I might just as well learn something new and challenging. I had never flown, but the Army Air Corps looked interesting and flying might be one of the better ways to fight this war. The camp commander, Colonel Selwyn D. Smith, agreed that I should move on.

So … I took the examination for aviation cadet and prepared to learn to fly. No big deal and soon I was accepted, but found myself on a long waiting list. In the spring of 1942 the U.S. was mobilizing with a capital "M." President Franklin D. Roosevelt, in a speech to a joint session of Congress on January 6, 1942, laid out production goals for the next two years … 185,000 planes, 80,000 tanks and 55,000 antiaircraft guns. Also, all men between the ages of 24 and 40 who hadn't registered for the draft were ordered to do so. Men volunteered by the thousands and training camps were overrun. Tent cities sprung up all over the country, and candidates for flying schools were backed up for months. It was nearly a year — January 1943 — before I entered preflight school at Ellington Field, Texas, near Houston.

I got my first view of a Marauder while I was learning the secrets of navigation at the Army Air Field Navigation School at Hondo, Texas. One day a Marauder from nearby Laughlin Air Base at Del Rio stopped over at Hondo, and we all stared in disbelief as it staggered into the air on takeoff. We all agreed that it was one plane that we wanted no part of.

We were having enough trouble with the twin engine Beechcraft C-45, our navigation training plane. It wasn't too bad except it was always hot inside, it smelled of old rubber, the wings sometimes rattled and it bounced all over the Texas skies. We really got shook up when we would go down to the flight line and find our buddy (who had just washed out of our navigation class) as

Aviation Cadet Moore (center) at Hondo Air Field Navigation School. Sextants in hand were for sighting stars during celestial navigation training flights. Beechcraft C-45 in the background carried three cadets, pilot and instructor who rode the copilot's seat (courtesy Army Air Corps).

General Jimmy Doolittle at the Martin plant just prior to going overseas. He said he wanted more B-26s with plenty of fire power. Left to right: Captain Hap Sahleneau, Air Corps liaison at Martin plant; Colonel Carl Ridenhaur, operations officer on General Doolittle's staff; General Doolittle; Peyton Magruder; Major Clair Bunde, base engineer officer on General Doolittle's staff (courtesy Peyton M. Magruder, Jr.).

crew chief for the plane scheduled for our next training mission. He was always very reassuring.

"I wired it back together, guys, so don't worry."

Our concern about these overworked C-45s was not entirely groundless. Returning from noon mess one fine Texas spring day, the sun was shining brightly as we marched along the road to our barracks. All at once, white parachutes started floating down from one of our C-45s as it passed over the field. One, two, three four — that accounted for three cadets and an instructor. We never learned whether the pilot brought the plane down or bailed out later.

Navigation school was interesting. The opportunity to fly was exciting even if we were too busy to see much country. I will never forget my first experience of climbing through the layers of puffy, low cumulus clouds — so typical of early mornings in South Texas — and breaking into the sunlight above. What a sight! Like a field of powder puffs! A dazzling white blanket. The clouds looked like you could walk on them.

Some features of flying were less beautiful—like the time I got airsick. At times the C-45 would drop a hundred feet, then bounce up a hundred. Maps, pencils, and other debris would suddenly be suspended in mid-air above the navigator's table. This was too much one day, and the inevitable happened—I became airsick. Back on the ground I would have chucked the whole thing and joined the ground crew. Who wanted wings anyway? To this day I can catch a whiff of the odor of those hot C-45s in a commercial plane and my body rebels. (I'm glad to say, that was the only time in nearly a thousand hours of flying that I was sick.)

The climax of navigation training was a cross country flight to Chicago's old Midway airport, an overnight stay in the Windy City, then graduation and home for leave in July 1943.

Marauders Go to European Theater

Meanwhile, in the Pacific Theater, Marauders continued to battle the Japanese, but their role was being taken over by larger planes and naval aircraft. By the end of 1943 they were withdrawn, and plans were made to concentrate them in the European Theater. In the meantime, General Jimmy Doolittle had called for medium bombers to help ground troops in the North Africa Campaign drive Erwin Rommel and the Axis forces out of North Africa. Accounts of the Marauders in this area matched those from the Pacific. The Marin Company's specialty was fast earning a reputation for safety and effectiveness.

In North Africa it was soon learned that the Marauder was more effective at medium altitude than on the deck. Yes, that was how it was originally designed, but in the Pacific, Japanese Zeros were more of a problem than anti-aircraft fire, and bombing accuracy was greater closer to the target. But the German anti-aircraft fire was deadly at low altitude. They would simply throw up a curtain of fire and let you fly into it. Although the Marauders played a significant role bombing supply ships and trucks at low level and doing reconnaissance work, it was at 10,000 to 12,000 feet altitude that they were at their best.

All of these facts I learned later, but in July 1943 I was only concerned with going home for two weeks, visiting friends and family then reporting to 3rd Bomber Command, 344th (M) Bomb Group, 494th Squadron at Lakeland Army Air Base, Lakeland, Florida. I had no idea what type of plane I would fly or what my assignment would be—a nice instructor's job would be okay in a B-17 or B-24.

Chapter 3

Operational Training: Getting Ready for Combat

Wearing my new tailor-made greys and crushed hat and carrying my briefcase of books, maps, and pencils, I reported to Operations at Lakeland Army Air Base, Lakeland, Florida, on July 28, 1943. As I completed the necessary forms and was assigned a room in the BOQ, I noticed several B-26s parked on the field. I casually inquired where they were from.

"They're ours!" proudly replied the sergeant.

Well, that wasn't the way I had heard it. Even in navigation school we had heard about "a plane a day in Tampa Bay" as pilots at McDill Air Base tried to learn how to manipulate this unstable critter. Anyone could tell from looking at the short wing and cigar-shaped body, it would be a better rocket than a plane.

"A plane that could not fly," "the flying prostitute," "widow maker," and a dozen other names — mostly derogatory — were given to this twin engine Martin medium bomber. It was a plane terribly unforgiving of pilot mistakes. What we navigators looked for was a nice, stable, comfortable Flying Fortress or wing-flapping B-24.

Introduction to the Marauder

The next day Lt. Richard S. Sliff, operations officer, invited me to go on a flight with him in a B-26. He showed no fear or concern. In fact, he seemed to be looking forward to flying this "rocket" from the Martin Company. As we approached the aircraft he carefully instructed me to always be aware of those big 12-foot props and to stay clear of their path, and also to stay out of line of their plane of revolution. An accident had occurred when a prop blade

"Pulling the props through" was standard procedure before starting engines. This removed any accumulation of oil that may have settled in the bottom cylinders. Usually several crewmen would line up and each grab a prop blade pushing it forward (courtesy Walker).

had broken loose and cut through a fuselage. Good advice, and immediately heeded and marked in my mind with italics.

After being certain that the ignition was off, each of us grabbed a blade of the props and moved them through about one complete revolution to clear the cylinders of any possible accumulation of oil (referred to as "pulling the props through"). Climbing up through the hole where the nose wheel retracted, we hooked on chutes and Lt. Sliff went through the preflight checks. Then, looking to be sure the prop on number one engine was clear, he pressed the switch for the inertia starter. When it was "whining" good (about 30 seconds), he engaged the starter, hit the choke switch once or twice, moved the throttle to about half open, and number one engine coughed, sputtered, and came to life with a roar. He went through the same procedure for number two engine and then taxied to the end of the runway. At this point he advanced the throttle on each engine in turn checking magnetos, making sure both engines were producing full power (seemed like a good idea to me), and tested the switch control to be sure it was okay. Poised at the end of the runway, he advanced both throttles, released the brakes and away we went. Just before running out of runway, he hauled back on the wheel, signaled for wheels up, and believe it or not, the thing actually flew — not easily or gracefully at this point. The pride of the Martin Company seemed to hang on the props, but it did fly and for me that was a reassuring revelation.

The confidence and pride of the B-26 crews at Lakeland soon convinced me that this ol' Marauder might be tolerable. A few flights further reduced my reluctance and I soon liked its clean lines and normal cruising speed of 200 mph. The twin 2,000 horsepower Pratt and Whitney engines supplied ample power. And I liked the idea of the firepower those eleven .50-caliber machine guns would give, if needed.

After seeing it fly on one engine and hearing about single engine landings, I even began to brag about this B-26. The navigator's compartment had all the necessities — table, drift meter, air speed indicator, altimeter, outside temperature gauge and even a bubble in the roof for taking star shots — assuming it would fly at night. (It would.)

I was too busy adjusting to the realities of flying a combat aircraft to give much thought to what was ahead. It was a lot more fun when you were not being graded on the flight. I liked the men in the squadron, and being an officer did have some advantages over being a cadet or a PFC. It was really a bit strange to me to be checking on the guards as I pulled my first duty as officer of the day.

It was fun to use my newly acquired navigation skills my way. I could look out the window and see where we were and not rely entirely on my dead reckoning. The last day at navigation school, our instructor who had shepherded us through dead reckoning and celestial missions admonished us, "Don't be afraid to look out the window. It might just let you know that you are over Dallas instead of Waco, as you thought from your star shots."

Building Flying Teams

New crew members were joining us almost daily, and the rumor was that we would become fully staffed and go overseas. In September, we moved to Tyler, Texas, and continued training as we participated in maneuvers with ground forces in Louisiana. We still trained at low level and played like we were strafing the troops. Crews began to take shape, and many flights were for orientation, including shooting landings, checking out equipment, and flying in formation. Colonel Reginald Vance, an escapee from Corregidor, joined us as group commander. Several pilots, including Tom Johnson and John Graves, former instructor pilots at Barksdale Field, Louisiana, joined the 494th Squadron. These pilots were exceptionally well trained and I was fortunate to fly with them.

Intense and disciplined training often is the key to the success of an operation. Flying the Marauder was no exception. As mentioned earlier, lack of training was the major cause of frequent accidents in training fields with the Martin B-26. Lt. Colonel Millard Lewis, already deeply involved in the story of the Marauder, was in charge of training at Barksdale when Tom, John and several other pilots in our squadron completed their indoctrination flying the Marauder and were assigned instructors' roles.

Millard Lewis was a determined man who believed in the potential of the Marauder in combat. He drilled his pilots mercilessly, but his major emphasis was on the development of a strong faith in the aircraft. He risked his own life and reputation on his belief that the Martin Company's fast flying, red hot, heavily armed plane was worth using. He required that his pilots complete at least 20 hours of ground study learning each part of the Marauder. He had a plane torn down and all the parts labeled so his students could see how and why each part functioned. In the air, 200 hours were required before a pilot could qualify as an instructor. He pushed his men hard but he turned out capable, confident pilots. I am thankful to him for doing so, for it was my privilege to fly with such men.

There is an interesting story told about the visit of an "inspection team" to Barksdale during Colonel Lewis' command of the training base. It seems that the Pentagon was not convinced that the Marauder was worth keeping, so they sent two experienced airline pilots with thousands of hours' flying time to Barksdale to inquire and make a report. It was apparent to Lewis that the inspectors had already made up their minds that the plane was no good even before they left Washington. To Lewis this was a golden opportunity to get the message to the top brass that this airplane was not only good but a valuable asset to the war effort.

Lewis took the inspectors for a ride. Takeoff was on a grass strip. He demonstrated single engine performance (over the objections of the inspectors) and brought the Marauder in for a perfect landing. That was the last time Colonel Lewis saw the inspectors and he never did learn what was in their report.

Odds and Ends of Training

Several interesting incidents occurred during this period of operational training. Pilots frequently discussed the best way to get a Marauder off the runway. The conventional procedure was to hold it on the runway until airspeed reached 125–130, then lift it off, retract wheels, and gain speed to 150 or 160 before executing turns or climbs.

Others argued that it was better to pull it off the ground as soon as possible — around 100 mph — to get the wheels up, then level off and pick up speed. Pushing this procedure too far, some pilots would even drag the tail on the runway. Colonel Vance objected to this procedure and ordered it discontinued. I was glad no one in the 494th tried this technique. Hanging the Marauder on the props while retracting the wheels exposed the plane and crew to unnecessary danger, as any loss of power would be disastrous.

Flight crews were an interesting mixture of men. Some were quiet, some were boisterous and loud, and most were carefree, but all liked to fly — except one navigator named Lt. Freeman. "Duck" (as he was called) came to the 494th following an earlier assignment to fly a Marauder to England via the northern route. Shortly after leaving the base at Presque Isle, Maine, one engine quit and the crew struggled to bring the Marauder back to land. Lt. Freeman reportedly walked into the CO's office of the base in Maine, threw his wings on the desk and said, "I quit!" Obviously he was talked into staying, but our routine operational flights didn't exactly thrill him. One day his crew was flying a training mission out of Tyler, and after an hour or two the pilot decided to return to base and called "Duck" on the intercom.

"Duck, we're ready to go home. Where are we?"

Startled from a sound sleep, Duck glanced at the altimeter and replied, "Three thousand feet over Texas."

One of the stories brought back from Barksdale by the pilots involved Lt. Bill Young. It seems that Lt. Young was a very skilled pilot but a bit bored with shooting landings and cruising over north Louisiana. For excitement he would see how close he could come to cattle, horses, or farmers on the ground. His buzzing became well known, and finally a complaint was filed. As a result, Lt. Young was hauled before a court-martial. During the trial his crew chief was called to testify. He was giving full support to Lt. Young's ability and finally the prosecutor asked, "Sergeant, what would you do if Lt. Young said he was going to fly through a barn whose doors were open on both sides?"

Without hesitation the crew chief replied, "How wide are the doors?"

Verdict? Send Lt. Young and his crew to Europe (which is what he wanted anyway). Leaving Barksdale with his Marauder loaded to the hilt for overseas, he climbed a few thousand feet, cut one engine, feathered the prop, and buzzed the tower on one engine.

My personal encounter with Lt. Young was much later at an air base in

France. He was up in an L-4 (Piper Cub) and caught four of us walking from operations to our quarters. He repeatedly had us "hitting the dirt" as he chased us with the L-4. We didn't really think he could hit us, but we couldn't be sure.

In retrospect, a flight from Tyler to Reading, Pennsylvania, reflects the progress we have made in our knowledge of weather. The father of a member of the ground crew was ill, and Tom Johnson was assigned to fly him to Reading, Pennsylvania. I went as navigator. We flew east to Atlanta, Georgia, then up the East Coast to avoid the mountains. On the leg from Tyler to Atlanta, I began to get unbelievable ground speeds — over 400 mph. Even with a good tail wind this was out of reason, but there it was. Returning, we encountered the reverse with ground speeds that seemed like we were standing still. Today, this would be no mystery. Apparently, we caught a jet stream that was much lower than usual.

This time spent flying out of Tyler had a special significance to me. It was while stationed here that I met Sue Watkins, a wonderful, beautiful girl from East Texas. We were married in 1945 when I returned from overseas.

A Winning Team

The assignment of men to the different crews was largely in the hands of the pilots working with the Commanding Officer and Operations Officer. I flew with several pilots and got to know them quite well, and even met some of their families. As time neared for our next move, I flew more and more with Lt. Tom Johnson and when we returned to Lakeland in December 1943, I was assigned to his crew.

Pilot — Johnson

This is a good time to meet the crew of *Tom's Tantalizer*, our plane as named by the ground crew. Thomas F. Johnson, pilot and "head honcho," was a first lieutenant when he joined our group in Tyler. About six feet tall, slender, quiet and soft spoken, Tom was an easygoing guy. Like most of us, Tom was in this war to get it over in a hurry and return to civilian life. His wife, Mary, and young son, Tim, were waiting for him back in Batavia, New York. Tom was an excellent pilot. He treated the Marauder with respect but never failed to ask it to do what was needed — more power, fly on one engine, fly with flak damage — or whatever the situation demanded. His steady hand on the wheel during bomb runs was a critical factor in our crew's success. While he obviously enjoyed flying, he exhibited none of the show-off or daredevil tendencies sometimes found in pilots.

Here's our combat crew: Back row, left to right: S/Sgt. Charles W. Calkins, turret gunner; S/Sgt. Joseph Castoro, tail gunner; T/Sgt. Dorr E. Tippens, radio operator and waist gunner. Front row, left to right: Major Tom Johnson, pilot; Lt. George Eldridge, bombardier; and Lt. Carl H. Moore, navigator.

Copilot — Willms

Lt. Frank Willms, from Coffeeville, Kansas, relatively new to the Marauder, joined us at Tyler. He stayed with us until he was checked out in England as "first pilot" and assigned his own crew. (On many of our combat missions a VIP flew as copilot.) Frank was a good pilot, young, eager and anxious to learn. Since he did not fly with us very long, I did not get to know him very well.

Bombardier — Eldridge

George W. Eldridge, second lieutenant and bombardier, hailed from Alma, Kansas. Of average height and weight, he was single and, like most bachelors, was interested in all pretty girls. His hobbies included motorcycles, and he had done his share of racing. George disliked mistakes with a passion but also had a sense of humor that tempered his conversation. As a bombardier, he was the best. He could spot aiming points unseen by others and zero his Norden in on them with unerring accuracy. He was the sharpest critic of my navigation and at the same time my most reassuring companion in the nose of the Marauder.

Navigation was strictly by pilotage and often we would have a margin of only a mile or two in our course to avoid flak. Visibility was sometimes limited, and from 12,000 feet it was easy to overlook a check point or to wander off course just enough to catch a blast from the enemy's 88s. George and I sometimes disagreed about our position. In fact, we often thought that if the rest of the crew could hear us arguing about our position, they would have bailed out. I appreciated George very much. With 36 planes carrying more than 200 men following my lead, I wanted all the help I could get.

Radio and GEE Operator—Tippens

T/Sgt. Dorr E. Tippens from Indianapolis, Indiana, was our radio operator on most of our missions. Dorr was tall and lanky and as a radio operator there was none better. He could get a message through any time and he amused himself by listening to other operators in the squadron trying to do the simplest tasks with the radio. He quickly learned to operate the "Gee" box—an early radar device—and assisted the navigator and pilot in determining the plane's position, particularly when cloud cover obscured the ground. Also, he was the only gunner in our squadron to score a "probable" on an enemy fighter and to win the Distinguished Flying Cross. T/Sgt. Tippens was not assigned to our crew until we were overseas. I became acquainted with Dorr (and his wife, Doris) after the war at Purdue University where we were both students.

Radio Operator—Thompson

For our flight across the Atlantic, Sergeant L.O. Thompson was our radio operator. He was assigned to another crew when we became operational.

An extra comment on Sgt. Thompson seems appropriate. Most men rarely admitted fear even under fire. It was not that each of us wasn't afraid at times and secretly wondered, "Will I ever return to the States and to those I love and who mean so much to me?" But these emotions rarely showed. Perhaps we built a wall around that feeling or pushed it back into our subconscious. To the world around us we were out to win the war and get back home as soon as possible. I do not remember consciously thinking that I might not survive the war. I have met many others who expressed the same thought.

Sgt. Thompson was one who showed his fear. He was a very religious man. He read his Bible often during the trip across the ocean. I don't know his background, but he never seemed comfortable. Perhaps it was a premonition, for when flying with another crew on an early mission, he went down in a mid-air collision as our planes moved through an overcast in formation over England. Another man in our squadron—a pilot—while happy-go-lucky on the outside, projected a sense of "something's going to happen." He later went down in his badly damaged plane after nursing it back from the target so the crew could bail out over friendly territory. At the last minute he directed the crippled Marauder away from a village and in doing so lost the necessary time to bail out. Perhaps within each of us there is a sense of direction that cannot be defined or described but that gives the assurance of survival or doom.

Crew Chief — Wren

Our crew chief for the flight to England was M/Sgt. W.A. "Willie" Wren. Again, we had an experienced man who had worked on the Marauders for several years. He knew those Pratt & Whitney engines like the back of his hand and could squeeze every last mile out of a gallon of gas. Also, he kept *Tom's Tantalizer* in top notch condition for our flights. The crew chiefs flew overseas with us for obvious reasons — to keep the Marauder running.

Gunners — Castoro and Calkins

S/Sgt. Joe Castoro from Brooklyn, New York, tail gunner, and S/Sgt. Charles Calkins, home town Corning, New York, turret gunner, rounded out our crew. They did not make the overseas flight with us but joined us in England. They were excellent men and performed their duties superbly.

Copilot — Graves

Another man who flew as copilot on several missions (and who had been at Barksdale Field with Tom) was John C. Graves. He was an excellent pilot and had his own crew. He respected the Marauder and made it perform like the sturdy ship that it was.

Now it was time to take one more leave, visit my family, return to Savannah, Georgia, and with the rest of the crew pick up a brand new Marauder and prepare for the flight overseas.

Chapter 4

The Long Way to England

New York to London in less than four hours? Impossible. But the British Supersonic Concorde began just such nonstop flights in 1978. That's a far cry from our experience in January 1944 with our Marauder. We had a top cruising speed of about 210 mph, service ceiling of around 14,000 feet, and a fuel supply that would take us about 1,800 miles at best.

A Brand New Marauder

Reporting to Savannah, Georgia, we picked up a new B-26B-50, serial number 42-95977. Tom and Willie ran up the engines and checked all the instruments. Then we took 42-95977 in the air and again checked for power, stability, and general handling characteristics. Tom tested all flight instruments for accuracy and response. Willie was particularly concerned with engine gauges, and everyone wanted to be sure the compass and radios functioned properly.

On our first takeoff, the fuel pressure gauge on the right engine kept going out. Also, the VHF radio was cutting out. For a while it looked like we would not complete the fuel consumption test or log the required three hours before time to go to West Palm Beach for our overseas flight briefing.

Tom and Willie were never completely satisfied with the right engine, but they couldn't find anything specifically wrong. It just didn't sound quite right. It did put out full power, so it was accepted.

As navigator, I was concerned about calibration of the magnetic compass and alignment of the drift meter with the horizontal axis of the plane. These were vital instruments to dead reckoning, and I wanted to personally check them.

Alignment of the drift meter was relatively simple. We stretched a line under the fuselage on the ground lined up with the longitudinal axis of the plane. This was done by sighting from the nose. Then a parallel line was placed on the ground directly under the drift meter. Sighting the line through the drift meter, zero drift on the meter was adjusted to the line. A little crude by modern navigation techniques, but the best we had in 1944.

Determining the deviation of the magnetic compass was more complicated. Two methods are available — one uses a compass "rose" drawn on the ground so the plane can be accurately pointed true north. The second uses a master compass to determine when the plane is pointing to magnetic north. I used the second method. People who have flown are well aware of "variation" and "deviation" in a magnetic compass, but for anyone who is not familiar with these terms, here's a more detailed description of "swinging the compass." (You old timers may want to skip the next few paragraphs.)

Variation is the difference between true north — the geographic north pole — and magnetic north, the center of the north magnetic field. It will vary from zero to more than 20 degrees and it may be either plus or minus. Thus, if you want to steer a true course of 90 degrees and the variation at your location is plus 10, you would steer a course of 100 degrees on the magnetic compass.

Deviation is the difference from magnetic north that a compass may read because of the influence of items such as radios, masses of metal (structure of the airplane itself), motors, and a multitude of other factors. To add to the confusion, the amount of deviation usually varies on each heading. In "swinging the compass," the aircraft is moved to at least four headings (north, east, south, and west) and the reading of the magnetic compass noted. Again, the compass "rose" on the ground or a master compass is used to be sure the plane is pointed to the desired heading. When it is in place, the reading of the compass is noted and compared with the true heading taking into account variation. Thus, with the plane headed south —180 degrees — and variation of plus 4 degrees and the magnetic compass reading 190 degrees, deviation on this heading is plus 6 degrees.

For maximum accuracy, the procedure should be repeated on eight or even 16 headings, and both with radio on and off. From all of this, I developed a card to place beside my compass in the navigation compartment like this:

MAGNETIC HEADING	DEVIATION	
	Radio On	**Radio Off**
360°	+1°	-1°
45°	+2°	0
90°	+3°	+2°

Magnetic Heading	Deviation	
	Radio On	Radio Off
135°	+1°	0
180°	-1°	+1°
225°	+4°	+2°
270°	+5°	+1°
315°	+2°	-2°

Accurate information about the magnetic compass in our Marauder was vital to me. Anyone using today's sophisticated navigation aids would find relying completely on the magnetic compass a bit primitive. But in 1944, flying the South Atlantic with partial radio silence and a limited number of radio direction stations for using the radio direction finder, the magnetic compass was the navigator's best friend. The pilot's gyro compass was helpful, but it frequently "drifted" and had to be corrected by caging and resetting.

With the compass and drift meter checked, I was ready to store my maps, protractor, E-6-B calculator (a circular slide rule), celestial navigation books, and other navigation aids in the navigator's compartment and head for England.

Reasonably satisfied with 42-95977, our next stop was West Palm Beach, Florida, for final briefing before jumping off on the long trip to England where the war was being fought. Several of the crews used bombardiers for navigators on the trip overseas. Unfortunately, our bombardier, Lt. Eldridge, contracted yellow jaundice at Savannah and spent several weeks recovering. Thus, he missed going with our squadron and had to cross the Atlantic in a troop ship. He rejoined the squadron in England weeks later.

An Old Story — Hurry Up and Wait

At Morrison Field, West Palm Beach, we suddenly were put on "hold." The following note is on my log sheet:

> Stayed at Morrison Field a week pending possible modification of the ships. Rumors were all over the place. Most persistent ones were that we would go to Mobile, Alabama, or Wright Field, Ohio, to have deicer boots installed. We were given back our AGO passes and allowed to go into West Palm Beach. George Washington Hotel was most popular hotel. Good food on the post and we could eat any time of day or night. We had drawn our maps and had courses plotted, but the most activity was one meeting a day at 1100 hours.

Many years later I learned that Colonel Reginald F.C. Vance, our group commander, convinced Washington that his men would not "talk" if they were permitted to leave the base during this delay. Some of the men had their wives living near the base, and Colonel Vance could not see any reason for restricting us. He assured his superiors that we could be trusted. Who would violate such a trust?

We never learned the reason for the delay. For my part, I was well satisfied to do without deicer boots. I had heard what ice could do to the flying characteristics of a plane, and flying the *North* Atlantic (which I assume we would have done with deicing equipment) in the dead of winter didn't sound nearly as pleasant as taking the warm southern route.

The southern route avoided all the cold and treacherous weather of the much shorter northern route via Greenland. But the Marauder, with only a I,460 gallon fuel supply (including 500 gallons in bomb bay tanks), wasn't entirely suited to the long flight from Natal, Brazil, to Ascension Island nor the flight from North Africa to England. Both of the flights would carry us well past the "point of no return." There was ample reason for fear and the incentive to prepare thoroughly. After all, engines did fail, there were few alternate fields, and we would be heavily loaded. One more thing—the Marauder was a lousy boat. We were told that we would have a maximum of two minutes to get out and launch a lifeboat if we had to ditch. We got our dry run drill down to 45 seconds.

How do you describe thirty days and a few thousand miles with a Marauder and its crew? Exciting? Challenging? Hard work? Monotonous? Yes, some of each. The endless and awesome sea, sleeping in a new place each night, stringing up mosquito netting, taking Atebrin tablets to ward off malaria, hearing the sounds of the jungle of Brazil at night, getting up early, being briefed for the next leg, waiting in line for takeoff, hoping the plugs on the engines wouldn't foul while they idled waiting your turn at the runway (there were at least 25 planes making the trip more or less together)—all these and many more experiences became a part of this unique venture.

Off We Go to England

Finally, on January 20, 1944, rumors were put to rest and we were briefed for the first leg of our flight to England. It was a short hop—only 872 miles—but it was a start. We were briefed on weather, radio beacons, and how to call for help if we ditched. Colonel Vance wanted the group to fly in formation for practice.

Morrison Field, USA, to Boringuen Field, Puerto Rico

Just at sunup January 21, 1944, we roared down the runway following Colonel Vance. We were to fly on his right wing. Notes from my log show takeoff at 1248 Greenwich Mean Time, 0748 Florida time. The following readings of inches of manifold pressure and rpm recorded in my log probably were made to give Tom an idea of how the engines would perform:

Time:	1256—35 inches	2300 rpm
	1257—31 inches	2100 rpm
	1308—30 inches	2100 rpm
	1412—32 inches	2000 rpm
	1430—32 inches	2200 rpm

About this time, formation flying was abandoned. It was using too much fuel and it was too tiring for the pilots. The flight was relatively uneventful and we came into Boringuen Field on the northwestern tip of Puerto Rico after four hours and forty-three minutes in the air. We were assigned to quarters, fed, and then relaxed; in the sack early though because we would be up early for the next briefing.

BORINGUEN FIELD TO ATKINSON FIELD, BRITISH GUIANA

Early breakfast and another briefing. This time we were reminded to keep radio silence unless we sighted a submarine. In that case, we should radio a report to the nearest station. Again the sun greeted us as we took our turn rolling down the runway. No talk of formation flying this time. The leg to British Guiana was not long—970 miles with estimated flying time of five hours and ten minutes.

Our course took us east over San Juan, Puerto Rico; then southeast past Beame Island, Galbero Point, Trinidad; then to Georgetown and Atkinson Field. Weather was good with only scattered cumulus clouds. To clear all clouds, Tom took us up to 11,000 feet. The air was a bit thin, so we occasionally took some oxygen from a portable tank just to keep us alert.

Sighted Sub—Reported Same

About four hours out I thought I saw a wake in the water below and to our right. I called Frank and asked him if he could see it. Sure enough, he could. "Do you think it is a submarine?" I asked. "Looks like one to me," he replied.

We told Tom what we saw and he said, "It's just your imagination. Probably a fishing boat." Not to be discouraged, Frank and I looked again and the object appeared to be submerging. "They said to report any sightings of submarines, Tom." "Someone else probably has already reported it," was Tom's reply. Frank and I finally persuaded him that he should call in a report. He reluctantly called Trinidad and told them we thought we sighted a submarine. "Proceed to Trinidad and file your report," came the reply. Now, no one had told us we would have to land and report.

"See what I meant," said Tom. "Now we've got to go down there and probably spend the night at some godforsaken air field."

An Unscheduled Stop

Down we went from 11,000 feet to Waller Field and reported in to S-2 (the intelligence officer). We said we weren't sure we had seen a submarine but it looked like one. "Oh yes. You probably saw one," replied the S-2 officer. "We've had several reports on one in that area."

"Good, can we go now?"

"Yes, thanks very much."

As we walked back to our plane, Tom's instructions to Frank and me were to keep our minds on flying and navigating and forget submarines. We told him that it was our patriotic duty and wasn't he glad his crew did something no others did. Anyway, no more submarines. We climbed aboard our Marauder and completed the hour and a half flight to Atkinson Field, two hours behind everyone else.

This incident illustrates the relationship that generally existed among crew members. Although Tom, as pilot and senior officer of the crew, was clearly in charge and had authority to say "go" or "stay," in matters less than critical to the success of a mission, there was a comradeship that made crew members a team. There was much exchange of ideas and even questioning of decisions, but when the chips were down it was the word of the man in the left seat that counted regardless of rank.

Atkinson Field to Belem, Brazil

This 812 mile, four hour leg was quite uneventful — the kind we liked. We skirted the coast going over Dutch and French Guiana, then southeast across the Amazon River to Belem situated on the southeast side of the Amazon Delta. Notes in my log indicated a solid overcast about one and a half hours out of Belem, which made it impossible to pick up check points visually. Also, there was some rain at this point and we were on instruments at the 9,000-foot level. Dropping to 6,000 feet, we made a position report to the station at Amapa. Stratus clouds at 900 feet did not seriously complicate our letdown and landing.

Belem to Natal, Brazil

By this time going to bed early under a mosquito net, taking Atebrin to prevent malaria, and getting up early (my notes do not mention wakeup time but takeoff was shortly after daybreak, so it must have been early) were almost routine. Not that I enjoyed it, because those tropics didn't do much for me. Nighttime noises of the jungle, a strange place, excitement of the previous day and anticipation of the next didn't make for a lot of rest. Probably we all were subconsciously looking forward to the big leg — Natal to Ascension.

The flight from Belem to Natal again skirted the coast. My notes show we passed Fortaleza seven miles right of course on a heading of 102 degrees — scattered clouds with tops of 6,000 feet but with unlimited visibility. We cruised at 9,000 feet with an indicated airspeed of 180 mph and a ground speed of 193 knots. Landing at Natal, after four hours and 58 minutes, was at 1525 Greenwich Mean Time, January 23, 1944.

Three days were spent at Natal to rest and to check the planes carefully. The next leg would be nearly eight hours in the air with no check points and only the South Atlantic for scenery. The distance was 1,200 nautical miles and there were no alternate fields. You either made it to Ascension or you ditched.

Natal to Ascension Island

This was a big one! Just fly east and hit that little 34-square mile island called Ascension. Joao da Nova Castella, the Portuguese sailor, gave the island this name because he discovered it on Ascension Day 1501. In 1956 there were only 390 inhabitants, and in 1944 there probably were at least 100 more, as it was a main refueling base for U.S. aircraft (ours included, we hoped). Pilots were warned that the runway (which was carved out of lava rock) was not absolutely level — there was a hump in the middle. If you were not firmly on the first half of the runway, better go around and try again. Also, when taking off don't be misled into thinking you were airborne when the second half of the runway seemed to be dropping away.

Briefing for the flight was very detailed. We were given winds at various altitudes, two radio beacons and emergency frequencies for distress. Oh yes, "And be careful that you are not misled by a radio beacon from a German submarine imitating the one at Ascension. It will be on the same frequency but just a few miles off so you will run out of gas and have to ditch." That was interesting. It put a little more pressure on my dead reckoning navigation. A head wind of 14 knots was forecast for the first 300 miles. It probably would increase to 18 to 20 knots the second 300, drop slightly the third 300, and swing behind us at about the 1,000 mile mark with velocity of 10 knots. These winds were at the 6,000 foot level. They were slightly stronger at 9,000 feet.

With a fuel supply of 1,462 gallons and an estimated consumption of

170 gallons per hour, we had about nine hours of fuel. My original estimate of flying time was seven hours and twenty eight minutes. This gave us a margin of a little over an hour, but there was no place to go in that length of time if we missed the island. The nearest land would be another three or four hours away.

With briefing behind it was out to the flight line, load up, crank those Pratt and Whitney R-2800s and get in line for takeoff. We were assigned in flights of five or six planes but there was no attempt to fly formation. I never was sure why they even made up flights. We were lead plane in our flight with numbers 5918, 5984, 5985, and 7565 assigned to our flight.

Takeoff was routine at 0634 local time, heading was 96 degrees. Tom put the Marauder in a gradual climb and leveled off at 7,200 feet at 0656. Airspeed in the climb was 165 indicated and 172 when we leveled off. I calculated ground speed at this point at 178 knots. Visibility was unlimited with light cumulous clouds at 6,000 feet — really a beautiful day.

As soon as we reached cruising altitude, Tom, Frank and Willie began to see just how little gas was required to keep 4,000 horses working for us. Tom eased the throttles back and reduced rpms. Willie worked on the fuel mixture. He would ease the mixture control back until the engine coughed, then move it forward slightly. At 1,900 rpm we could almost count the revolutions of the props. Tom had cut power to 26 inches and that seemed to be the best we could do. The Pratt and Whitney engines purred like kittens and everything appeared to be in order. I had picked up the radio station at Ascension about as soon as we leveled off. It was faint at first but was growing stronger by the hour and the radio compass pointed straight ahead.

So far so good. What do you do for eight hours flying straight and level with nothing but water beneath you? Tom was watching the flight instruments; Frank was helping him. Willie was wondering if he couldn't cut the mixture "just a little," and Sgt. Thompson, radio operator, was listening to his radio and reading his Bible from time to time. (Seemed like a good idea — we wanted everyone on our side.) I amused myself by taking drift readings on the waves and rechecking my dead reckoning calculations. I had picked up one radio fix when we leveled off but with only one station it wasn't very conclusive. It did confirm my dead reckoning position, which was reassuring.

Two hours out I decided that I could use sun shots to check ground speed. We were flying directly into the sun and with good luck these shots could be useful. Repeating a sun shot an hour later, I estimated ground speed at 170 knots compared with 168 by dead reckoning. This also was reassuring. An hour later a line of position from the sun gave a ground speed of 165 knots — still okay. This kind of celestial navigation wasn't very accurate but helpful. There really wasn't much to do except to keep checking the waves to be sure the wind was still as predicted. The radio beam from Ascension was very strong now and the radio compass still pointed dead ahead. Both engines droned steadily and fuel consumption was less than the 170 gallons per hour expected.

I moved my last two sun shots forward — not a very accurate means of determining position but the best I could do at the moment. It showed us eight miles right of course. Not bad. The radio compass continued to point straight ahead. By keeping busy it gave less time for my mind to conjure up such things as, "Suppose one of the engines quits?" Or, "Suppose we have picked up the wrong radio beam?" Actually, I don't remember having doubts about the safe completion of our flight.

Where Is That Island?

About thirty minutes before my ETA (estimated time of arrival) of 1362 Natal time for Ascension, Tom began a gradual letdown. There were scattered clouds at 5,000 feet, so visibility was not perfect but the radio compass continued to point straight ahead. We all began to strain to get a glimpse of an island. Every cloud threw a shadow on the water and every shadow looked like an island. As we began to break through the scattered fluffy cumulus clouds, Tom wanted to stay in the clear and not go on instruments even for a minute. So he asked which way to dodge around the clouds. I wasn't positive and my confidence began to shake just a bit. The radio compass still said "straight ahead." Therefore, I directed him around the clouds so we would not stray very far from our course. When we broke in the clear at about 4,000 feet, there was no island in sight!

It's at times like this that pilots, copilots, engineers and everyone else aboard looks at the navigator and silently says, "I hope you know what you're doing." And the navigator replies — silently — "I do too!" Holding to my course — remembering a time in navigation school when I didn't and missed the destination — we flew on probably two or three minutes that seemed like hours — and then we saw a shadow at about two o'clock! Was it the island? It could be a cloud shadow. It grew and grew, and when Tom called the Ascension tower, back came a clear quick reply with landing instructions.

We all relaxed, and I made notations in my log and gathered my maps, pencils, etc., together and put them in my briefcase. Tom and Frank made preparations for landing, and Willie pushed the fuel mixture to "auto rich." We made it and without incident. That 34-square-mile oasis in the South Atlantic looked mighty good.

Ascension Island to Roberts Field, Liberia

After the long lonesome flight from Natal to Ascension, the rest of the trip should have been "duck soup"—just a short 886-mile jump to the coast of Africa and on to England. But we were to learn that there was much ahead of us. Haze was very heavy out of Ascension and especially at Roberts Field. Most of the flight was at 9,000 feet, and after hitting Ascension Island I felt like I could do anything.

The flight was routine and Tom let Frank bring us in to Roberts Field. The thing I remember most was my first glimpse of the ground as we circled for landing. Right out of my old geography book were the thatched huts of the villages. As we landed there were dozens — maybe a hundred — black men mowing the grass on the field with machetes. Slowly it dawned on me that there really were places different from my home country. The world was big and I was seeing only a small part of it, but my perspective was changing fast.

Roberts Field to Dakar

Another short flight — 700 miles — but we were to have an experience that was an omen of things to come. On the takeoff run, the right engine would not put out full power. No obvious reason, so Tom brought our Marauder around again, and this time the engine behaved and we were on our way. Colonel Vance wanted to fly formation again, but after he tried to join up above the haze layer he called everyone and said to forget it. We approved. Weather was good and visibility was unlimited after we cleared the haze two hours out from Roberts Field. Ground speed was about 190 knots as we took advantage of a 15 knot wind from the east. Our course was 308 degrees, which took us clear of neutral territory and mostly within sight of the coast.

Dakar to Marrakech in French Morocco

Up again early and off at 0825 — a bit later than usual. The Atebrin tablets finally got to Tom. He was sick as a horse but was not about to be left behind. He sat in the left seat but as soon as we were on course he turned the plane over to Frank and went to sleep. Well, not exactly asleep, but he leaned back and closed his eyes.

Our course took us over Mauritania, skirting neutral Spanish Sahara, through the pass in the Atlas Mountains and to Marrakech in French Morocco. We were briefed not to try the pass if it was closed in with clouds but to go west around the end of the mountain range and then back to Marrakech or to the alternate field at Casablanca. Most of the flight after crossing the Senegal River northeast of Dakar would be over the Sahara Desert. The first check point was the little village of Atar about two hours out of Dakar. My log note says, "What a hole in the desert." I guess I wasn't impressed. As we cruised along at 9,000 to 9,500 feet, we were making good time, estimated ground speed at nearly 200 knots. Not bad for the 01 Marauder. Tom was dozing. Frank was manning the controls and I was riding the nose so I could see my check points.

Right Engine Losing Power

About 125 miles from Tindouf, our last check point before heading for the mountain pass, the plane began to pull to the right. Tom got well immediately. He came up out of the seat like his mother had called him to supper. The right engine oil temperature was going up and the oil pressure was going down, causing the engine to lose power. Tom's decision was calculated but not slow in coming. Hours of experience in the Marauder came into his evaluation of the situation, and he didn't hesitate to cut the right engine off and feather the prop, but not before giving the good left engine full power. In view out the window, there was that prop still and straight!

Again the hours of experience came into play as Tom prepared to keep the B-26 in the air on one engine. The Marauder flies well on one engine but not at 9,500 feet. And not with an extra load of fuel in bomb bay tanks and miscellaneous equipment including a "putt-putt" (small gasoline engine to provide auxiliary power to start the engines when away from base) and our personal belongings.

Number one — salvo those bomb bay tanks. I opened the bomb bay doors and let the tanks go, watching them as they dropped toward the desert floor some 9,000 feet below. Next, "Willie, go back and throw *everything* out of the back end." It was already certain that we could not maintain altitude or power to make the pass over the mountains. Tom asked me for the nearest landing site. "Could we return to Dakar?" A quick check confirmed that Tindouf was the nearest landing field — more than 125 miles ahead. We were still losing altitude and slowed to about 150 miles per hour. This was one of the few times I remember Tom showing any anger. His instructions to the radio operator about getting an emergency message through to Tindouf were clear and pointed.

I had a good look at the desert floor beneath us before leaving the nose compartment. Tom had me stay there to give additional weight to the nose until he could stabilize our altitude. The idea was to get the tail up.

What would we do if the other engine quit and we had to crash land on the desert? It gets cold in the desert at night. We had only limited emergency food and clothing—and Willie probably had already thrown that out. While the desert looked even from 9,000 feet we all knew that it would be very difficult to find a smooth place for a crippled Marauder to land. It would be a wheels up landing with the danger of fire. Tom had wisely kept the bad engine so it could be used to assist in a crash landing if necessary. How low would we have to go before the plane would hold its altitude? These and many other thoughts went through my head, and I am sure the rest of the crew had some thoughts about such a landing too.

Soon Willie returned to the cockpit and asked Tom how we were doing. "She's beginning to hold," replied Tom. And at about 6,000 feet our sick Marauder settled down to flying along on one good engine. I recalculated our ETA to Tindouf using the slower speed and passed the information to Tom and the radio operator. Nothing to do now but sit back and pray that good engine would remember what it was made for. The manual said, "Do not maintain full power for more than five minutes." It would have to do better than that. It would take at least an hour to reach Tindouf. (Later, in combat, pilots ran those great engines at full power from takeoff to landing in order to keep in formation.) Tom settled for 2,600 rpm and 42 inches—less than takeoff power but more than the manual called for.

A quotation from T.O. 01-35EB-1 "Pilot's Flight Operating Instructions" is interesting.

> Single Engine Flight:—The best attitude in which to fly the airplane with one engine operating is at zero yaw with a small degree of bank. However, there is no instrument or set of instruments which will indicate that the airplane is flying at zero yaw. Optimum conditions must be derived from the resulting performance. For example, if the airplane is banked too greatly for the amount of yaw it will slip and lose altitude, recording such a condition on the rate of climb indicator, altimeter and turn and bank indicator. If the airplane is not banked sufficiently it will yaw and hence lose altitude because of the increased drag. The optimum condition will be found between excessive bank and insufficient bank where the airplane will be at a zero yaw, will perform best, and will maintain level flight for the charted engine and airplane conditions.

The chart calls for maximum allowable continuous cruising engine settings of 32 inches of mercury and 2,100 rpm. Nice if you can afford it but not with the Sahara Desert looking up at you.

As we approached the field at Tindouf, I heard Frank ask Tom if he had ever made a single engine landing before. Tom's reply was to hold up five fingers. I liked that answer and relaxed. Anyone who has flown a twin engine plane can imagine the yaw created when one engine is dead. It is difficult to hold enough rudder to correct it for any length of time. The answer: crank in enough trim to hold it. The only problem is that when you throttle back on the good engine to land, the trim must be reduced accordingly. Also, in landing, the pilot has two hands full with the throttle and the wheel. Solution: "Frank, as I nod my head you crank out the trim as we make our final approach." Here we go! Wheels down and locked. And as pretty a landing as Tom ever made with *two* engines.

With the ailing Marauder towed to a parking stand, Willie and the base engineer began the job of trying to find out what was wrong with the uncooperative engine. They expected to find metal filings in the oil pan, indicating a burned out bearing. Tom, Frank and I sat in the plane making small talk but subconsciously wondering, "What happens next?" Tom took a few emotion-releasing kicks at the cockpit and suggested that we take the fire ax to ol' 42-95977. I happened to glance back through the bomb bay and saw something in the rear area of the plane.

"Aren't those our B-4 bags [personal belongings]?" Tom took a quick look and yelled at Willie, "I thought I told you to throw out everything!"

Willie managed one of his ear-to-ear grins and replied, "Captain, I figured government property first, and when that 'putt-putt' went overboard, the tail came up and I figured we had it made." Needless to say, we all agreed. At the time we would have gladly lost our clothes, but now that we were on the ground, we were very glad to have our personal property intact. Our B-4 bags and the plane were literally our home.

Goodbye to Ol' 977

No evidence of damage in the engine, so it was take it up for a test flight, taking the base engineer and the base commander (a first lieutenant) with us. After just a few minutes in the air, the right engine began to heat up and the oil pressure dropped. Tom immediately turned onto an approach to the runway. The engineer said, "There is obviously something wrong with that engine, but I can't ground this plane because I can't find anything wrong with it." The base commander, showing a bit of concern about his own safety in this misbehaving Marauder, spoke up quickly with, "*I* can and I *do* as of right now!"

After a night in the desert at this tiny oasis once made famous by stories of the French Foreign Legion, we hitched a ride in a C-47 on to Marrakech and joined the rest of our group.

One more jump and we would be in England. The 1,337 mile, seven and a half hour flight was well within the range of the Marauder. But there were other conditions that posed some problems. First, the prevailing winds

Here's our hard-working crew at Tindouf in the middle of the Sahara Desert without an airplane. Ol' 977 had deserted us and we were ready to hitch a ride on to Marrakech in a lowly C-47. Left to right: Sgt. L. O. Thompson, radio operator; M/Sgt. Willie Wren, crew chief; Lt. Carl H. Moore, navigator; Lt. Frank Willms, copilot; and Captain Tom Johnson, pilot. Willie was later assigned to another crew.

were from the north, giving us a head wind. Second, we would be over water (nothing new to us) and within range of fighters from occupied France (this was new).

Arriving in Marrakech, we learned that weather was not favorable for our flight to England. We would have to wait until the strong head winds subsided or shifted. Okay with us. We had to check out a new airplane anyway. No telling when someone would fix up ol' 977, down in the desert at Tindouf. We were assigned a B-26C-45 Serial 42-107573. Tom, Frank and Willie took it up for a spin and found everything okay. I looked over the navigation instruments and they were in order. Someone had already checked the compass and drift. Since it had been ferried over from the States, it should have been well checked.

A Fortnight in Marrakech

Days stretched into weeks and still we were delayed. One of my "exciting" experiences was learning to eat cooked cabbage. We had three meals each day, but no snacks in between — no PX, no stores — and I got hungry. So whatever they had on the menu, I ate. Amazing how good cooked cabbage tastes when you are really hungry. Another thing I learned was the value of human life in some parts of the world. We were told to be careful not to hurt a goat but running into a person was okay. Or rather, if we had to choose, avoid the goat.

We were free to go into the town of Marrakech but were told to avoid the "old town" called Medina. It was reported that a crewman had gone there and was never heard from again. It was assumed he had been killed. Just like little boys told to stay out of the cookie jar, we *had* to see Medina. Several men went and told us just how to do it. How to get a "cab"—a horse-drawn vehicle—and where to go. All went well at first. We strolled into the narrow, dimly lit street and didn't see anything so dangerous. Soon a young boy asked to be our guide. That seemed like a good idea, so we said okay. As we went down one street after another, a second boy began to tag along. All at once our guide grabbed him and with a rock in his hand pushed him against the wall, drew back his arm and aimed it at the intruder's head. Tom stepped between them and said quickly, "We'll pay both of you! Don't hit him!" The older boy stopped then and we began to figure a way out of that place. We had seen enough. We were convinced that the boy would have seriously injured the intruder—maybe killed him as he threatened. We told our guide that we were ready to leave and, if my memory is right, we found some other men from our squadron and together we left.

Tippens and a group of his friends also yielded to temptation and made the journey to Medina. Here's his account of their "Mission to Medina":

> A group of six of us decided we had to see the "forbidden city" of Medina in Marrakech. We proceeded to dress ourselves as much like Arabs as possible and hailed a cab. The "taxis" were old model cars, heaps as it were, usually pulled by one or two horses, mules or a variety of other beasts. We paid the "cabbie" who sat on top of the vehicle his fare, a reasonable amount, and off we went.
>
> We drove around seeing the sights. A horrible picture really. The streets were narrow, but all kinds of creatures sat or lay in their gutters—drunks, lepers, and other filth—a real mess. We drove or walked around for maybe an hour, our cabbie staying right with us.
>
> When we were ready to return to base, we stuffed back into the "cab" and signaled the driver our intentions. After probably forty-five minutes' driving within the walled city, we knew we were not taking the direct route home. We had not gone that far into the town. There was no way we could have found our way out of this labyrinth. Finally the driver volunteered he could find a shorter route for an additional fee—as I remember about $60 a head. In just a few minutes we were at the gate leaving the town. At that point our

greedy cabbie asked for more money to take us the last mile to the base. We paid him and the horses started trotting along toward the base.

Yankee ingenuity had to prevail, so when we were well outside the gates of Medina, one by one we slipped out of the "cab" until only one was left. He, being a rather large fellow, proceeded to recover our "extra" fares. He left the driver all that we had paid to go to the town and what we had paid to get back, but not the extra.

Wake Me When You Fill Those Tanks

While in Marrakech, Tippens had another "exciting" experience that could only happen to a sound sleeper. The enlisted crewmen were assigned on a rotation basis to guard the planes. This meant that they had to sleep in the planes at night to keep anyone from taking equipment or sabotaging them. Here's his personal account of one such night.

As usual, there were the bonfires off the end of the runway and frequent chanting by dancing natives. This encouraged the guarding, as who knew what these strange people might be planning? This particular night my bed was made in the bomb bay with my sleeping bag spread out on the keel between the two bomb bay tanks. When I finally fell asleep, I dreamed—and what dreams! In them, friends, both new and old, would float around and become globs! By some miracle, I awoke and put my hand out to my side. It became immersed in liquid.

What had happened was that word had finally come down that we would take off for England the next morning and the ground crews were out refueling the planes. They had filled the bomb bay tanks where I was sleeping and these tanks had overflowed. I was practically floating in gasoline! What to do? Should I open the bomb bay doors or go forward and get out? One thing I wouldn't do was light a cigarette! Finally, I crawled forward and got out of the plane, and was I sick! And did I smell! We sometimes used the high octane gas to do our dry cleaning, but this soaking took care of me for the next six months!

Marrakech to England

Finally, on February 16, 1944—18 days after we arrived—we were told that the winds were okay and we could take off the next morning. Good! Now we could get on with this business of war.

After the thorough briefing we realized we were closer to the real war than appeared from our uneventful layover in Marrakech. For example, we were told to load our guns but not to charge them (put a cartridge in the chamber), observe radio silence, turn off all lights 10 minutes out from Marrakech, and activate the IFF detonator after takeoff. If forced to land in a neutral country — Portugal or Spain — we were to destroy all secret material, give only our name, rank and serial number, say we were on a nonoperational flight and ask to see the military attaché. If forced to abort and fuel permitted, we could return to Marrakech but should be careful about homing on the signal at Marrakech. Oh yes, and we should be alert for enemy fighters coming out from the Brest Peninsula of France.

Upon reaching the British Isles, we must make our approach to Lands End (England) only from the north. If we couldn't make visual contact at 800 feet, climb back up to 5,000 feet and make an instrument approach. Fat chance we could do that with the margin of fuel we would have by the time we got to England.

There were a few more goodies about radio frequencies, how to call for a heading to the base in England known as Odd Job, how to call "Darky" for a heading, how to call for air sea rescue, and so forth.

We were to fly a relatively loose formation as protection against enemy fighters — if we were attacked. We flew on the left wing of Colonel Vance, who led the group. Major Hale rode the left seat while Colonel Vance was in the right seat. Major McKool, group navigator, was with Colonel Vance and thus led the group.

Once in the air and in formation, we headed for the coast of Africa on a course of 345 degrees, which would skirt the coast of Portugal. Later, we swung almost due north heading for the southern end of Ireland. When we were abreast of Lands End, England, we would turn east and make landfall from the north side of the point. Although we were following the lead plane, I kept careful notes and plotted our course using dead reckoning and a few visual check points. We leveled off at 9,500 feet, crossed the coast of Africa several miles right of course, and almost ran into the coast of Portugal, making a quick correction to the left.

About an hour out and well over the Atlantic we encountered scattered clouds with tops estimated at 6,000 feet. I could still see enough of the water to take drift readings, and during the first two hours I recorded a ground speed of 200 knots. We were indicating about 180 to 185 mph and I was estimating the wind at 16 knots from 290 degrees. So far so good. Those great Pratt & Whitney engines purred like they were supposed to. We had had enough of engine problems, and Tom and Willie liked the sound of these better than those on that lousy 977 back at Tindouf. Sergeant Thompson was monitoring the radio and everything seemed to be going according to plan. It was still too soon to expect any fighters, as we were not far enough north to be within their range.

Ground Speed Drops Drastically

We had left Marrakech at 0710 hours and by 0945 my estimated ground speed had dropped to 183 knots. Thirty minutes later it had dropped to 173 knots — not a good omen. I estimated the wind at 22 knots and from 330 degrees — nearly a direct head wind! I had moved my ETA ahead 20 minutes and if these winds continued that would not be a good figure.

Flying formation, we were only about 60 feet from the cockpit of the lead plane. Major Hale waved to us and obviously was trying to convey a message. Soon he picked up the Addis lamp and began sending a message by blinker. Now we had all ﬄpassed a test in reading Morse Code, both audio and by blinker, but we were far from experts. Finally, utilizing the talents of Sgt. Thompson, we understood that he wanted to know our estimate of ground speed. We told him and apparently it agreed with theirs — way too slow!

It is very difficult to be sure of the wind and the ground speed flying straight with no visual check points or reliable radio fixes. I told Tom we could take an abbreviated double drift and check our ground speed. It would take us away from the formation but we could catch up. Tom agreed that it would be desirable, so he turned 45 degrees left of course for one minute. (Usually we would take two minutes to get a more accurate reading.) Then 90 degrees right for one minute, then back to the original heading.

My drift readings confirmed the strong head wind. In fact, it indicated a wind of 35 knots from 360 degrees. Our true course was 349 degrees. Ground speed was calculated at 160 knots! It took us fifteen minutes to rejoin the formation. We learned later that the other planes thought we had left the formation because of trouble. An hour later my calculations showed a ground speed of 170 knots — an improvement — but fuel consumption now was a critical factor.

At 1245 —five hours and 35 minutes out of Marrakech — I plotted our position 40 miles left of course. Colonel Vance certainly wasn't taking any chances of getting too close to the Brest Peninsula of France. We were warned not to turn east too soon. An hour and a half later we still hadn't turned east toward England. Well, they said to approach from the north. We surely were going to do that. Finally, we turned east toward Odd Job, the code name for the airport at Lands End. We were at 10,500 feet altitude when we changed course and the cloud layer at about 6,000 feet was now broken rather than scattered. Although we had a radio fix showing us in position to proceed to Odd Job, in order to stay visual rather than go on instruments it was necessary to dodge around through the clouds. The radio compass continued to point to our destination.

England at Last

At 1534 hours — nine hours and ten minutes after leaving Marrakech — we landed at Odd Job and taxied to a parking stand. Some of the planes had left the formation because of a critical fuel supply. Two of them did not even have enough fuel to taxi to the parking stand. We all heaved a sigh of relief that our long journey was now ended.

Tippens, flying in another plane, had an even more harrowing experience. To begin with, as his crew walked to the aircraft for the flight to England, he observed the new pilot (the regular one was ill) reading the pilot's manual. Tippens asked if anything was wrong. Imagine his feelings when the pilot replied, "No. It's just that I've never been in one of these critters before." Running low on fuel as they approached England — the empty bomb bay tanks had been jettisoned to lighten the plane and the main wing tanks were already empty — the crew was unable to find the field at St. Mawgen (Lands End). Finally they spotted a landing field and proceeded to set their Marauder down. It wasn't the usual paved bomber runway but a grass one used by Spitfires. Not only was it short but at the end was a concrete operations building! The pilot used everything available, including the emergency air bottle, to bring the Marauder to a halt only a few feet from the concrete building. After landing they discovered that they were only about two miles away from St. Mawgen. But they were thankful to be on the ground.

Now came a bigger problem — how to get their speedy Marauder in the air again. Describing their procedure, Tippens said, "We unloaded that plane of everything possible. We took out radio equipment, machine guns, the ammo, even the seat cushions and Plexiglas gunner's dome. Then the pilot all by himself with only an 'eye dropper' of gas, brought the Marauder around to the end of the runway. We put chocks under the wheels and at his signal as he revved up the engines, we pulled out the chocks. He shot off the runway like a rocket."

The next day we all headed for our permanent base at Stanstead, England, about an hour's drive north of London. Weather forced us to return to Odd Job the first day, but on the second day we arrived at what we would call "Station 169."

So this is where the war is? We were assigned to quarters — Quonset huts — issued blankets and told how to find the mess hall. That evening we were treated to another evidence of the war as the Germans bombed London. It was for real! We could hear the German planes and hear and see the antiaircraft fire. This was close enough!

Chapter 5

What Good Are These Marauders?

Bombs rained on London and on England's industrial cities to the north of London. Hitler was sending his Luftwaffe into the air daily, believing that he could break the spirit of the British people. My arrival on this island bastion was February 20, 1944. Was it a quirk of fate? A movement of the stars? Or was it the will of God, who had other plans for me than to be on a fateful low level mission on a Marauder?

I believe it was the latter. I was older than most of the men in my squadron. I had been delayed in my training as a cadet for nearly a year. I was assigned to a squadron with some of the best pilots in the Army Air Force. During those years of delay the problems with the Marauder were being resolved. I will always believe that the God of the universe was guiding my destiny. Why I was spared the problems of the early crews in England flying the Marauder I do not know, but I am grateful.

Disaster at Low Level

Let's go back less than a year before my arrival in England to those fateful missions to the Dutch town of Ijmuiden on May 14 and May 17, 1943. Major General Robert M. Stillman (Retired) rode the right seat of a Marauder on the first low-level mission and led the second. Let's listen to his story as told to me in 1979.

General Stillman, I believe you led the group of 11 Marauders from the 322nd Bomb Group that were sent to Ijmuiden on May 17, 1943.

STILLMAN: Yes. I had been on the mission three days earlier to the same target, and as Commander of the 322nd I wanted to—at least felt I should—lead this second mission.

I understand that you had some misgivings about returning to the same target.

STILLMAN: I damn sure did! I knew we had hit the target on the first mission. I saw the bombs go into the building. Why they didn't cause the desired damage wasn't the fault of the Marauders or the crews. To go back to the same target so soon, attacking with bombs utilizing the same fuse, over the same route, would simply be repeating the initial error.

Did you express your concern to higher command?

STILLMAN: Yes sir. I questioned it with Brigadier General Francis Brady, commander of the Third Wing, and he expressed my concern to General Longfellow at 8th Bomber Command. But General Longfellow said it was part of the plan for the day, and since I could not live with being relieved of command after one mission. I said, "Okay, we'll go."

Was there some question as to whether the bombs detonated on the first mission?

STILLMAN: Yes, there was. But the reconnaissance pictures showed a great number of bomb craters alongside the ash dump of the power plant, strung out in a line perpendicular to our line of attack and well inside our turn into the target. It was my belated contention that the Germans, familiar with the type of fuze employed by the Allies in attacking targets in occupied countries, and knowing that you could beat on these bombs with a sledge for twenty minutes before the chemical fuze would detonate, forced employees of the plant to load all exposed bombs into the ash dump carts for a run to the ash heap. They knew they would be safe for eighteen minutes.

Major General Robert Stillman (retired) reminiscing about his experience with the Marauder.

Were you directed to carry the same type bombs and fuzes on the second mission?

STILLMAN: Yes. The Allies had repeatedly assured the occupied countries that whenever targets involving their nationals were attacked, twenty minute delay fuzes would be employed.

What position did you fly on the first mission?

STILLMAN: I flew on the right wing of Captain Roland Scott, operations officer of the 450th Squadron, who led the first flight on the mission.

You led the second mission and I believe you carried a crew of six—yourself, copilot, bombardier-navigator, radio operator, top turret gunner and tail gunner.

Colonel Stillman, center left, briefing crews for the second mission to Ijmuiden. Crews are gathered around a sand table model of the target area. Use of the sand table was critical for briefing on low level missions. There was little time to look for landmarks and crews had to be quick to pick out silhouettes of check points and the target. Others in the photograph include Lt. Colonel von Kolnitz, intelligence officer (next to the window) (courtesy General Robert Stillman).

STILLMAN: Yes. In the ten planes that crossed the Dutch coast (the eleventh plane aborted before we made landfall) we had 30 officers and 30 enlisted men. Ten officers and 11 enlisted men ended up in prisoner of war camps. The remainder were killed, except for two gunners who managed to get into a life raft and were picked up in the North Sea by the British. The rest were lost — a 60 percent casualty rate.

Would you describe your experience on that second mission?

STILLMAN: I "bumped" Lt. E. J. Resweber's copilot and had Lt. Resweber fly with me as copilot. We headed east over the North Sea on the deck to avoid detection by German radar. We were right on top of the waves and indicating about 200 mph, until we made landfall, when we opened up to 240. The heading was nearly due east. As we approached the coast of Holland we spotted a convoy of ships and veered to the south to avoid them.

I assumed they were armed. We made landfall several miles south of the intended route over the heavily defended Maas Estuary leading to Rotterdam. Enemy fire was intense even before we crossed the coast. As we were turning toward the target area, our ship took a jolting hit somewhere in the tail section. Maybe the entire tail came off. I really don't know. The control column flopped back and forth and the rudder did not respond. The plane did a snap roll to the right and then recovered momentarily. I had aileron control but it was of little help. The next reaction of the plane was a half roll and we saw the sand of the beach coming at us. The only thought I can recall was, "Well, the Air Force is losing a good man."

Other crews reported that we hit the beach upside down, blew up and burned. The first thing I remember was looking up from the ground at a toothless old German grinning down at me as they opened the doors to a "meat wagon." His comment—"Yah. For you the war is over."

Your experience during the next two years is a story in itself. At the moment I would like to go back to some of your earlier experiences and how you happened to be in England commanding the 322nd Bomb Group. You were in the West Point class of 1935 and soon after graduation joined what was then known as the Army Air Corps. Where were you when the war broke out?

STILLMAN: I was at Bolling Field but was soon requisitioned along with five other lieutenant colonels to Air Force Headquarters. I was there about ten months when I learned that field grade pilots with tactical experience were urgently needed for B-26 units being activated. I had tactical training in Hawaii in B-12s and B-18s, so I felt qualified for such an assignment. A friend, Colonel Tom Hall, was already at McDill Army Air Field, Tampa, Florida, seeking a like assignment. I asked him to give my name to the personnel people at McDill who secured my release from AAF Headquarters, and I was soon headed for McDill and my first ride in a Marauder.

This was in February 1943. Colonel Carl Storrie gave me this first ride and checked me out in the B-26. He was in command of the 387th Group, then in its first stage of OTU [Organizational Training Unit]. He took this group to England where they joined the fray on August 15, 1943. Colonel Tom Hall, my intermediary, later took the 394th Bomb Group to England, and the group earned a fine reputation for "bridge busting." One war later, Tom was killed while leading another B-26 Group in Korea. These were Douglas B-26s originally designated A-26s.

I guess the Marauder was your first and last combat aircraft?

STILLMAN : Right. I did check out in the Douglas A-26 after the war and also flew the P-51 and F-100. But as far as actual combat was concerned, the Marauder was my first and last.

Did you ferry a Marauder to England?

STILLMAN: Yes. I flew one over the southern route going by way of Natal, Ascension Island, Dakar, and Marrakech.

Did you have any contact with the pilots who were flying Marauders in North Africa?

STILLMAN: Yes, I did. In Marrakech I ran into General Joseph Cannon and he asked me how we were going to operate in England. I said I understood we were going to go low level. His reply was in very colorful terms that that would be stupid and advised me to refuse to fly missions that way. He said in North Africa low level had been fairly successful against shipping and some desert targets where flak was light but over enemy held parts of the European continent it would be suicide.

That didn't give you much encouragement, did it?

STILLMAN: No, but again as a soldier you follow the command of those who are directing things.

Putting it mildly, General, your experience with the Marauder was short and not very sweet. I understand that after the war you flew a Marauder again.

STILLMAN: Yes. In order to find out if I could still fly they sent me to Laredo, Texas, where they still had some B-26s. This was the last plane I had flown and they thought it would be easier to start with one that was familiar to me. After checking out in the Marauder they also checked me out in the Douglas A-26, which was a fine airplane.

More Background of Early Operations in England

Lt. Colonel Glenn C. Nye, former group commander of the 322nd Bomb Group, was in the tower that fateful May 17 waiting for the return of the Marauders from Ijmuiden. Brigadier General Francis M. Brady, commander of the Medium Bombardment Wing of the Eighth Air Force, was with him. Their watches told them the Marauders should be roaring into view any minute. They waited. They waited until well past the time the bombers should have returned.

Finally, Brady said, "Let's go."

They drove to Wing Headquarters and the talk soon got down to fundamentals. Should any more Marauders be sent on low level missions? If not, where could they be used? If the Marauders were not of value in the European Theater, the War Department should be told.

It was decided that the strategy of low level attack was still valid. But first the morale of the crews had to be rebuilt. Lt. Colonel Nye took over the group and began to rebuild. In the meantime, Millard Lewis (remember him from Barksdale?) reviewed the entire operation of the two fatal missions. He concluded that there was nothing wrong with the plane but it was being used in a manner for which it was not designed.

In retrospect, it is hard to understand why it took so long for the Air Force to learn a lesson that should have been evident from the beginning. Weren't the specifications put out in 1939 for a bomber to be used for medium altitude? Hadn't the experience in North Africa demonstrated that it was too costly to use the Marauder at low level? Weren't two disastrous missions in Europe enough to convince the most skeptical? But then, hindsight is always 20/20.

New Tactics — Medium Altitude

Colonel Samuel E. Anderson was appointed to lead the 3rd Bomb Wing. A veteran of missions in the Pacific, Colonel Anderson was a quiet, cool, brilliant officer who gradually saw the possibilities of using the Marauder at medium altitude. He consulted the British and their reaction was negative for any daylight bombing at medium altitude. Too dangerous. The German fighters would blast you out of the sky. They suggested night missions. But the Marauder was not well designed for night formations and besides there was not a suitable bombsight. Would the British provide fighter escort for a daylight mission? Yes, if the number of bombers was limited and they kept a tight formation.

During the next two months, Colonel Nye continued to practice low level tactics with the 322nd Group. The 323rd Group under Colonel Herbert Thatcher trained for altitudes of 8,000 to 12,000 feet. The 323rd had had some experience with the Norden bombsight — that mysterious black box that could pinpoint a target and was being used by the "heavies" (B-17s and B-24s). Strategic bombing was still the big thing and the heavies had priority on Norden bombsights. But by cajoling, begging and reportedly outright "borrowing," enough Nordens were made available for training.

Colonel Thatcher's group training with the Norden soon discovered that this was a whole new ball game. Their bombardiers couldn't hit the broad side of a bam. The navigators couldn't find a check point in broad daylight. Gunners, who until now had been concerned only with a ride, had to learn to hit German fighters flying at different altitudes and speeds than their plane was traveling.

On July 16, 1943, Colonel Anderson was ready to send his Marauders across the English Channel, this time at medium altitude and with fighter escort. The briefing was detailed. The British furnished spitfires for fighter escort and it looked like the whole Royal Air Force went along. More than 100 German fighters challenged the mission but were driven off by the spitfires. The navigators did a good job, and the pilots flew excellent formation, but the bombs didn't hit the target.

But the point had been made. The Marauder could be effective at medium altitude. Now to train the bombardiers and get some accuracy in the missions. Soon the Marauders were proving their effectiveness in driving off fighters. Teaming with British intelligence and knowledge of the German anti-aircraft guns — basically the 88mm gun — the Marauder crews learned to take effective evasive action from flak. Through the late summer and into the fall and winter, the Marauders hit German air fields in France and Belgium, gradually driving the Luftwaffe back from the coast. It was not without cost as fighters swarmed up to challenge these pesky B-26s. But the value of the Martin Company's pride was not questioned again.

A New Adventure

When I arrived on the scene in February 1944, there was no question about how we would operate. One of the ironies of the war was that we arrived in England with little practice at medium altitude. We had practiced at low level. However, our bombardiers had trained on the Norden sight. Our pilots

Flight of six from 496th Squadron, 344th Bomb Group, returning from target. Must have been a "milk run" or they would have tightened up the formation (courtesy National Museum of the U.S. Air Force).

had practiced formation flying so we were not completely unprepared. Our gunners had been trained in aircraft identification and firing at moving targets.

I consider myself very lucky to have arrived on the scene at this particular time. Losses were minimal. In the 494th Squadron we lost the two planes and crews in a midair collision over England mentioned earlier. But I am aware of only one crew lost to enemy action and that was due to poor judgment in making a second run on a target already destroyed by other flights in the squadron. Several planes were so badly damaged that they were no longer serviceable, but they brought the crews back. Losses of Marauders in the 9th Air Force were less than one percent.

The big battle with German fighters was about over. We even went in without fighter escort sometimes — not intentionally, but sometimes it was not available. The evasive action against flak worked. We learned that it took the German gunners about 30 seconds to track, load, and fire, and for the shell to reach our altitude. We didn't fly straight and level for 30 seconds.

Flying formation in a plane like the Marauder that was not very sensitive to the pilot's touch on the controls was tiring. Fighters and other lighter planes responded much quicker when ailerons or rudders were moved. At cruising speed the Marauder did okay, but it was still hard work to hold a plane in formation through constant turning. The tighter the formation the easier for the pilot, as each wingman became almost an extension of the lead plane. Pilots kept their eyes glued on the wing of the lead plane, manipulating their controls to imitate the movement of the leader. Much of the time this meant one hand on the wheel, the other hand on the throttles and, of course, both feet on the rudder pedals.

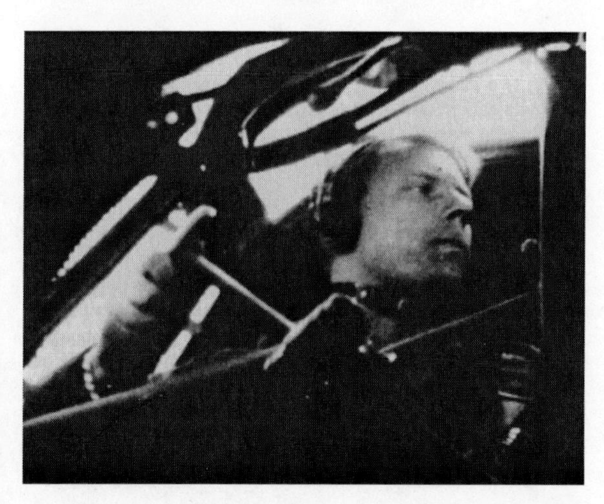

Copilot flying formation. Note concentration. Photograph taken from bombardier's compartment, 344th Bomb Group, 494th Squadron, but copilot is unidentified.

A very loose formation gave wingmen more latitude for error and they could relax some, but on the bomb run or when flak appeared or fighters were sighted, it was amazing how quickly the formation tightened up — like chicks gathering around a mother hen. It was the stray from the formation that was most likely to catch a burst of flak, and fighters looked for the plane slightly away from the concentrated fire of 66 machine guns that a flight of six Marauders provided. Add 132 more guns from the other two flights of the "box" of 18 and it is no wonder fighters looked for easier prey. A tight formation on the bomb run concentrated the bombs in the target area, as only the lead bombardier sighted. Others dropped when they saw bombs leaving the lead plane.

Can you imagine zigzagging across France for two hours in formation? Time after time we would turn the formation and see the sky blacken with anti-aircraft fire in the spot where we would have been if we hadn't turned. The pilots came home with shoulders aching from horsing their Marauders back and forth — but they came home!

Chapter 6

Combat Mission Procedures

"Left, left."
"Right."
"Right."
"Left, left."
"Right."
"I've got it now, Tom."
Click.

Doesn't make much sense, does it? To Tom, our pilot, George, our bombardier, and me it was a precision approach to a successful bomb run. Teamwork was critical on a combat mission. Each crew member had specific assignments, and their performance of any duty could determine the success or failure of the mission. As a navigator, my responsibility was to direct evasive action and to bring the formation over the initial point. George's job was to line up on the target and release the bombs. Tom's job was to fly the Marauder steady and level and command the formation. Gunners were to scan their area of vision for fighters and report flak bursts (except on the bomb run).

Intercom communications in the Marauder were less than perfect. All of us used throat microphones, and, especially in the excitement of enemy fire, conversation was frequently garbled and indistinct. We quickly learned that some type of abbreviated signals would be much more effective. As far as indicating turns to the pilot, we found that saying "left" or "right" could easily be confused, so our solution was to say "left, left" for a left turn, and "right" for a right turn. Thus, if the pilot heard only one word, he knew it would be a right turn. The amount of the turn was left to the discretion of the pilot, but it was usually a minimum of 30 degrees. Acknowledgment of the message was a click on the microphone made by depressing, then releasing the mike button.

Getting ready to fly the Marauder on a combat mission required careful attention to details. Here is a description of a typical mission in which *Tom's Tantalizer* participated.

Planning

At Group Headquarters, a squadron navigator, a pilot, and a bombardier will have been "on duty" through the night. When targets have been assigned for the next day, word comes down from Wing Headquarters giving the target, time over target for the mission, time and place of rendezvous with fighters, type and size of bomb load, and number of planes to be involved.

Beginning with the time over target, the duty navigator plots the course (place of landfall is usually given) using information on winds and normal airspeed. He works back from the time over target to arrive at takeoff time, engine start time and wake-up time. He also prepares a detailed flight plan showing headings, ground speed and turns.

The duty bombardier gives instructions to the armament crew as to bomb loading. Everyone prepares maps for briefing and notes any other useful information such as location of troops, unusual features of the target, etc.

Our crew is listed on the "loading list" at Operations, so we know we will be flying if a mission is called for the next day. About two hours before takeoff time we are awakened (if it is an early flight) by the C.Q. (charge of quarters). Dressing, but still half asleep, we stumble out to the mess hall for breakfast. Dried eggs, reconstituted powdered milk, bread and jelly, maybe sausage or bacon, and coffee get us started. Conversation is light with only a hint that we are concerned about which target we will hit. Breakfast over, we pile into a jeep or mount our bicycles and head for Group Headquarters and briefing.

As we enter the briefing room, all eyes go straight to the large map on the wall. There a red string indicates the target and route to be flown. Red circles show the location of known antiaircraft guns. By now we know where the hot targets are and where the "milk runs" are, so one glance is enough. If it's a hot one, a few appropriate remarks are exchanged about the ways of fate and how at least it's one more mission and we're that much closer to being rotated back to the States.

Today the target is a railroad bridge southeast of Angers, France. It will be a four-hour mission and we will lead the second box of 18 planes. Flak doesn't look like it will be too bad, and we will have fighter cover. Nevertheless, we plan our approach to the target carefully. As navigator, I quickly begin copying the flight plan prepared by the duty navigator. With the bombardier and pilot, I plan our approach to the target in great detail, including evasive

A group of Marauders from the 597th Squadron of the 397th Bomb Group over England heading for another enemy target. These planes with all paint removed to reduce wind resistance were sometimes referred to as the "Silver Fleet." Most Marauders were originally painted a dull green. Later some were painted with a variety of patterns as crews attempted to make them less visible to the enemy. Some were green on top to make them less visible from above and silver on the bottom to make them less visible looking toward the sky. Some green paint was on the upper side of the nose of all planes to prevent glare in the pilot's eyes (courtesy U.S. Air Force).

turns from the I.P. (initial point) to the exact spot where I will turn the plane over to the bombardier. The hotter the target, the shorter time he will take for the bomb run.

Keeping in mind that the flak gunner needs 30 seconds of straight and level flight to get his 88mm shell to us, we reduce the bomb run to under 30 seconds, if the target is a hot one. This requires careful planning. George presets windage and ground speed in the Norden, and if we roll out on the proper heading over the correct check point on the ground, he will have almost no corrections to make. It is a tribute to Tom's ability to hold the plane steady, rolling out on the correct heading, and George's ability to pick up the aiming point in the Norden quickly, that a bomb run of 25 seconds can be effective. These skills enable us to avoid losses over the target. A straight run of a minute or more gives the German gunners time to put their shots right on the formation — and those 88s are deadly. However, on this mission we will give George nearly a full minute since no flak is expected over the target and bridges look very small from 12,000 feet high.

Briefing

The briefing officer explains the mission, giving any available information about the route or conditions likely to be encountered. Since it is in support of ground troops, the "bomb line" will be marked clearly and the briefing officer warns everyone not to drop too soon and, if our plane is hit, make every attempt to bail out behind our lines (which seems logical enough). The weather man gives all information on weather likely to be encountered going out, over the target, and returning to base. This includes clouds, visibility, and any fronts likely to be along the route. Pilots are given code words for the mission and where the fighter cover will be picked up. Ordnance men explain the type of bomb being used and what damage is needed on the target, i.e., anti-personnel for troop concentrations, delayed action for gun placements, or contact fuses for bridges.

Turned at 45 degrees to the taxi strip, pilots "run up" engines checking for full power and also checking generators and other instruments waiting their turn to take off.

Major T. F. Johnson, commander of the 494th Squadron, 344th Bomb Group, in 42-107573. It was a pleasure to fly with this talented pilot.

With all this information, we load into a jeep and head for our Marauder. By this time the ground crew has loaded the bombs and the machine guns and checked out the entire plane, including radio, instruments, fuel, etc. As navigator, I fold my maps and flight log so they can be read easily. I go over the route again with the pilot and bombardier, taking special note of known anti-aircraft gun positions.

As time to start engines approaches, everyone climbs aboard and checks his equipment. I have everything I need in my maps and flight plan. I cannot use the radio, and I surely have no need for celestial navigation equipment. I have already given the pilot the compass heading to use leaving our base. I check my watch and give the pilot an indication of when to start engines. All around the field, 2,000 horses in each Pratt and Whitney engine begin to sputter and then roar as they spin 12-foot props, grabbing for air!

Execution

Commanding the lead plane, Tom waves the ground crew away and leads the second group of 18 Marauders away from their hard stands and out toward the runway. Just before reaching the runway, Tom swings the Marauder at a 45 degree angle to the taxi strip and with the copilot goes down the check list. This includes checking both magnetos, power from each engine, propeller pitch governors, position of cowl flaps, and, of course, movement of all controls. The fuel booster switch is turned on, right rudder trimmed 2-3 degrees, and wing flaps ¼ to ½ down. Moving onto the end of the runway, our Marauder takes a position on the right side. The next plane takes the left side and will be 20 seconds behind us. Waiting for the time for takeoff, the copilot checks the flare gun in the roof behind him in the event we have to abort. Unless there are further instructions there is no conversation between the tower and the pilot during this time. Everyone keeps one eye on the tower, as the signal to delay or abort the mission will be a flare from the tower, yellow to delay and red to abort.

Thirty seconds before takeoff time, I signal Tom and count down the last 15 seconds. As I reach about 10 seconds, Tom eases the throttles forward and the plane begins to roll. Fuel mixture is at "auto rich," prop governor at 2700 and engine cowl flaps are partially closed to keep engine temperature at about 70 degrees. Tom's eyes are glued to the runway, with his left hand on the control column and right hand on the throttles. Frank has his left hand on the "wheels up" lever and watches the engine gauges. As the Marauder

Grabbing for altitude, a Marauder clears the runway. Note doors of nose wheel well just closing. An M.P. is stationed at the end of the runway as security. This was part of the 344th Bomb Group in England.

rolls forward, Tom quickly moves the throttle to 52 inches and is particularly sensitive to the power those Pratt & Whitneys are putting out.

Airspeed picks up — 50, 60,70, 80 — the nose comes up and the ship thinks about flying! Now, 110, 120 — the Marauder bounces slightly — and as airspeed reaches 130, Tom pulls back on the wheel and the Marauder reluctantly leaves the runway. As soon as Tom is sure we're in the air and the props won't hit the ground as the ship settles slightly, he jerks his thumb up to signal the copilot to retract wheels. The sturdy Marauder seems to hang on the props. These are critical seconds, as one cough by an engine and the Marauder is in trouble. (One of our planes once lost an engine about two-thirds of the way down the runway. The pilot slammed the control column forward, forcing the plane onto the runway, and cut both engines. As the plane came to a stop, crewmen scrambled out of every available opening and ran for their lives. In less than one minute the load of bombs exploded and the biggest piece of the plane left was one bank of cylinders from one engine. Miraculously, no one was hurt.)

Airspeed picks up to 150, 160, 170 and everyone consciously or subconsciously breathes a sigh of relief. At least we are airborne. Tom relaxes as I hand him a cigarette.

Box of 18 Marauders of the 344th Bomb Group on the second pass over the field forming up for flight to target. Lead flight is in center with the middle plane of the front three carrying the lead crew for the box. Formation will "tighten" greatly as it approaches enemy held territory. Flight on the left is the "high flight" and will fly about 200 feet above and to the right of the lead flight. The "low" flight will be on the left and about 200 feet lower than the lead flight. If bombing is by "box" rather than by flights, all planes will fly as close together as possible to insure a concentrated pattern of bombs on the target and to evade flak and defend against enemy fighters.

Take off with a full load of bombs and fuel is probably the most critical time in any flight. The possibility of mechanical malfunctions is always present, and there is very little that can be done once the pilot has committed the plane for takeoff. Marauder crews visiting the pubs in London sometimes run into criticism from crews of the "heavies" about our short missions, 3 to 4 hours, when theirs are 8 to 10 hours long. Our reply is, "How many takeoffs and how many landings did you make?" We sometimes flew two missions a day and the takeoffs and landings are always critical.

Two minutes after takeoff, I indicate to Tom that it is time for his first left turn. From now on he will time the turns, depending upon the report of gunners as to how the rest of the flight is moving into place. Within about 18 minutes, the entire 36 plane formation is on its way to the target.

Precision Navigation Critical

When the formation is on course away from base, I nudge the copilot, and he slides back his seat so I can crawl into the nose compartment. There I check the folding of maps to be sure that I can follow the route carefully. I have already marked on the map all known anti-aircraft gun locations. In some areas I will only have a few miles' margin to avoid picking up their fire. I have learned to look directly below the aircraft to determine our position because at 12,000 feet what appears to be very close may be several miles away. To avoid ground fire I must know our exact position while directing the pilot in route to the target. As the formation climbs to altitude over the English countryside and the English Channel, the bombardier joins me in the nose compartment and checks his equipment.

Now, there are no seats in the nose compartment of the dear ol' 26! It is about 30 inches wide, about the same in height, and maybe five feet long. This space is shared with a .50-caliber machine gun, a Norden bomb sight and a control lever for operating the bomb bay doors. But this is the "workshop" for the navigator and bombardier. Get the picture? The pilot and copilot comfortably strapped in their upholstered seats, the tail and dorsal turret gunners reasonably comfortable, the waist gunner trying to get comfortable between two .50-caliber machine guns and two open hatches, and the navigator and bombardier on their knees, shoulder to shoulder arguing about the plane's position. At least it is quiet in the nose with the noise of the engines behind us. Together George and I verify landmarks and check points, and notify the pilot when landfall is sighted. This is particularly critical as there are only a few spots along the coast of Europe where there are not several 88mm gun emplacements — our most accurate and destructive enemy.

Approaching the coast, I assume direction of the flight. Remember, for effective evasive action, we cannot fly straight and level for 30 seconds. With one eye on the sweep second hand of my watch and the other confirming our position visually, I give instructions to Tom as to which way to turn, being careful not to follow a set pattern. In other words, I might give a left turn twice and right once, using any sequence to avoid a pattern and yet staying within the limits of the prescribed ground course. Gunners are instructed to report any fighters, of course, and also any flak. The German 88mm gun does not have a proximity fuse. The altitude at which the shell explodes is preset at the time of firing. The exploding of the shell, usually four in a group, is evidenced by a large black cloud. It is important to know where and when the formation is being fired upon in order to know the critical need for evasive action.

As we approach the I.P. we establish our exact position by looking straight down and picking up railroads, rivers, highways and other reference points. As mentioned, if the target is a hot one, George and I will have also marked a point on the map which will be the latest point that control can be turned over to the bombardier for sighting in on the target. Here again, evasive action is continued and the formation rolls out on its last evasive turn on the desired heading for the bomb run. As soon as George indicates he has sighted the target, he takes over for the rest of the bomb run. Today he takes over at the I.P. but continues evasive turns.

Teamwork on the Bomb Run

The Marauder does not respond well to flight control linked to the bomb sight, so directions to Tom as George works the bomb sight are transmitted to a vertical needle on the instrument panel called a PDI (pilot direction indicator). Every movement of the Marauder affects the trajectory of the bombs as they are released. On the bomb run, Tom has his eyes glued to the instruments keeping altitude, speed and attitude (wings level, no pitch or yaw) steady and following the directions of the PDI. All this while trying to ignore the flak bursting all around. Quite a trick and Tom does it very well.

One of the interesting things we found by experience was that we had to ask all crew members not to say anything on the intercom once the bomb run was begun. (One time we were on the bomb run and a gunner reported flak. The pilot thought it was the bombardier saying "turn" and we almost missed the bomb run completely. Since then, there is no conversation once the bomb run is started.)

The Norden bomb sight has two marks on its face. One is the preset

A Marauder over Europe. Tail markings indicate 344th Bomb Group and letters on fuselage are of 497th Squadron (courtesy National Museum of the U.S. Air Force).

Copilot's view of lead plane as bombs tumble out of bomb bay on bomb run. 344th 80mb Group, 494th Squadron.

Tail gunner's view of number four ship in the formation. Pilot is Major John Graves, operations officer, 494th Squadron, 344th Bomb Group (courtesy U.S. Air Force).

point at which bombs will be released, and the other is tied to the operation of the sight by the bombardier and moved gradually forward. When those two meet, the bombs are dropped. The actual dropping of the bombs from the plane takes only 2 to 5 seconds. The bomb bay doors are opened just before the bomb run starts. As George takes over, I watch those marks intersect and feel the bombs drop away, then hit the salvo switch just in case a bomb has "hung" in the racks. No one needs to say "bombs away"—although we usually do—as you can feel the ol' Marauder give a sigh of relief as she sheds 5,000 pounds of her load. George watches the bombs hit and in his modest way says it looked good. (The recon photos will prove him right.)

The first turn away from the target is a predetermined turn, and the pilot and all the wingmen know which direction the first turn will be, as it usually is a rather sharp maneuver. (If anti-aircraft fire is particularly heavy, the pilot will usually lose 1,000 feet in altitude in order to pick up some speed.) Returning from the target is a repeat of the incoming flight with turns every 20 to 25 seconds until safely across the coast of Europe or enemy lines. At that time, the bombardier usually leaves the nose compartment, and unless visibility is very poor, I turn the flight back to the pilot, who leads the formation back to base.

Combat Mission Emotions

What did I think about on a combat mission? Was I scared? Did I flinch at every unusual sound or movement? Every crewman had his own set of emotions and reactions, and the less activity you had to perform the harder it was to avoid thinking thoughts that could be upsetting. The gunners, for example, had little to do except scan the sky for fighters and report flak. Fortunately, I was busy most of the time. Climbing to altitude and before reaching enemy territory, there was little to do and too much time to think. If we were approaching a particularly hot target, I might mentally review the briefing for survival if shot down, hoping I would not have to test my knowledge.

The survival kit I carried in my flight jacket included a map, sulfa pills, a first-aid kit, a compass, and some concentrated candy. Sometimes my mind would wander and recall stories of crewmen being shot down by enemy fighters as they parachuted from a crippled aircraft. But usually I could push such thoughts back into my subconscious and concentrate on the activities at hand, whether it be reviewing the flight plan or watching other formations that might be within sight. I strongly suspect that most men offered a prayer or two during this time. I know I did.

The hardest part of any flight was the 20 to 30 seconds of the bomb run. During this brief period, there was the greatest danger from ground fire and the necessity for maintaining a steady "platform" for the bombardier, and virtually nothing you could do if anything happened. With "bombs away," tension relaxed, and I was again busy with things to do to occupy my mind. More zigzagging and home interrogation; then on to more interesting things such as eating, sleeping or going to London or Cambridge.

Chapter 7

Pre-Invasion Targets: Noballs, Rail Yards and Bridges

"Has anyone seen or heard from Johnny Eckert or Smokey Miller?" excitedly shouted Lt. Rivers as he burst into our Quonset hut returning from one of our group's early combat missions. Wondering at his concern and excitement, we replied that we hadn't. "They didn't join up with the formation above the overcast," Rivers replied with deep concern in his voice.

The tragic news that they had collided in midair and crashed, killing all aboard both planes, was soon confirmed. They were our first casualties and the war suddenly became very real. Sgt. Thompson, Eckert's radio operator, had been on our crew for the flight overseas. I had visited Johnny and his wife in their home in Lakeland, Florida. They were expecting their first baby in a few months.

People do get killed in these airplanes. So what do you do? Get scared every time you get in the plane? Refuse to fly? Cry?

No, the human mind has great capacity for absorbing jolts. I think most of us simply accepted this shock to reality as part of our destiny at the time and proceeded to live life as best we could. It is interesting that our base chapel was filled to capacity the Sunday following the loss of two crews.

This tragic accident caused a re-evaluation of the group's procedure for taking a formation through an overcast. Why the elaborate technique used on that early mission didn't work we will never know. Entering the overcast, wingmen were to turn away from the center ship 45 degrees for 30 seconds and then resume the original heading until clear of the overcast and then reform. Whether one pilot misread his compass or his clock or whether he had a defective compass are pure speculations.

One of the quirks of fate occurred as the medical team searched the wreckage for identification of the bodies. All had been accounted for except Johnny Eckert, and the squadron medical officer had given up and started to walk away. As he glanced at the ground one more time he spotted one of Johnny's dog tags. Thus, Mrs. Eckert and other members of the family were spared the report of "missing in action" and the suspense of wondering for months or years whether he was really dead.

My First Combat Mission

My first combat mission was on March 19, 1944. Our crew had been on the "loading list" for 11 consecutive days; however, bad weather had prevented any mission being flown. But now the weather had improved and we were called for briefing. The target for the day was a Noball east of St. Omer, France. Lt. Arthur Curmode was our bombardier, as George had not yet joined the squadron. (Time in the hospital with yellow jaundice and then crossing the Atlantic in a troop ship delayed his arrival in England.) Captain

Marauders over France prior to D-Day. Note the patchwork pattern of the fields on the ground. Top plane is 42-95864, *Valkyrie* (courtesy U.S. Air Force).

Two Marauders of the 344th Bomb Group, 495th Squadron. White triangle on the tail is the mark of 344th Bomb Group and the Y 5 on the side of the fuselage designates the 495th Squadron (courtesy National Museum of the U.S. Air Force).

John Graves flew copilot with us. It was a short flight—two hours and 45 minutes—and my log indicates that although some flak had been expected, we did not encounter any nor see any fighters. It was exciting to actually be over enemy held territory. The patchwork pattern of fields, the small villages and the bright sunshine gave no hint of the struggle for survival in which we were engaged. Crossing the English Channel, that treacherous body of icy cold water and unpredictable currents at 10,000 feet, looked as calm and peaceful as a swimming pool. My reaction upon returning to our quarters was, "If this is combat, I believe I can take it." Later missions were to shatter this unruffled concept. But like a rookie in his first big league game, the first apprehension and nervousness were behind me.

Noballs and V-1s

What were these Noballs that we were supposed to hit with our bombs?

All we were told at the time was that they were important targets. They were usually located in the corner of a small patch of woods—not a very big target. Later we were to learn that Noball was the code name for the launching sites of the German V-1 rocket. The sites consisted of a launching ramp only a few hundred feet long and little else. Sometimes we would drop a perfect pattern of bombs on them only to have Intelligence tell us that after reviewing the films of our hits that the launching ramp was still intact. (Films were taken automatically by certain planes in each flight.)

The V-1 was not a true rocket but a small drone plane powered by a pulse-jet engine and carrying a large explosive charge. The thing flew at an altitude of about 1,000 feet and, of course, had no pilot. When the engine ran out of fuel, controls were activated that caused it to nose down. As it hit the ground it exploded like a bomb.

It wasn't long before we saw V-1s coming over our Quonset huts where we lived. They were awesome! We never knew when the motor might stop and the V-1 would come crashing down. Crazy Americans that we were, we would stand out in the open areas watching and cheering them on "Don't stop yet!" "Keep going!" If they passed over we knew we were safe. The one we didn't see coming that was gliding toward us would be the one to worry about.

Flight of six from 344th Bomb Group. Note the mottled paint on upper surfaces for camouflage effect (courtesy National Museum of the U.S. Air Force).

I have no idea how many V-1s the Germans fired at the British countryside. In total, their damage was probably far less than that of some of the earlier manned bomber raids. But the uncertainty of when or where they would hit had a strong psychological impact on the British people — and on those of us stationed near London, which seemed to be the principal target. They were difficult to shoot down, and if they were, they still caused a big explosion wherever they hit. It was rumored that the Royal Air Force finally developed a technique of flipping them over as they crossed the English Channel, causing them to fall harmlessly in the sea. A fighter pilot would fly alongside the V-1 and maneuver the wing of his plane under the wing of the V-1, then lift the wing quickly, causing the V-1 to go out of control and crash. But there were so many V-1s that it took a lot of planes and pilots to perform this operation who could otherwise be carrying out offensive missions.

Later — in the fall of 1944 — the Germans began firing their true rockets, called the V-2. These were fired nearly vertically and came down out of the sky with no warning. You could be standing next to a building in London, and all at once that building would disappear. These V-2s carried a heavy charge of explosives and also were a powerful psychological weapon. Our squadron had moved to the Continent before these started hitting England, but we were exposed to them some as we went back to England on flak leave.

Preparing for the Invasion

With our mode of operation stabilized and with several groups of Marauders in England, including the 322nd, 344th, 394th, 386th, 387th, 391st, 397th, and 323rd, during the next ten weeks — right up to and including D-Day — we flew missions like there was no end in sight. We hit Noballs, bridges, rail yards, gun emplacements, and even returned to the E-boat pens at Ijmuiden. In 72 days I flew 24 missions. I even began to think about getting enough points to be rotated back to the States.

The Allied strategy for opening the second front was obvious in retrospect but cleverly handled at the time. Marauders knocked out virtually every bridge over the Seine River from the coast to Paris, but at the same time struck at heavy gun emplacements in the Calais and Dunkerque areas to give the impression that the landing from England would be across the Straits of Dover. Interrogation of German officers after the war showed that Hitler suspected that the invasion would not be in the Calais area, but most of his staff were fooled. A series of events and minor decisions caused the Germans to believe that the invasion would not come when or where it did.

Among the targets our crew hit during the pre-invasion weeks were

Noballs; rail yards at Creil, at Hirson, at Montigvies-sur-Sambre, and Charleroi; the E-boat pens at Ijmuiden; a gun position near Le Havre; rail marshaling yards at Cambrai; and 288mm guns northeast of Boulogne. (George was the only one to see the target. We climbed to 13,500 feet and George got a good hit. Other flights returned without seeing the target.) Also hit were the airport at Cormeilles-en-Parisis and engine sheds at Amiens (a hot one).

Did flying combat missions ever become "routine?" No! A thousands times no! Each mission had its own dose of adrenalin and its own hazards, questions and doubts. I don't recall taking any flight over enemy territory as "routine." Missions in direct support of troops close to the front line gave us less to worry about as we were over enemy territory only a few minutes; however, all missions had the possibility of tragedy.

Hit by Flak

I have mentioned the missions to Dunkerque and the fact that Sgt. Tippens was wounded. His account of that mission reflects some of the emotion and the trauma of such experiences.

> I was not flying with my regular crew but was filling in for a gunner who was ill. Flak over the target was intense and I sat at my waist gun watching for fighters and seeing the sky full of black clouds of flak. Suddenly, I felt a sharp pain in my right hand! At the same time, my right glove flashed into a ball of white. A piece of flak had ripped through its sheepskin, exposing the fleecy white interior. It looked horrible! I was terrified. I gingerly removed the rest of the glove and discovered the wound was only a piece of skin off the knuckle of my finger.
>
> What a relief! No big deal, so I hurried forward to send the usual message that we had dropped our bombs on target. I had already reported over the intercom that my hand was hit, and Lt. O'Connell, the bombardier, came back from the nose to assist me.
>
> As I was beginning to tap out the message, Lt. O'Connell suddenly yelled, "My God! Look at your leg." There was a large red spot appearing through my heavy flying suit! Despite the intense cold at the altitude we were flying, I ripped off my flying suit and sure enough a piece of flak had entered my leg!
>
> It was really a superficial wound but a very messy one. The flak sharpnel was still embedded but when we got back to the base the squadron physician required only a pair of tweezers to remove it. The interesting thing about the whole affair was that I wasn't even aware of the leg wound. The shock of seeing the ripped glove together with experiencing pain sensation in my finger effectively masked the unseen problem. It is no wonder I would always hurry to my little concealed radio compartment after bombs-away. There I was blinded from the sight of the war raging on the other side of the fuselage!
>
> The end of the story is that I was awarded the Purple Heart and given a three-day pass to London.

Parachute Built for Two

What do you do if you forget your parachute?

First you hope and pray that you won't need one. But on a combat mission that's not quite enough. You try to make some alternate plan. Tippens relates his "make do" arrangements under such a situation. He had been asked to carry the gear for a VIP who was flying with the crew, and in the process of carrying all the chutes, flak suits and other gear, felt that he had forgotten something. Going down the runway on takeoff he confided to Joe Castoro, the tail gunner, that he had forgotten his parachute. No way to go back and get it. So Joe agreed that if they had to bail out they would both hook on to his Joe's chest pack. Tippens had the harness, as that was no problem to carry and really hard to forget.

That was the plan. Well, it turned out to be a rather hot target and included some strafing at fairly low level. At one point Tippens and Joe were both hooked onto Joe's chest pack and had their feet out the waist window so they could get out in a hurry. Who knows — it might have worked!

Chapter 8

D-Day and Support of Ground Troops

"We'll go." With those simple words, General Eisenhower set in motion Operation Overlord — the invasion of Europe.

Originally scheduled for June 5, 1944, the invasion had been delayed because of what old timers called the worst weather in 50 years. Heavy cloud layers, 40 mile per hour winds, seas that would swamp landing craft and the impossibility of air cover dictated a delay. But delays could be disastrous. A full moon and favorable tides were needed and several days' delay would mean further delay until early July. Troops were already assembled. Many were already at sea.

Early on the 5th, Captain J. M. Stagg, chief meteorologist, told General of the Armies Dwight D. Eisenhower that there might be a break in the weather during the next 24 hours. At the staff meeting, opinion was divided. After hearing all the advice and facts, it was up to General Eisenhower to make the decision. It proved to be a sound one.

Around the 494th Squadron everyone knew something big was coming. As a potential lead crew, we had been briefed as to the type of target we would hit, but no times given. On June 4, Major Bill Hale and Tom invited me to go with them to visit friends of Major Hale's. It was a short flight of about 30 minutes, but when time came to return to our base, weather had moved in and we could not take off. Weathered-in, we would have missed D-Day if it had gone on schedule. On the other hand, if weather had permitted the invasion, we would not have been weathered-in away from our home field.

No problem getting home on June 5. We were immediately told to go to briefing where we were given all the details of our part in opening of the "Second Front." Excitement, apprehension, relief that we were finally going to open the second front, and yes, fear, were emotions felt by all. But now, on with the invasion!

D-Day 1944

Final briefing was early — about 3:00 A.M. on June 6, 1944 — as we were due over the beaches at 6:20 A.M. *exactly.* We already had most of the necessary information — aiming point, bomb load, etc. Our Marauders were loaded with twenty 250-pound bombs, and crew chiefs had every plane ready to go. Weather was our major concern. Clouds were everywhere and we were told that we must drop visually. We would assemble at 10,000 feet, above the cloud layer, but be prepared to descend to whatever altitude was necessary to bomb visually. Thoughts of that disastrous second low level mission to Ijmuiden by the 322nd on May 17, 1943, came to my mind, and I expect to others'. But this was the big one, and we were going.

We were to fly deputy lead to Colonel Robert Witty, deputy commander of the 344th Bomb Group, who was leading the 48 Marauders of the 9th Air Force which would hit Utah Beach. We would be number four in his flight and would take over the lead if he was forced to abort, or — perish the thought — was shot down. Under no conditions was the group to abort the mission. It had to go on even if we went down on the deck. Also, we had to be over the target within one minute of the briefed time.

As we walked to our aircraft that morning, I looked up at the sky and in the semidarkness and partial cloud cover I could hear a sky full of airplanes. An occasional running light would appear momentarily then disappear behind a cloud. I thought to myself, "How many mid-air collisions will we have today?" But there was nothing I could do about it, so as we often said, "*C'est la guerre.*" (That's the war!) And so far as I know, there were no collisions, thanks to the advanced planning, careful scheduling of flights and skill of the pilots. As we took off and headed south past the coast of England and over the channel, the sky was alive with airplanes — thank goodness most were ours!

George told me I could stay in the navigator's compartment and he would ride the nose. I would join him if we had to assume the lead. I think he just wanted more room, but it was okay with me. He was a good navigator and he would have to be there to drop our bombs with the leader. Besides, the navigator's compartment was right next to the only emergency exits — it might be impossible to get out of the nose in time.

Below the Clouds

Shortly after assembling above the cloud layer, Bomber Command radioed, "Proceed below the cloud deck!" Down we went through the layer of broken clouds. As we moved out over the Bay of Seine, I looked out of the side window of our heavily loaded Marauder and could hardly believe what I saw. Ships of all sizes and shapes from huge battleships to fragile landing craft literally blackened the surface of the English Channel and the Bay of Seine off the coast of France. We always knew the invasion would be big when it happened, but never had I seen so many ships — you could almost walk from England to France on the fleets of cruisers, destroyers, battleships, LSTs and carriers.

We were at 5,320 feet under a heavy overcast sky — 7,000 feet below our usual reasonably safe bombing altitude — not our favorite place in this war. Why do I say 5,320 feet instead of "about 5,000 feet" or "nearly 5,400 feet?" My memory suggested 4,500 feet and my notes made no mention of altitude, so I wrote George hoping he would remember. Back came a letter with the

Marauders over the invasions fleet in Bay of the Seine. Note the 24-inch black "invasion" stripes on the wings and fuselage. Stabilizer marking indicates 323rd Bomb Group, 555th Squadron (courtesy National Museum of the U.S. Air Force).

casual comment that our altitude was 5,320 feet. Not "I think it was" or "It was about this high," just the simple statement that our altitude was 5,320 feet. Knowing his ability to retain details and that as bombardier he would had to have been monitoring the altitude for use with his sighting operation if needed, I accept this figure as fact. But what a memory—that mission was in 1944!

It was now D minus 20 minutes and we were to drop our bombs at D minus 10 on the section of the Normandy Beach, labeled Utah on the east coast of the Cherbourg Peninsula. Our twenty 250-pound bombs had to be dropped before the ground troops landed. The bombs were to blow enough holes in the beach to give some protection for troops on foot—predug foxholes so to speak. This didn't seem like much, but this was all we could do for the men in green as they pushed ashore under enemy fire.

What an experience! The largest military operation in history, and we were a part of it! Hours earlier paratroops had landed on the Cherbourg Peninsula, and we hoped were assembling and moving toward the sea to meet thousands of troops storming up the beaches.

Over Utah

Over the beach at exactly 6:20 A.M. and "bombs away."

What a sight! History records that more than 4,000 ships participated in the assault. I can believe it! As we passed over the beach the first wave of troops were poised to jump off. Guns from hundreds of naval ships belched flames as they fired on shore batteries. Our gunners spotted a German fighter but he apparently wasn't interested in us. It was almost too exciting to be scared but we really were flying into the unknown.

Immediately after bombs away, we turned inland away from the beach, climbed above the overcast, and with a sigh of relief returned to England. Back in the sack in our barracks finally—we had been up since 2:00 A.M. We had been briefed the day before on what to expect, so sleep had been more of a dream than a reality. Now we dozed off and on, listening to radio reports waiting for news of Allied troops opening the second front on the beaches of Normandy. It was not long in coming. Soon the whole world knew of Operation Overlord and the Allies' invasion of Europe.

Progress of Ground Troops Now Critical

All attention now shifted to the progress or lack of progress of ground troops. It was soon obvious that while the enemy had been surprised by the

This before and after picture of an enemy bridge illustrates the tight pattern of bombs that a flight of six Marauders could lay on the end of a bridge. The bursts visible at lower left may have been from a flight that had a different aiming point or they may have missed the target (courtesy U.S. Air Force).

location of the invasion, he was far from defeated. Coastal defenses were stubborn and weather was about as bad as could be imagined. The time of events now was frequently expressed as D-plus the number of days after 6:30 A.M., June 6, 1944. D plus 2 brought heavy winds, storms, and seas that swamped boats and tore up temporary docks. The British troops were stalled outside of Caen and the Americans fought bitterly for a foothold on Omaha Beach.

A tribute to Peyton Magruder by the officers of the 397th Bomb Group. Magruder rode with this group on D-Day over the beaches of Normandy (courtesy Peyton M. Magruder, Jr.).

Marauder crews were eager to give support to the ground troops. We welcomed targets such as gun emplacements and troop concentrations where we could see and know that we were helping our infantry and artillery move inland. Our fast, sturdy Marauders were well suited to this task. We could go in by flights of six and bomb gun emplacements or bridges with precision or we could go in by boxes of 18 and saturate an area with antipersonnel bombs. With the enemy busy defending against advancing troops, we encountered less and less flak. Fighters were not a problem, as they apparently had more pressing tasks than challenging our Marauders with all those .50-caliber machine guns. We could carry small 100-pound bombs or if necessary, huge 2,000-pound block busters. And because of our speed we could be briefed and over a target more quickly than any other bomber. Many of our missions were less than three hours from takeoff to landing.

Our squadron flew a second mission on D-Day, but my crew did not participate. On D plus 1, we led the second box of 18 to a gun position near Cherbourg. Because we would be over land only a few minutes, I operated the "Gee"—a prelude to radar—and George again had the nose compartment to himself. Weather was bad with heavy clouds and we went in at 6,000 feet.

More Bridges to Hit

On D plus 6 we again led the second box, and the target this time was a vital bridge at Conde-sur-Noireau about 40 miles south of Caen. Bombing by flights of six, we left the bridge still standing, but the town was no longer useful. The next day I flew with Major Hale and the target was a road junction at St. Pierre south of Caen. Swinging inland over the beaches, we turned back toward the sea and made our bomb run. Our bombs were left of target but still effective. Lt. McConnell was Major Hale's bombardier. We circled the target three times waiting for the first box to drop their bombs.

It was about this time that Tom decided I should not fly with any other crew because I was building up points too fast and might be rotated home before he accumulated enough missions — 65 — to earn a trip to the States. That was okay with me. I didn't care for the idea of flying with different crews, especially when it resulted in two missions a day.

On D plus 18 our crew led a box of 18 Marauders on a mission to knock out a gun position south of Cherbourg. It was on a hill, and George laid our bombs right on the target. We were told that the ground troops took the hill immediately after our strike. These missions close to the coast were short and we flew down from England over the Bay of Seine and then swung inland for the bomb run. The steady flying of the pilots and the careful sighting of the bombardiers resulted in effective action against the enemy. Navigation was not difficult, as we had learned the details of the coast by heart. Visibility had improved and the weather began to cooperate. Ground crews kept our Marauders raring to go, and enemy action against us was almost nonexistent.

On July 8, we led our squadron on a mission to destroy a bridge north of Chartres, about 50 miles southwest of Paris. Since we were over enemy territory for much of the mission, we continued our evasive action, although most of the 88s were busy with ground troops. Clouds obscured the target, so we circled three times and finally George found a break in the clouds and picked up the aiming point. The bombs were slightly short but still caused much damage. After dropping our bombs, we circled again, as one flight had failed to pick up the target, then joined up for the flight home.

A railroad bridge southeast of Angers, France, was our next target, as the 9th Air Force continued to harass enemy transportation. Leading a box of 18 planes, George laid our bombs on the bridge and one more obstacle was placed in the path of the enemy's movements.

Our bombardier, 1st Lt. George Eldridge, showing his skill at "bridge busting" as we attack a railroad bridge at Wolksmarsen, Germany, on March 19, 1945. The first bomb from our plane hit the aiming point; this photograph shows the pattern engulfing the end of the bridge and the abutment when we dropped all our bombs. This concentration of bombs was made possible by six Marauder pilots flying almost as one plane. Each flight of six planes in the box formation would move into a trailing formation at the initial point, then the lead bombardier in each flight would sight for his flight of six. The group reassembled into the box of 18 formation after leaving the target (courtesy U.S. Air Force).

This war was now beginning to show real progress. The beachhead was well established. Cherbourg had been captured and supplies were flowing to ground troops. General Patton was sweeping across France almost unopposed. It seemed inevitable that Germany must surrender soon. Our crew continued flying missions in support of ground troops. In late September, the 344th moved to Pontoise, France — a short drive northwest of Paris. Pyramidal tents pitched in a patch of woods became our quarters and Paris became the place of diversion in place of London. Tippens soon made friends with a French family and quickly mastered the language. He was to learn later that his French was quite different from that his mother had been teaching for years. They really had trouble communicating in French when he returned home. Most of us were content to sightsee and shop in Paris and learn only the necessary phrases of French to get by.

Life on the Base

I had a sweetheart waiting for me in Texas. My day to day goal was to finish this war and get sent home. If that meant flying two missions each day, so be it. In the Mission Logs that accompany this book I often used the phrase "let's go home" or we will cross the coast and "go home." My real home was a few thousand miles away. But being with friends and those who had similar reasons for being here created a temporary home, however.

The camaraderie of these men provided the comfort of home and substituted for kinfolks and close friends. We all slept in tents or temporary housing. We ate the same food. I remember watching a healthy airman watching the cook unwrap a recently arrived package of meat. It was several pounds of choice T-bone steaks.

"Are we having steaks for supper?" asked the airman.

"No, we don't have time to prepare steaks so we'll grind them up for hamburger."

"What a shame! I could fry one in my tent."

Wrapping four steaks in a newspaper, the chef handed the package to the airman, "You just found this but not here."

"Thank you, it must have fallen off a delivery truck."

The airman and three buddies had a steak dinner. But most of us had glorified hamburgers.

Flak Leave

Away from black bursts of anti-aircraft fire, away from sweating out fighters, away from powdered eggs and milk, cold meals, and all male company — that's "flak leave."

The Air Force probably called it R&R for rest and recuperation but we knew it as flak leave. It was a pleasant change from the pressure and routing of fighting the war.

We spent our leaves either in Aberdeen, Scotland, or at large castles and estates in western England. I don't remember names, if I ever knew. We usually stayed a week and spent our time sleeping, eating, playing croquet, shooting skeet or just loafing. Red Cross girls were hostesses and provided an excellent change from talking and looking at only males. I can't say that we returned to the fighting war with renewed vigor and enthusiasm, but flak leaves did provide a break and a chance for nerves to relax.

Tom's Tantalizer's crew was on flak leave at the time of the breakthrough of ground troops at St. Lo in July 1944 and again just before VE Day in May

Another view of "Headquarters" and entertainment while on flak leave.

1945. In fact, we were in London the evening of VE Day and witnessed the celebration in Trafalgar Square.

Bomb Line Watchers

"Let's go up to Group [Headquarters] and check the bomb line" was a common suggestion of our crew as the ground troops pressed on across France and toward the Rhine River. The large map in Group Headquarters had a red string (sometimes a grease pencil mark) that showed both the front line of our ground forces and a line slightly behind this which indicated the line before which we were not to drop our bombs under any condition, thus avoiding hitting our own troops. We became avid "bomb line watchers." Every mile the army advanced brought us closer to the end of this ugly war and a chance for us to go home.

Can I Borrow Your Plane?

Marauder crews usually flew together and in the same plane. Sometimes crews were shifted, and when necessary a crew would take a plane other than the one assigned to them. For example, we flew Major Hale's plane *Suzzane* on D-Day for reasons lost in my memory. We had become well acquainted

Returning from a mission, a Marauder prepares to set down on the runway. Note nose high attitude of plane and M.P. for security. This was part of the 344th Bomb Group.

with 42-210573. Tom knew its little flying peculiarities. George and I had made little modifications to the nose, like adding a piece of armor plate on the floor and arranging our flak suits along the side. It was "our ship."

One bright October day, Corky took 42-210573, better known to us as K9-B (the designation painted on the side in huge letters), on a mission since his regular plane was being repaired. Being generous, we were glad to loan his crew a good Marauder, but we were really upset when the 494th returned from the mission and Lt. Korkowski told the control tower the wheels on K9-B would not lower.

"Use the emergency hand crank," instructed the tower.

"Will do," replied Lt. Korkowski.

About 20 minutes later, Lt. Korkowski reported, "No can do, nothing works."

"How's your fuel supply?" inquired the Tower.

"We will have about 30 minutes left."

"What do you want to do?"

"We'll burn up more fuel; then request permission to bring it in, wheels up, on the runway."

"Roger. Give us a call when you're ready. Runway will be clear and emergency vehicles standing by."

"Roger."

By this time we were all watching and fussing at Lt. Korkowski for messing up our airplane. Flak had not been heavy on the mission but apparently ol' 573 had taken a hit in a vital place.

As we gathered at a safe distance and yet with a good view, we watched Lt. Korkowski bring the Marauder around on final approach. He came in high until he was sure he would make the runway, then dropped the nose sharply. Fully committed and over the end of the runway, he cut both engines. Fire was the big danger and by cutting the engines the manifold would cool and reduce the chance of a fire if gas tanks ruptured.

The Marauder looked like a duck coming in for a landing. Props slowly windmilling and Jack holding the nose up as long as possible, 573 settled on the runway tail first, and quickly skidded to a stop. Beautifully done! The crew scrambled out and the emergency vehicles, not now needed, rolled away.

There sat our beautiful Marauder on its belly with the tips of the props bent. No other damage was apparent. Investigation by the ground crew found one flak hit — on the hydraulic cylinder controlling the lowering of the wheels. One lousy hit and a ruined airplane. Engineering would not okay it for flight without a structural test and that would take time and there was no shortage of planes. It is interesting to remember that the first Marauders in combat flying out of Australia didn't let a belly landing stop them. One Marauder survived four such landings and kept on flying. Ground crews would jack up the plane, repair it, and a crew would take it up in the wild blue yonder again. There were no replacement planes then.

The generous Army Air Corps soon found us another plane — a B-26G (serial number absent from all my records) and we began test flights and familiarization with the new Marauder. It had increased wing incidence of 3½ degrees and several electrical features, including bomb bay door operation not used on the B-26C. Tom did not find the flying characteristics much different on the G model. It would take off and land at a slower speed, but Tom didn't change his routine appreciably.

Battle of the Bulge

Suddenly in mid–December we were jolted from our routine and made vividly aware that this war wasn't over yet. Reasonably comfortable in our tents a short distance from Paris with our potbelly stove helping us to tolerate some miserable winter weather, we suddenly found ourselves digging foxholes and checking our .45s.

"Germans in American uniforms have parachuted near Paris and could

A snowball fight in France. It was fun at the time but we were soon to learn that this storm was cover for the enemy's last offensive of the war — The Battle of the Bulge. Heavy snow and thick overcast skies were to keep our Marauders on the ground when the infantry and artillery were in desperate need of air cover and support.

invade our base at any moment," was the word from Group. What a horrible turn of events! But nothing compared to what was happening in the Battle of the Bulge. Only later were we to learn of the heroic struggle and huge losses among the ground troops.

We flew one mission on December 23 — a pathfinder mission — and then our crew was briefed on operation Clarion and grounded from combat missions until that all-out mission was flown. The 494th flew many missions as the enemy was stopped, pushed back and badly beaten in the Battle of the Bulge. Again, bridges were primary targets to hamper the movement of retreating German troops. But the crew of *Tom's Tantalizer* watched from the sidelines. We flew training missions and dropped practice bombs but supposedly we knew too much to risk being shot down and interrogated. We waited nearly two months to fly this mission, as near perfect weather was needed. Tom, George and I had about decided that they had forgotten it and that was all right with us. But more on this later.

We flew four more missions in March and April, going deep into Germany on four-hour missions again hitting transportation facilities. We had almost no opposition, but we were briefed to surrender only to the Luftwaffe, or if that was not possible, to surrender to the Wehrmacht. It was very dangerous to be captured by civilians or the SS. It was reported that emotions were running very strong against any airman, partly because of the intense bombing, but we were told also it was because some pilots had strafed civilians. It was a bad situation. A hopeless one for the Germans.

Why wouldn't they give up?

Chapter 9

Missions I Won't Forget

The human mind is a marvelous machine. It can erase from our memory events and facts that we don't like and it can recall in every detail other events that took place years ago. For example, my mind will let me forget which tool I walked to the garage to pick up. Yet it will help me recall a target we hit years ago. I have a vague idea of what route we took on many missions, but for others I can trace the exact path we traveled on today's map, even to locating the heavy flak areas. The missions I remember most vividly were not necessarily the most spectacular or the most dangerous, but they were the ones that apparently made the deepest impression on my mind's memory bank. Of course, D-Day will always remain as the most spectacular and the most historic. It may have been the greatest military event of the century. The missions to Dunkerque were remembered for the intense enemy fire. Here are some more that are etched in my memory.

The Bridge at Koblenz

Even if I could forget this one, George wouldn't let me. It was a hot one and my performance as a bombardier's aid wasn't up to George's standard. We were flying out of the airport at Cormeilles northwest of Paris, and it was after lunch when our crew was called to lead the second mission of the day for the 494th Squadron. There was a heavy overcast and to add to the confusion our regular plane, *Tom's Tantalizer*, was down for repairs. We were assigned a late G model with more electric controls for the bomb bay doors than we were accustomed to.

Climbing up through about six thousand feet of overcast, we emerged on top to find that our flight of six was the only one of three in our box of 18 still with us. The others had aborted for one reason or another — mostly because they lost us in the overcast. In addition, fighter escort was nowhere in sight. Tom's call to Bomber Command brought the reassuring answer, "Don't worry, fighters are above you. Proceed to target."

Ground troops were within 100 miles of the target, which greatly reduced our time over enemy territory, so on we went, all six of us, to "strike a blow for democracy." Leaving the I.P., we begin to pick up flak, and it was intense on the bomb run. Black bursts of 88mm shells filled the sky around us. The new ship had bomb bay door controls on my side of the nose compartment so following George's instructions, I flipped the switch to open the bomb bay doors. As soon as the bomb sight indicated that the bombs had dropped, I hit the salvo switch just to make sure all bombs were clear of the bomb bay.

Ground fire continued to be intense even as we turned off the bomb run. We could hear shrapnel peppering the Marauder. One burst broke a hole in the Plexiglas in the nose and I saw a piece of shrapnel on George's wrist. "You've been hit." "You have too," he exclaimed as he picked a tiny bit of metal from my eyelid.

We zigzagged back across enemy lines and our gunners reported that the number six plane piloted by Lt. Webster S. Allen was leaving the formation, apparently hit. We learned later that it had taken a hit in the bomb bay that started a fire. The copilot, Lt. Fred Fubel, put out the fire but the pilot was barely able to nurse the crippled Marauder back across our lines. All but one gunner who "froze" and would not jump and the pilot, who stayed with the plane too long in order to steer it away from a village, parachuted safely.

Back at our base, we learned that the mission was an exercise in futility. Our bomb bay doors didn't open until I hit the salvo switch (how was I to know that I had to *hold* the bomb bay door switch down until the doors were completely open?), so everyone salvoed bombs all over that part of Germany as we were in a sharp turn at the time the bombs were released. George never let me forget how I fouled up a perfectly good bomb run.

Operation Clarion

Probably the most memorable mission other than D-Day was on February 22, 1945. Germany was near defeat. The Battle of the Bulge was over and Allied troops were advancing almost at will. SHAEF (Supreme Headquarters Allied Expeditionary Forces) had decided that an all-out attack against transportation facilities would deal a death blow to the enemy. Our crew was to lead our group. We were to bomb targets by flights of six, then peel off and strafe the target! Shades of Ijmuiden and no Marauders returning! This is the mission our crew was briefed on late in December 1944 and then pulled off all combat flights so we couldn't be made to talk if shot down.

Well, bad weather was the order of the day and, as mentioned earlier, we sat around the base for nearly two months while the other men were logging missions and accumulating points for rotation to the States.

One bright morning about 3:00 o'clock, the charge of quarters shook me and said, "Time to get up." I sleepily mumbled, "You've got the wrong bunk. I'm not on the loading list. " "Your name is Moore, isn't it?" "Yes, but I'm briefed on another mission." "I know," he said with a smirk, "and that's the one they're flying today."

ANOTHER IJMUIDEN?

They're really going through with this thing, I thought to myself as I hurriedly dressed. It was supposed to be an all-out effort with every available plane in the 8th and 9th Air Forces participating. Almost every rail yard, bridge and cross road in Germany was to be hit. Here we were with the war almost over and me with nearly fifty missions and points enough to be discharged if this silly war was over, and we were going out on a mission that called for our "slow" Marauder to strafe. The last time this was done, the Marauders were cut to ribbons.

B-26G on the ground at Martin's Baltimore plant. Note the .50-caliber "package guns" on the fuselage between the cockpit and the wing. These could inflict awesome damage on strafing targets (courtesy Lockheed Martin).

Briefing was thorough and explicit. Our target was deep into Germany. Not many gun positions in route but peeling off and strafing was an unknown, or rather, all we did know was bad. As Tom led our group down the taxi strips past the ground crews and other flight crew members, the expressions on their faces were not very encouraging. And the sincerity with which friends wished us well was not a morale booster. After all, everyone knew what happened at Ijmuiden.

Remember I mentioned that it was best to stay busy so you didn't have time to think? Well, on this mission we had about thirty minutes straight climb on course over friendly territory—and I hand plenty of time to think. You've heard that men pray in the face of danger. I prayed many times, but I think this time I put more urgency in my petition to God to let me return from this mission alive. Stories of answered prayers occurred throughout the war, and I assure you on this occasion I had an immediate feeling of security and lost all doubt as to my safe return.

A Norden in My Lap

The flight to the target was uneventful. All guns were test fired, including the fixed forward ones operated by the pilot. George picked up our target—a rail junction—and dropped our bombs. I knew he had been dying to use that .50-caliber in the nose since he started flying the Marauder, and he had given me specific instructions about what to do to stay out of the way after he dropped the bombs. The Norden bomb sight was in the way of effectively using the nose gun. So as soon as he dropped the bombs, George unhooked the Norden and handed it to me—with the gyros in it still spinning at about 3,000 rpms. As a result, my experience of using the nose gun consisted of holding a wildly spinning bomb sight while George fired away.

When our ammo was gone we climbed back to our comfortable altitude of 12,000 feet and headed home. We saw no enemy, had no fire returned and saw no enemy fighters. All of our Marauders returned home safely and all in the 9th Air Force, except one. Another group lost one plane to ground fire as they strafed. Operation Clarion was over, and life returned to near normal. Friends welcomed us back to base with a big smile and rousing cheer. The mighty Marauder had done it job again.

Round House at Calais

More than 200 P-47s went with us on this one. What a show! The target was less than 100 air miles from our base and just a stone's throw from the point of England nearest to occupied France.

As part of the continuing diversion to make the Germans think the attack of the Continent would be by the shortest route — across the English Channel — the 344th was ordered to bomb the railroad round house at Calais on May 9, 1944. I was to fly with Major Hale, with Major Smith as copilot and Lt. McConnell as bombardier.

The flight plan called for swinging south of London across the channel and making landfall between the mouth of the Somme River and the little town of Berck. We would then swing north, avoiding the heavily defended area around Lille, and make our bombing run toward the channel on a northwesterly heading. The flak guns were so thick around Calais that the briefing map was solid red in that area.

Enter the P-47s. As we began our bombing run and the enemy's 88s opened fire, the P-47s were to dive bomb the gun placements, enabling us to make a safe and accurate run.

Did it work? You bet it did! No sooner had we sighted flak than those beautiful, wonderful P-47s peeled off and headed down toward those enemy gun positions. And that was the last we heard of flak on that mission. It is my recollection that no planes — either Marauders or Thunderbolts — were lost. Our bomb rack malfunctioned and we had to salvo the bombs, thus hitting slightly over the aiming point. We were all ready to sign up the fighters for every mission.

Pillbox on Utah

Drop 2,000 pound bombs from 3,000 feet? We had never done that, but this German pillbox on the coast above Utah beach east of Valognes had been holding up ground troops for eight days. Naval guns — even those from the battleships — had been unable to silence fire from this vantage point over the beach. So SHAEF called on the Marauders to see what they could do.

For sheer excitement this mission takes the cake. Here was an opportunity to really give the ground troops a hand. But we had never dropped 2,000 pound bombs from 3,000 feet — the altitude clouds dictated that we fly. How strong would the bomb blast be? Would it bounce us out of formation? Could the bombardiers pick up the target soon enough at this low altitude? Could they use the Norden sight?

These were unanswered questions, so Tom, who would be leading the 494th, worked out a procedure with our flight. We would approach the target from the sea and drop by flights of six. Each Marauder would be carrying two 2,000-pound bombs. George calculated the time it would take the bombs to reach the ground after releasing, and it looked very much like the formation

Marauders of the 344th Bomb Group lined up waiting their turn for takeoff (courtesy National Museum of the U.S. Air Force).

would be directly over the impact area when the bombs exploded. To avoid this, Tom told the pilots in our flight, especially our wing men, that he would count to three after bombs away, then bank sharply to the right. This meant each bombardier in the other planes of the flight would have to be sure and drop as soon as they saw George's bombs drop and the pilots would have to be ready to make that sharp right turn. Tom told the right wing man, "Just get out of my way." The formation would reform after leaving the target and return to England.

It worked beautifully! Eighteen planes dropped thirty-six 2,000-pound bombs on the pill box. We had no opposition, and although the pillbox was still standing, Intelligence reported that all personnel in the fortification were causalities from the concussion. We were all proud of the following commendation from our group commander.

> 1. On 14 June, 1944, Major THOMAS F. JOHNSON, 0-659307, with 1st Lt. CARL H. MOORE, 0-685694, as his navigator and 2nd Lt. GEORGE W. ELDRIDGE, 0-741494, as bombardier, led a box of eighteen airplanes in an attack against a gun position on the Cherbourg Peninsula within our own lines, and which was causing much trouble to ground forces.
>
> 2. The importance of this target could not be overemphasized, and the results obtained by Major JOHNSON and his flight; Captain CURTIS S. SEEBALT, 0-727270, his bombardier, 1st Lt. EDWARD E. HARRISON

0-429587, and the members of his flight were excellent with several direct hits scored on the briefed MPI. The attack had to be perfectly timed and carried out without error. The results obtained by this flight and others, resulted in this highly fortified position being captured by the ground forces immediately following the attack, after its impregnable stand for a period of eight days under constant Naval shell fire.

3. Therefore it is my desire to commend these members of your squadron for the excellent results achieved by them in helping to destroy their briefed target....

REGINALD F.C. VANCE
Colonel, Air Corps, Commanding

Toome Field, Ireland, and Aberdeen, Scotland

This was not a combat mission but a flight on which I was as scared as on any mission over enemy territory. The things men will do against their better judgment is amazing. On June 26, 1944, Lt. Wilber Kolberg and Lt. Fred Schnubel invited me to go as navigator on a trip to take some men on flak leave. En route to Aberdeen we were to stop over in Ireland and drop off one man there for his leave.

The weather over England was not good. Lots of clouds and no sign of improvement. But we were taking an AT-23, the stripped down model of the B-26, so we didn't think we would have any problem. Besides, the men were eager to go. Flying time to Ireland was less than two hours and another hour and half would put us in Aberdeen, where we would spend the night.

The flight to Ireland was uneventful. We put Sandy out with his gear and went into operations to file a flight plan for Aberdeen. Weather was getting worse. Ceilings were less than 300 feet and visibility only fair with some fog and rain. That should have been enough to stop anyone with good sense, but we were young and we had a crew that was anxious to get to Aberdeen. Besides, we didn't want to spend the night at Toome. So, we took off.

I decided to ride the nose so I could pick up check points easily. The flight across the North Channel to Glasgow was okay. But then things got worse. The ceiling dropped to almost tree top level, and Lt. Kolberg had to go on instruments. Undaunted, I said I would direct him, so up a valley we went. Fortunately, I had a good map. We often couldn't see the tops of the hills on either side but I could still see ahead and the map showed that we could make it up the valley.

We had almost crossed Scotland when we came to a fork in the valley. Which one to take? There was no turning back now. We could not go up on instruments in the clouds, as we didn't have clearance. We couldn't go up in the clouds and out to sea because we didn't have clearance to cross the coast from the North Sea. And the British were very fussy about letting unidentified planes cross the coast.

"Which valley do we take, Moore?"

"Ah — the right one, Willie."

No sooner had he committed the Marauder to the right valley when it became obvious that I had made a mistake. We were heading into a dead end!

"Wrong one," I shouted. "We have to take the left one!"

Willie wheeled the Marauder in a left turn at about an 80 degree bank, nicely clearing a church steeple. Back on the correct valley, we soon broke out of the clouds enough that it was possible to see Aberdeen and land.

Reporting to operations, we commented that we had encountered some bad weather and had flown pretty low.

"Ah, yes, we've been plotting you," was the Scotsman's calm reply, just as though it wasn't unusual for them to keep track of those crazy Americans and their Marauders.

Two days later weather cleared and we went back to A-169 a wiser and a thankful crew. I don't know who had been the most scared on the flight — me (who hoped the map was right and that I could direct a plane going 220 miles an hour around the hills and church steeples), the pilot and copilot (who were on instruments), or the other crew members (who didn't even know what was going on).

Marauders Are Tough

From the summer of 1943 to VE-Day, May 8, 1945, Marauders and their crews did the impossible. Holes in the wings, engines shot out, wounded crew members, landing gears stuck, and shattered controls, and still they flew home after hitting critical targets. Every squadron had its own library of "you won't believe this" stories. We had a pilot abort a mission when one engine quit. Spotting a fighter field, he approached the runway only to get a red light from the control wagon at the end of the runway. So he poured the coal to the good engine and went around again with a 5,000 pound load of bombs and nearly a full load of fuel. Approaching the runway the second time, he got a green light to land from the tower. When the plane was safely on the ground, it was discovered that the only problem with the other engine was that someone had hit the switch controlling the flow of fuel to that engine and shut off the fuel.

Another time our returning Marauders found our home base with visibility and cloud ceiling too low for landing. "Go anywhere you can find a

Captain Curtis Seebalt, 344th Bomb Group, 494th Squadron, bringing his wounded Marauder home from a mission to a target on outskirts of Paris. The left engine was hit and caught fire. The Marauder's fire extinguishing device put out the fire but the engine was "through for the day." Note prop of left engine is feathered.

Truman Committee **returned from a Noball mission in February 1944 with numerous flak holes (arrows) and a shattered nose glass. The plane was named in "honor" of the Congressional group that investigated the combat fitness of the Marauder in 1943.** ***Truman Committee*** **was written off in May after flak damage caused a crash landing; the crew was shaken but safe (courtesy Peyton M. Magruder, Jr.).**

field open," was the control tower's instruction. Two of our pilots found the same field and proceeded to put their Marauders on the runway—one from each end and passing each other in the middle. Is that why they trained pilots to always land on the right side of the runway?

This overmodified output of the Martin Company's production line, in the hands of skilled and disciplined crews, survived incredible damage. As we turned off the bombing run on a mission to hit rail engine sheds at Amiens, France, we noticed one of the planes in our formation swinging wildly from

Opposite, bottom: **Damaged but not defeated! Somewhere behind the enemy lines in Normandy, Nazi flak gunners had torn to shreds the tail of this Marauder from the 573rd Squadron of the 391st Bomb Group. Using his engines to control turns, Lt. Col. John S. Samuel of Hinsdale, Illinois, brought this crippled Marauder home and made a safe landing (courtesy National Museum of the U.S. Air Force).**

one side to another. The pilot headed for Maston, England, the emergency field just across the Straits of Dover. We learned later the plane had been hit heavily. The pilot had rudder control only, with trim tabs and limited elevator control. Both engines appeared to be hit but continued to run. As the pilot approached the field at 9,000 feet (that's what he said), one engine quit. Dropping rapidly, he made a turn to line up with the runway and the other engine quit. Tower personnel estimated the plane's speed at over 200 mph as it passed the tower. Crashing off the end of the runway, it finally came to rest and all crewmen scrambled out safely. The pilot's comment to the squadron commander as he stopped by Operations on his way to Cambridge for a date was, "Sorry about losing that airplane, Chief."

The mighty Marauder continued to make friends with crewmen as she demonstrated an amazing ability to absorb damage and still fly home. Coming home on one engine, while not routine, was expected; holes in wings as big as a football; damaged controls; shot out cylinders on the engines; and blown tires all failed to halt this solid, determined defender of freedom. It was even reported that they would be good dive bombers, as one fearless pilot took one up a few thousand feet, dropped the nose into a power dive (thrilling a group of friends on a nearby airfield) and pulling out at the last moment. He didn't even notice that his Marauder knocked the antenna off the control tower.

Chapter 10

VE Day and Home

At last, the war in Europe was over!

How do you describe the end of nearly five years of bitter fighting that had seen disastrous defeat (at Dunkerque), bombing of civilians, recovery and ultimate victory? Relief? Joy? Thankfulness? Numbness? I do not think the mood in Trafalgar Square, London, the evening of May 8 was typical. It was a boisterous, noisy, celebrating crowd. But to the U.S. and British soldiers and airmen it was a quiet feeling of relief and thankfulness. Each had his own thoughts, but I suspect that common to all was the thought of those who had paid the ultimate price for this moment of victory and a silent "thank you" to them. Why were we spared? Only God in His wisdom would know, and behind it all there must be a purpose.

Our crew had been on flak leave in England and was in London when news of the surrender of the Germans became generally known. Many of the details of that night are vague. Etched in my mind is the scene in Trafalgar Square in the heart of London. Crowds milled around singing, shouting, climbing up the side of buildings and generally whooping it up. I do not recall seeing any men in uniform in the crowd. Probably there were some but most were civilians. They tried to turn on the lights in the buildings. But after four and a half years most of them would not function. We watched from our hotel room and went to bed early, thankful for the end of a struggle that had claimed millions of lives and changed the quality of life of many who survived.

The next day we returned to our base near Brussels and waited for the word that we would be sent Stateside. As a safety measure, all planes were grounded for two days. I do not recall any great celebration among the crews, but headquarters wasn't taking and chances of crew members taking to the wild blue yonder in an inebriated condition.

Volunteers for the Pacific?

Remember Colonel Vance — the escapee from Corregidor? He was now wing commander and had often mentioned that we should hurry up and finish the war in Europe and get on to the Pacific "where the *real* war was being fought." It was only a few days after VE Day when word came through the grapevine that Colonel Vance was forming a group of volunteers to go directly from Europe to the Pacific. That was farthest from the thoughts of any crew member I knew. But how do you say no to a wing commander — especially if you are a squadron commander like Lt. Colonel Tom Johnson? The simplest way is to avoid being asked. So the control tower at our base had instructions to call all squadrons and alert them as soon as they recognized Colonel Vance's plane approaching the field. Surprisingly, Colonel Vance could never find any of the crews around to invite to the "real war." We had only one thought — going home. Tom learned that orders had been cut at least once sending us to Paris for transportation home, but someone pulled our names off the order. George didn't have enough points to leave yet, but Tom told me and John Graves to have our bags packed ready to leave at a moment's notice. We were all for that.

We had been flying a few pleasure trips in our Marauder just for fun. Not long ones — just an hour or two. On one trip we flew over the Ruhr Valley to see the damage. I will always remember flying over Cologne, Germany, and seeing almost total destruction of the city but with the famous cathedral still standing apparently undamaged. What a tribute to the accuracy of bombing crews and artillery!

Tree Top Level Again

A tragic and useless event occurred about the third day after VE Day. Orders came to have crews practice low level flying!

Would we never learn?

Why such an order was issued I do not know, but a replacement crew that had just arrived from the States went out on a low level training flight, taking several crew men "just for the ride." Flying the Marauder at tree top level (and below) required thorough knowledge of all the plane's flight characteristics and a steady and alert hand on the controls. Experienced pilots had great respect for the Marauder and what it would and would not do. One characteristic was well known — this medium altitude bomber was slow to respond to a tug of the wheel in clearing objects at low level. In other words, it tended to "mush" when the pilot hauled back on the wheel.

This crew never made it back. The report said the plane failed to clear a tree and crashed, killing all aboard. I did not learn whether orders were changed, as we left soon after that, but it certainly took the edge off of our celebrating the end of the war.

Homeward Bound

June 15, 1945 (about mid-morning, if my memory is correct), Tom came running into our Quonset hut waving a piece of paper and said, "Grab your bags and let's go." In his hand were orders sending us to the States! It didn't take but a few minutes for us to be out the door, into a jeep and out to the waiting Marauder for a flight to Paris and transportation home.

The trip back to the States lacked the excitement and suspense of the flight to England 18 months earlier. Twenty-one days aboard a Victory ship with a top speed of eight knots was a far cry from flying in a Marauder, but it was a welcome change. VJ day occurred while I was on R&R leave, and it was back to the life of a civilian for me, a wiser and more mature young man. Two years with the Marauder, 18 months of it in combat, had given me a new sense of values, a greater appreciation for life, and friends and experiences that would last a lifetime.

My journey into civilian life began with a commercial airline flight to Detroit. The first bus back home to Quincy, Michigan, left the next morning. When I arrived in Detroit it was after midnight so I took a nap in the park. On the bus the next morning we stopped at every crossroad along the way before finally arriving in Quincy. A telephone call to Mom and I was home.

Author receiving the Distinguished Flying Cross from Major General Samuel E. Anderson.

Dad was in the midst of harvesting the wheat and oat crops. The weather was good but it was critical that the harvest be completed before it rained. I decided to stay three days and help Dad. I called Popsy, my Texas sweetheart, and she said it would be o.k. to stay and finish. What would I have done if she had said she would be "busy" after three days? I would have found the fastest way to Tyler.

Popsy and I had parted July 22, 1945. The time through October 17, 1945, was a period of high intensity for the nation and for the world — the end of four and a half years of bitter and devastating war. For me, it was a welcome relief that I could resume life as civilian. Would it mean Popsy and I would resume our courtship? I fervently hoped so.

I took the next train to Tyler, anticipating an emotional reunion with Popsy. It bad been eighteen months since we had seen each other. The train did not go to Tyler but stopped at the small town of Troup, 20 miles southeast of Tyler. Passengers for Tyler made the final miles by bus. Popsy met me at the bus station, but her greeting was less expressive than I had built up in my mind. Then I remembered, Popsy did not like to reflect her emotions in public. She had her car so I took the driver's seat.

"Do we go to Mary Lee's [Popsy's aunt] house or to your apartment?"

"To Mary Lee's. I didn't renew rent on my apartment. I didn't think we would want it this year."

"You are right. I hope we will have our own home this year; like maybe next month!"

Things were looking up.

"1 know the rest of the family wants to greet you. Then I want to take you into Mary Lee's sun room and give you the welcome I didn't want to give you while the world looked on at the bus station."

I thanked Caroline Jo (Popsy's cousin) for her support during my absence and Popsy told the family that we would be in the sun room and not to bother us. She took my hand and walked us into the sun room, where we had spent many happy hours. Putting emotions and actions into words is not easy. We embraced each other and found that our kisses were as thrilling as ever.

Tom's Tantalizer Crew Following the War

Tom Johnson, pilot, squadron commander and recipient of the Distinguished Flying Cross (DFC), Croix de Guerre (French), and Air Medal with eight oak leaf clusters, returned to civilian life following the end of World War II and was involved in several business operations. Tim, his oldest child, was born during World War II and subsequently Pat, Peg, and twin girls,

Jane and Joan, were added to the family. He boasted 11 grandchildren. He and his wife, Mary, resided in Batavia, New York.

George Eldridge, bombardier and also recipient of the DFC, Purple Heart and Air Medal with eight oak leaf clusters, remained in the service following World War II and attained the rank of colonel. He attended Air Tactical School and was a member of the first full class of navigator bombardier-radar operations trained for the B-47 bomber. After teaching in the school for four years, he flew as crew member in the Strategic Air Command for five years. Another five years in headquarters of the 8th Air Force and six years as a missile squadron commander were enough, and he retired in 1969. He moved to Nampa, Idaho, where he sold cars, built racing cars, and did some racing himself. He and his wife, Elena, have five children. As of the date of this writing, George and the author are the only known surviving crew members.

Dorr E. Tippens, radio operator and gunner, and recipient of the Purple Heart, DFC, and Air Medal with twelve oak leaf clusters, and the only one in our crew to score a "probable" on an enemy fighter, returned to school following World War II and obtained a bachelor of science degree in chemical engineering from Purdue University. Following an additional year of graduate work, he joined the American Sugar Refining Company with which he has been associated since. Professionally, he has developed several improvements in operation of plants, plus a U.S. patent for a new process in the production of dry brown sugar. He was married to the former Doris Willsey, with whom he had three children and two grandchildren.

In his own words, he was an "incurable hobbyist" and listed the following among those which he pursues whenever possible: photography; wine and beer making; camping; fishing; exotic aquarium fish breeding; music; cabinet building; horticulture; real estate development; and just for fun — skiing, sail boating, dancing, hiking, jogging, and golf. No wonder he got bored on our dull missions!

We have all lost contact with the other gunners, **Joseph Castoro** and **Charles Calkins**, and have been unable to obtain any information on their post–World War II activities.

A man who was not a regular crew member (he had his own crew) but frequently flew copilot was **John C. Graves**. He and Tom served together as instructors at Barksdale Field prior to going overseas. John remained in the military service after the conclusion of World War II. He received a regular commission during the first postwar integration program, and later attended the Air Tactical School, Royal Air Force Staff College (Bracknell, England), and Air Command and Staff School at the Air University. When he resigned his commission in the U.S. Air Force in 1954 to enter the construction field, he was Director of Operations and Training at Headquarters, Air Proving Grounds Command. Last he served as a construction analyst in the loan guaranty division of the Veterans Administration in Houston. He had two daughters and one son.

Chapter 11

After the War

When the earlier version of this book was published in 1980 there was one Marauder left that was restorable to flying condition. When I went down to look at it, I had not seen a Marauder in nearly 30 years. Visiting the Confederate Air Force in Harlingen, Texas, I saw that familiar cigar-shaped fuselage standing in the comer of the hangar. Resembling a lost child in the corner, my old friend was minus its left engine, an ugly black nose had replaced its smooth clear Plexiglas front window of the bombardier's work shop, the top turret was missing and there was a door cut through the radio compartment. But there was no mistaking the clean lines of the fuselage and the high tail. It dwarfed the P-51, P-38, and several restored Navy fighters sharing the hangar. This was not the "combat model"

Restored tail gunner's turret on a Marauder at the Confederate Air Force (now Commemorative Air Force).

Nose of the Marauder at the Confederate Air Force (now Commemorative Air Force). Much work yet to be done.

that I flew, but its survival marked an important link to the history of this great plane.

Memories of people and places flooded into my mind — Dunkerque — Utah Beach — Koblenz — the never ending sea — crew members and friends whose skill and sound judgment under fire were the difference between life and death. From the depths of my mind, events long forgotten sprang to life. Walking around to the nose of the Marauder I could almost see George and me crouched over the clear Plexiglas, maps in hand, carefully checking highways, rivers, towns, and a hundred other check points as we picked our way through the flak free paths over France and Belgium.

Did I want to again climb up through the nose wheel well and soar into the wild blue yonder with my friend of hundreds of hours? Not really. Fifty combat missions and hours of training are enough for one lifetime.

Visiting the Confederate Air Force again in 1979, I asked the colonel at the reception desk (everyone in the Confederate Air Force is a colonel) if I might take some pictures of the Marauder being restored. He readily agreed, and I strolled out into a hangar sheltering a P-40, a twin Mustang, a Hellcat, and a Bearcat. Over in the corner waiting to be dressed in its combat clothes

Turning a Marauder into an executive plane has really made the restoration job difficult for the Confederate Air Force. Sponsors for the restoration had already completed plans for closing this ugly door and another Pratt and Whitney R-2S00 engine sat nearby ready for mounting.

was the Martin B-26. Her tail turret had been restored and two mock .50s protruded from the tail "stinger." The dorsal turret was in place and several electronic harnesses were being rewired.

The ugly black nose cone was gone and strange (to me) radar equipment was sitting where George and I had knelt as we led our group over Europe. The door was still cut through the radio operator's compartment, and much of the right wing skin was off and the left engine was missing. But over to the side sat two Pratt & Whitney R-2800 engines ready to be mounted—one obviously for a spare, as the right engine was in place.

Talking with Colonel Jerry Harville, project officer for the restoration of the Marauder, and with other persons at the Confederate Air Force, I learned the story of the airplane.

The Confederate Air Force's Marauder

Built at the Omaha plant in 1943, serial number 41-35071 was assigned to this plane when it was accepted by the Army Air Corps on May, 24, 1943.

The "41" prefix to the serial number denotes the year in which the contract for that plane was awarded. There were 175 Marauders built under this contract. The story of this plane during the next two years is lost in the records of the Air Force. Almost certainly it was used for training purposes, as no Marauders were returned from the war zones.

Decommissioned on April 23, 1974, number 41-35071 shuffled around looking for a home. At one point it was even raced in the Bendix air race under the name *Valley Turtle* while owned by Allied Aircraft Company in California. One race apparently convinced everyone that the Marauder was not a racer, as that is the one and only time it was reported in such an event.

Next stop appears to have been in Houston with the Tennessee Gas and Transmission Corporation, where it was converted into an executive plane. That was in the 1950s. During the next several years it went from one owner to another, including a tour with Pemex, the Mexican oil firm.

Almost Deserted

In 1967, officers of the Confederate Air Force learned that this plane was for sale by the State Bank of Greeley, Colorado. The bank presumably had loaned money to the owner of the plane and, unable to collect the loan, had taken title to the Marauder. With a check for $12,500 in hand, Colonels Vernon Thorp, Gary Levitz and Lefty Gardner went to Colorado, bought the

In gleaming white paint, Colonels Vernon Thorpe, Gary Levitz and Lefty Gardner bring the Marauder to Rebel Field, Harlingen, Texas, to add to the stable of World War II planes already restored and flying. Note that cover for the left main gear is missing. The plane had been badly neglected passing from one owner to another with little maintenance being done (courtesy Commemorative Air Force/ Confederate Air Force).

plane, and after a day checking it out, flew the Marauder to Harlingen, Texas, where it took its place with the other war birds of World War II. The plane was in very poor condition and to add to the problems of restoration the right landing gear gave way a few months later during a routine engine run-up. The main spar of the right wing was damaged, and it has been necessary to have a new one forged.

Restoration continued and this plane indeed flew again, but its story came to an abrupt end on September 28, 1995. The reconstructed B-26 owned by the CAF crashed, killing five aboard and totally ending any thought of further reconstruction. Vernon E. Thorp, who piloted the restored B-26 on its fateful flight, told a reporter of the *San Angelo Standard-Times* that he would be working on stalls and steep turns. The National Transportation Safety Board report of the incident stated:

> Witnesses observed the aircraft approximately 250 feet above the ground heading toward the southwest. As the aircraft passed overhead, the "engines were sputtering." Approximately ¾ mile from the witnesses, the aircraft made a "sharp" right turn, nosed down, and impacted the ground. The engines "quit" prior to the aircraft turning right. According to the operator, the flight was in preparation for a flight evaluation for the pilot-in-command by an FAA inspector. The pilot reported to Departure Control that he would be "working on stalls and steep turns," and the pilot was instructed to "maintain VFR at or above five thousand five hundred." The pilot-in-command had accumulated approximately 500 hours in the B-26. Prior to the accident flight, he had flown the B-26 once since October 8, 1993.

Shortly after being delivered to the Confederate Air Force the plane's right landing gear collapsed during a routine engine check (courtesy Commemorative Air Force/Confederate Air Force).

That flight was on September 26, 1995, for a duration of 30 minutes. Prior to the flight the fuel tanks were "sticked" and the total fuel was approximately 720 gallons of 100 octane low lead avgas. Examination of the airplane and engines did not disclose any pre-mishap discrepancies. Due to the extent of damage, flight control continuity could not be established.

The Marauder that had served brilliantly as it brought crews safely home with holes in its fuselage, engines and hydraulic lines and with an injured crew member aboard, if it could talk, would have complained: *Don't make me do those maneuvers. I'm not built for them. Keep me straight and level and I will bring you home. If you violate my limitations I cannot promise to keep you safe.*

Number one in official flying instructions for the Marauder says "all acrobatic maneuvers are prohibited." The National Transportation Safety Board reported that the cause of the crash was at least in part failure of the pilot to maintain minimum air speed for flight, resulting in an inadvertent tail-spin." The crippled Marauder was forced into a sharp right turn and impacted the ground nose first. Thus, five lives were lost, thousands of dollars of donations for restoration and hundreds of volunteered man hours of labor were gone forever.

I have thanked the Lord many times for my privilege of flying with Tom Johnson as my pilot of our sturdy and reliable Marauder. He had learned

A front view of the crippled Marauder at the Confederate Air Force. The folding door cut into the radio operator's compartment is clearly visible. Despite discouraging accidents like this and much needed repair throughout the plane, restoration continues (courtesy Commemorative Air Force/Confederate Air Force).

what the Marauder could do and demanded it do its part, but he knew its limitations and respected them. As a result, we flew safely the thousands of miles from Florida to England despite an uncooperative engine over the Sahara Desert and an unpredicted head wind over the North Atlantic. During fifty combat missions over France and Belgium evading anti-aircraft fire and the ever present possibility of enemy fighters, there was never a doubt in my mind of Tom's ability to bring us safely home.

The Confederate Air Force, now known as the Commemorative Air Force, is still in business with headquarters in Midland, Texas. At last count, it had 167 planes in various stages of restoration.

One Last Marauder?

Fantasy of Flight in Polk City, Florida, likely has the last B-26 Marauder that will ever be flight worthy. This is what they have to say about their plane:

Martin B-26 Marauder
Year built—1940
Wingspan—65 feet
Cruise / Top Speed—210 mph / 315 mph
Gross Weight—27,220 lbs.
Engine—2 Pratt & Whitney R-2800s (1850 hp each—original) (2000 hp each—current)
Armament—2 – .50 caliber machine guns in Martin turret
3 – .30 caliber machine guns in nose, ventral and tail 3,000 lbs. of bombs

General History

The Marauder was designed to meet the U.S. Army Air Corps demand for a high-speed medium bomber. Martin's proposal was considered to be so far in advance of other proposals that the company was awarded an "off the drawing board" contract for 201 aircraft in 1939. The first production B-26 flew by year's end. Testing confirmed that performance had been achieved, but at the expense of low-speed handling characteristics. Training accidents multiplied and an investigation was set up to consider whether or not to stop production. It was decided to introduce modifications that would improve its slow-speed handling qualities. Later aircraft were built with longer wings, a lengthened fuselage and larger vertical fin and rudder. B-26s saw combat in the South Pacific as well as in North Africa. Over 5,000 Marauders were built and it went on to have the lowest combat attrition rate of any American aircraft in the 9th Air Force.

Personal History

This particular aircraft has a fascinating history. It was one of the 201 early short-wing aircraft built and was #103 off the production line. Months after the attack on Pearl Harbor, the Americans were deeply concerned that there

Sitting on jacks, number 41-35071 awaits more funds for complete restoration.

might be an attack on Alaska. Many aircraft were flown up for defense, including B-26 bombers. In February of 1940 this aircraft was leading two other B-26s from Edmonton through the Yukon Territory on their way to Alaska. Lost with marginal maps and deteriorating weather, the decision was made to force land while they still had fuel and light. This aircraft was the lead aircraft and landed first. The decision was made to land on what looked like a smooth valley floor with the landing gear down. This proved to be a serious mistake. What had looked like grass protruding out of the snow turned out to be the tops of bushes protruding out of deep snow! Touching down, the aircraft came to a very abrupt stop. The nose-gear collapsed, the pilot was thrown out the windshield and co-pilot Howard Smiley was left trapped in the wreckage. Realizing the mistake, the other two aircraft made smooth belly landings with their landing gears in the up position. Co-pilot Smiley was cut out of the wreckage and, after a few days, the crews were found and provisions were dropped off. Smiley was flown out for medical treatment by a bush pilot while the others trekked several days to safety.

The three aircraft sat in the "Million Dollar Valley" until the early 1970s when collector David Tallichet sent a crew in to retrieve them. Built up from the best parts, this aircraft was restored over a 20-year period by volunteers. In 1992, with less than 30 hours total airframe time since factory-new, it flew again for the first time in over 50 years. In 1994, Kermit acquired the aircraft along with Tallichet's B-24. Not content with the condition of the aircraft, Kermit hired Aero Trader in Chino, California to do a major inspection on it. Two years later, and after an additional 6000 man-hours of work, the aircraft was flown to Fantasy of Flight in 1997.

Soon after its arrival, a very historic reunion took place. Co-pilot Howard Smiley, who just happened to live in Tampa, Florida, came to Fantasy of Flight and met up with the old friend he had crashed in, 57 years ago! Howard passed away in 2000.

Kermit Comment!

There are only six B-26s left in existence and this is the only one capable of flight.

Because of its small wing area, the B-26 was nicknamed the "Widowmaker" and the "Flying Prostitute" (i.e., no visible means of support)! MacDill Air Force Base in Tampa was the main training base for B-26 crews during the war. Because of a short series of training accidents after take-off, the undeserved phrase "One a Day in Tampa Bay" came about. In 1998, I flew this aircraft into MacDill for their annual air show. This was the last B-26 to ever leave a MacDill runway. We departed without a problem so hopefully the curse has been broken [courtesy of Britani Taylor, Fantasy of Flight, e-mail to author on May 21, 2012].

These B-26 Marauders, lined up at attention near Landsberg, Germany, march one by one to the salvage pile to be blown up for scrap after still-needed parts have been removed by the mechanics of the United States Air Force in Europe. This is only one of several such scenes in Germany where obsolete combat aircraft of the Army Air Force were salvaged (courtesy National Museum of the U.S. Air Force).

These war weary B-26 Marauders were headed for the scrap heap at Landsberg, Germany, one of several salvage depots of the U.S. Air Force in Europe where obsolete aircraft were scrapped to save American taxpayers a tremendous bill for storage, maintenance, and guarding. Explosive breakup saved thousands of man hours of labor and material (courtesy National Museum of the U.S. Air Force).

What a pity that at least one of each of the World War II planes was not placed under protective custody of a museum. Hundreds were literally blown up and used for scrap. All Marauders overseas at the end of the war were destroyed, and those in the States soon became fuel for the scrap furnaces. But in 1945 no one was interested in anything but getting the men back home and beginning the rebuilding of areas blasted by the war and our own civilian economy. Preserving the now surplus fighting machines was farthest from most Americans' thoughts.

This is my story. My relationship with the B-26, known as the "Marauder" is finished. To cite a quote of a survivor of D-Day, "It was worth a million to be a part of the war of the century but it would take several million to get me to do it again." The crash of the last B-26 reminds me of the age old saying, "The sea is terribly unforgiving of mistakes." The same can be said of the air.

Part II : Logs, Specifications, Charts and Miscellanea

Chapter 12

Mission Logs

In telling my story, I gave more details about three missions; D-Day, Clarion and Pill Box at Utah. This was not to imply that the other missions were not important. Every mission was important. Reviewing old files I discovered a stapled file that had hand written notes and a rough diagram of each mission. These were written after each mission and are supported by a pilots' log and my memory of the events. A discussion of these missions is shown on the following pages. Though I still have the maps, they were hand-drawn, in pencil, and thus impossible to reproduce here.

At the start, we were flying out of Stansted Mountfitchet, a Royal Air Force (RAF) base just North of London. The army designation for the base was Army Air Base #169, though it was commonly referred to as simply "Stansted." We lived in Quonset huts and flew off of parallel paved runways. Since the Marauder had an effective range of around 500 miles, one way, most of our missions were aimed at Northern France and Belgium.

Mission #1

Date: 19 March 1944
Target: NOIS de HUIT RUES (Noball) (N.E. of St. Omer)
Crew: Johnson, Graves, Curmode, Moore, Castoro, Calkins, Tippens
Position: Number four in first flight of second box.
Length: 2:15

Our first combat mission. We had been on the loading list for eleven consecutive days and had loaded in the airplane seven of those days only to have the mission scrubbed. We were flying deputy lead so we had little to do except to stay in formation. The target was in an area where flak could be expected but we saw none, and immediately decided this war wasn't so bad after all. It was strictly a milk run with no flak and no fighters. Our reaction at the first view of the continent of Europe—France in particular—could best be described as a mixture of curiosity and fear.

From our few map study classes we knew what the coast line would look like and were a little surprised that it looked exactly like we expected it to. We saw nothing whatsoever on the ground and passed within sight of Dunkerque where for a fleeting moment we remembered the fateful days a few years ago when we first heard of Dunkerque.

Mission #2

DATE: 20 March 1944
TARGET: CRIEL MASHALLING YARDS (Thirty miles north of Paris)
CREW: Johnson, Willms, Curmode, Moore, Castoro, Calkins, Tippens, Vellesco
POSITION: Deputy to Hale in first box.
LENGTH: 3:45

We were flying deputy to Hale again so we more or less went for the ride. The extra radio man stayed at the radio and the other man went to the waist gun—a new wrinkle in our routine. This time we made landfall near Dieppe, another place that looked so innocent from 12,000 feet but would be a place of fierce fighting later. Some flak was thrown at us as we crossed the coast but very little, and from my position in the navigator's compartment I saw none. It was a beautiful day and we could see for miles. Making our turn on to the target we were only about 15 miles from Paris but could not quite see the town. Our bombing run was good and Curmode did a good job. Hudgins up in the high flight released early and quite by accident hit a bridge. Other bombs hit in the area and the second box hit a surface mine of some sort of down to the left of the target. An uneventful trip and one more mission on the chart.

Mission #3

DATE: 25 March 1944
TARGET: HIRSON MARSHALLING YARDS (in northeast France)
CREW: Johnson, Wills, Curmode, Moore, Castoro, Calkins, Tippens, Campbell
POSITION: 1-1-4 deputy to Hale, who led group.
LENGTH: 3:20

We flew deputy to Hale and we followed the 322nd group. Weather was good and we saw a lot of France. I'm afraid there were times when all the towns looked alike to me. Coming out the 322nd went over Bandidier and lost two ships from flak. I didn't see either of them but heard the gunners describe them. The war immediately took on a more realistic aspect. Prior to this time Tom and Willms had not put on their flak helmets because they were a little uncomfortable. But when those ships went own I immediately saw two arms reaching back for helmets. Our evasive action increased 100% from that time on Ackerman (Sam), who was navigating for Hale, took us on out. We didn't see any more flak thrown at us but the mission had made the war much more real and made us all firm believers in evasive action.

Mission #4

DATE: 26 March 1944
TARGET: E-BOAT PENS
CREW: Johnson, Willms, Curmode, Moore, Castoro, Calkins, Tippens
POSITION: 3-1-4
LENGTH: 3.35

This was a maximum effort mission and all medium bomb groups in the 9th Air Force—including 700 Marauders—were sent to the same target. Personally, I wasn't interested because I was coming down with a case of ETO [European Theater Operations] laryngitis. We were flying deputy to Hale in the third box so I didn't bother to work very hard. We were briefed that the target would be well defended. On the bombing run (made from the sea) I wrapped in a flak suit and watched the bombs drop. They hit short and right. They said there was a solid cloud of flak. I did hear and feel some of it but didn't get up to watch it. No one was hurt and we made it home o.k. All 14 direct hits were made on the pens by the attacking forces. No apparent damage was done to them. Surrounding buildings were hit and destroyed.

(I went to see Dr. Seelinger, squadron doctor, after the mission and he put me in the hospital for a week. Must not have been serious, I was flying again after the week.)

Mission #5

DATE: 8 April 1944
TARGET: HASLETT MARSHALLING YARDS
CREW: Johnson, Major Smith, Curmode, Moore, Sgt.
POSITION: Led second box behind Norgard.
LENGTH: 2:55

What a day. Strictly a tour of Belgium. We were following Norgard and

Offenburg—an arrangement we were later to become quite familiar with. Weather wasn't very good and we made landfall at only 10,000 feet. Norgard wasn't any higher so we could not get any higher. Just after landfall we started evasive action and some flak started coming up. To be honest, I wasn't sure where we were but I noticed the compass read almost south for too long a time. Finally we left the first box and turned left planning to pick them up on a turn. About this time we went on instruments in a cloud layer and decided to go home. I told Tom to turn left and we would go north to the course out and back.

We soon broke out of the clouds and by some miracle we had our box still intact. We zigzagged north hunting for an air field where we could drop our bombs and came out close to Antwerp. Major Smith saw the air field first and called our attention to it so we headed west. I wasn't doing very good job at pinpointing myself up to that time but had a pretty good idea of our location. As we came out, we flew parallel to the Schelde Estuary and it appeared that we were paralleling the coast. Major Smith's map had been cut off just below the Estuary and he was sure we were paralleling the coast. He called every few minutes to ask if I knew where we were (by this time I did for certain) and was I sure I knew where we were. I must have made it convincing because Tom flew my heading (he always did) and we soon saw the coast. We made evasive turns to the right to avoid Blankinberg, a heavily defended naval base. They threw up a little flak but we were out of range. We returned to base, bombs and all, without further incident. We were mighty thankful to be home but highly P.O. not to have dropped our bombs.

This fact continued to be a sore spot for several days, as the first box had continued east down and around Brusells and finally dropped their bombs on Goxyde air field on their way out. Five other boxes had gone on to the target and bombed. Hell was raised about us all the way from General Anderson. (We were just happy to be home again.) It later developed that we had gone over Gourtral and Lillie and by all rights we should have been shot up badly. I'm not sure who was scared worst, me or the rest of the crew who thought I was lost, or myself who knew I wasn't sure where we were. Flak was as thick as clouds. The sky between us would turn black with flak. How we got through it and back home without serious damage, I'll never know.

Mission #6

Date: 11 April 1944
Target: MARSHALLING YARDS—Montique
Crew: Hale, Aultman, McConnell, Ackerman, Moore (Gee operator).

POSITION: Hale led group.
LENGTH: 3:20

I was "Gee" [Gee was a prelude to radar] man and saw practically nothing except the Gee screen. I learned considerably by listening to the conversation on interphone between Hale and Ackerman. I took fixes as far as possible but the signals faded out soon after getting over enemy territory. There was a cloud layer below us but Mac got his away just as clouds covered the target. We couldn't see where they hit. Second box got lost joining up and went by the "Hook of Holland." They finally found themselves and bombed the target. From the pictures they took over the target, the bombs looked good.

Mission #7

DATE: 13 April 1944
TARGET: LE HAVRE COASTAL GUNS
CREW: Seebalt, Sandstrum, Eldridge, Moore
POSITION: 2-2-1
LENGTH: 2:45

We were leading the high flight and Tom was riding with Aultman leading the second box. The target was covered with clouds and we were unable to drop. However, landfall was a little unusual. In fact, the whole trip was a series of ups and downs — literally. We climbed to 14,500 to go over a cloud bank even before we reached the coast. Just at the coast we had to go up or down so down we went — 230 mph to 9,500 feet and we went on to the I.P. [Initial Point], a point on the Seine River below LeHarve, getting a little flak from a field division. From the I.P. we climbed up on top of the clouds at 11,500 but could not see the target. It would have been suicide to go under the clouds.

We had three A-20s with us which went in a few minutes ahead of us with window [chaff] and the flak became quite inaccurate. Coming home we went back to 14,000 feet to get over the cloud bank again. Later we learned that one of the A-20s got lost in the clouds and made an approach to Cherberg thinking it was England. Cherburg almost let him land but when they started shooting at him he got out of there.

Mission #8

DATE: 18 April 1944
TARGET: MARSHALLING YARDS — Monseau-sur-sambre Charleroi
CREW: Johnson, Sandstrom, Eldridge, Moore.

POSITION: Deputy lead to Hale
LENGTH: 3:00

Target was on SW side of town and the run was uneventful. We bombed as briefed with excellent results. On return to our field we left the formation because the left engine was losing power. Nothing serious. No fighters. No flak.

Mission #9

DATE: 20 April 1944
TARGET: COASTAL GUNS SW OF LE HARVE TROUVILLE
CREW: Johnson, Smith, Eldridge, Moore
POSITION: Led second box behind Pathfinder
LENGTH: 3:10

This was our first experience following a Pathfinder and we were quite skeptical of the results we would obtain. The Pathfinder crew was at the briefing and explained what we should do. The boxes were going in fifteen minutes apart and one Pathfinder was assigned to each box. We loaded in our Marauder and paused on the end of the runway timing our take-off. We faced the same emotions each time. Join up and the trip down were uneventful. They flew number two position until we left the English coast, then we dropped back and followed in a number 4 position on them. We knew they would take a long bombing run and we were praying for no flak. It was uneventful.

The weather wasn't too good with some middle clouds and it looked like it might be closed over the target. George followed the Pathfinder all the way down and all of us did all the way back. The clouds broke at the target and we could have bombed visually.

The Pathfinder bombed the wrong target and missed it a mile.

Mission #10

DATE: 20 April 1944
TARGET: NOBALL NW OF ST. OMER
CREW: Johnson, Smith, Eldridge, Moore
POSITION: Led second box.
LENGTH: 2.30

The weather cleared out during the day and we were sent out in the late afternoon to get this Noball. It was so close to St. Omer we knew it would be hot. We tried to plan our evasive action to avoid as much as possible. Join up was o.k. and we spaced ourselves far enough behind the first box led by Norgard so that we could take our own evasive action.

Visibility was not over four miles because of haze and we had some trouble picking up check points. We turned a little past my ETA [estimated time of arrival] to turn and started for the target. Finally George said he saw it and took over. In the meantime, flak started coming up and it was pretty accurate. All the enemy gunners must have been on "active duty." George saw the bombs hit and they were o.k. I got a glimpse of target as we passed over it. The ship had been hit some but not seriously. Tom made a screaming left turn then back to the right. We made for the coast west of Dunkerque and we came home in one piece. However, one piece of flak came in just ahead of the co-pilot and knocked the light off the control column and gave Major Smith a good scare.

Tom said he thought Major Smith was hit at first. The piece of flak was found in the doorway to the nose so it must have glanced off my back. The ship had eight holes in it — none serious. Capt. Johnson, Harvey Johnson of the 496th, went down out the first box. The first box had been crowded off the target on their bombing run and nearly ran over Calais. They were shot up considerably and did not drop. Results of our box were excellent, putting a good concentration in the target area; one side of our bombs failed to release. George salvoed them. They made a direct hit on a buzz-bomb ski. From now on we felt like veterans.

Mission #11

DATE: 22 April 1944
TARGET: NOBALL (north of Dieppe)
CREW: Johnson, Sandstrum, Eldridge, Moore, Sgt. Diery (that's all)
POSITION: Led high flight of first box.

This was one for the books. It was milk run but if the truth had been known at the time, what fun there would have been. Everything was o.k. until we got to the airplane and found no gunners. A quick mental check revealed that they were on their day off. What a surprise. Too late to get more gunners even if there had been any extras. We finally borrowed Sgt. Diery, who was flying as an extra radio operator with Captain Steen, who was flying deputy to Hale. No escape kits and no candy bars, and with one gunner off we went unto the wild blue yonder. We finally decided that Diery would take the turret, I would take the tail guns and George would stay in the nose. I gave Tom my maps and flight plan and Diery briefed us on emergency radio procedure. Fortunately, it was a milk run with no fighters and no flak record straight.

Mission #12

DATE: 22 April 1944
TARGET: NOBALL—SERRA COURT (near Poix)
CREW: Seebalt, Peters Eldridge, Moore.
POSITION: Led high flight in first box
LENGTH: 2:15

This time we were sure there was a full crew so I didn't ride as tail gunner but instead carried a K-20 camera and rode back in the camera hatch. I gave all my maps to Peters and briefed him on our way back. I scrambled back of the waist guns to keep out of the way of Sgt. Tracy at the waist guns. I had my chamois liners to my gloves but they proved to be inadequate at that altitude and being almost in the slip stream. My hands soon started to freeze and it was a battle all the way over and back to keep them from freezing completely.

I would take a picture and make sign language to Tracy, and he would call it up to George on the interphone. It was really fun taking pictures of anything military. Flak was heavy over the target but I didn't get any good picture of that. I missed a strike photo of the bombs because of the evasive action. Kieslowski, in the second box, went down. Gorski was with him. Ship caught fire and doubtful if any up front got out. We had a hole in the tail that cut the top of Sgt. Griffith's cap. It was a rough one and bombs were just over. Some, in fact most, of the damage was done by one flight. We were out of position so our pattern was behind the others.

Mission #13 (or 12-A)

DATE: 25 April 1944
TARGET: CRISBECQ C/D GUN (on Cherbourg Peninsula)
CREW: Johnson, Col. Vance, Eldridge, Moore
POSITION: Led second box.
LENGTH: 3:10

We had to be good this morning. The "Old Man" was with us to watch. It was a very difficult target to pick up because there were no nearby reference points. George and I studied the target photos and found one object—a long terrace-like affair that showed up in the picture. The trip down was o.k. but it looked like the target would be covered with mid-clouds. We came around on the I.P., which was the inlet to the base of the peninsula and started on a heading to the target. We couldn't pick up the A.P. [aiming point] I finally saw the terrace but not in time for a bombing run. George saw the target as we passed over it and quickly turned to make another pass at it. The first box was doing the same thing so we followed around. This time we took a long run and knocked the target out. Going back, "Bandits" were reported to be in the vicinity and some gunners reported seeing them follow us. We decided it would be best to let down over south England. Tom started circling through hole in the clouds. Col. Vance said, "Hold a straight course," so we went down on instruments. We made it o.k. and proceeded back to base.

Mission #14

DATE: 27 April 1944
TARGET: CAMBRAI MARSHALLING YARDS
CREW: Moore, Sgts. Castoro, Calkins, Tippens
POSITION: Led second box.
LENGTH: 3:00

Not very exciting but a long ride.

Mission #15

DATE: 30 April 1944
TARGET: NO BALL—RUSSELLVILE
CREW: Johnson, Seebalt, Eldridge, Rivers, Moore
POSITION: Led second box.
LENGTH: 2:30

As usual we caught the Sunday morning ride. The target didn't look too bad but we were briefed that there was a field division north of Berks-Sur-Mer which was on our course. We went in far enough behind the first box to take our own evasive action. Visibility was good and George picked up the target quite a ways out, although it was very difficult to see. It looked very much like any one of the small villages near it.

We took a good run and I saw the place the first box had bombed pass under the nose and George had not dropped yet. He insisted he had the right target so I didn't argue with him. We made a hard 180 and headed back for the coast. We turned short of Berks-Sur-Mer to cut off Norgard and get back with him. This was a mistake, as someone took a few shots at us. No one was hit but it stepped up our evasive action.

Back at interrogation the fight was on as to who hit the right target. Both Parrish and George insisted that they did and Offenburg swore they were within five miles for sure. (They were.)

The picture proved George was right and Parrish wiped out a French village. Our bombs were on the target but missed vital areas.

Mission #16

DATE: 2 May 1944
TARGET: VALLENCIEMS MARSHALLING YARDS
CREW: Hale, Graves, McConnell, Rivers, Moore, Sgt. Castoro, Tippens, Calkins.
POSITION: Led the group.
LENGTH: 3:00

The mission started out as a mid-day affair but with a three hour delay, it ended up a late afternoon one. It was delayed because of cloud cover over the target. We kept hoping it would open up because it looked like a milk run.

It was my first trip with Hale and I was a little concerned about how we would get along. Having flown as G operator once with them, I was familiar with their procedure and everything went o.k. We were two minute early at #7 and by dog-legging, we came around and finally made fighter rendezvous at N. Foreland only a minute early. Rivers checked my landfall with the Gee box and we came in just west of Nieport near Farness. The route into the target was quite long as we went in north of it and circled down east and south coming in on a heading of 315 degrees. Visibility was good. It was rather easy to pick up check points along the way. As we passed north of the target, the 386th was just hitting the target and a large cloud of smoke was rising to about 8,000 feet. We passed over several "juicy" marshalling yards and made a note for S-2. Mac took over as we passed the I.P. and came within sight of the target. Since we were bombing by flights, numbers 2 and 3 broke off to make their own runs. There was no flak at the target and Mac set everything up on a long bombing run. As we approached we could see large fires burning in the yards, and just before we released a large oil dump exploded with a large ball of flame.

Mac laid 'em in right on the engine shed and the other flights added their bombs to the "party," blowing the place sky high. Tippens reported that he could see debris dropping into the canals long after we had passed the target. By making a few turns we picked up the other flights and headed home. The trip home was without incident except for a few balloons that were loose in the London area. We saw two or three in the distance but none close.

Mission #17

DATE: 7 May 1944
TARGET: MESZIERS — CHARLEVILLE M/YDS

CREW: Johnson, Seebalt, Eldridge, Moore Tippens, Castoro, Calkins
POSITION: Led second box.
LENGTH: 3:35

This was one of the deepest-yet penetrations by Marauders. And our deepest, going within 20 miles of the Luxenberg border. As usual we led the second box and followed Norgard. There was almost solid overcast over the Continent and by luck we found a hole enough to navigate by and bomb the target. Laon threw some flak at us but not much. We bombed by flights and George hit o.k. but flight #2 was left and over. (Dick Hynes and Cather put 'em in the middle of town. Doolittle — the general's son — was riding with him and watched the bombs hit.) Coming out Norgard almost took us to Lillie. But by good fortune we made it back home. A group of 109s attacked the 322nd who were behind us and shot down one 26.

Mission #18

DATE: 9 May 1944
TARGET: CALAIS ROUND
CREW: Hale, Smith, McConnell, Rivers, Moore, Sgts. Tracy, Griffiths.
POSITION: Led our group.
LENGTH: 2:00

This was one of the biggest shows we had taken part in. We followed the 391st and 322nd while about 150 P-47s dive bombed the enemy flak positions. They did a beautiful job and our group had no flak. The ground was almost covered with bomb bursts as the 47s went after the guns. We made a long bomb run and Mac had it on the button, but the racks failed to release and he had to salvo throwing our bombs 600 feet over. We think a few hit in the target area. The second box hit left but they think they got one flight in on the target. I had some trouble with my timing and getting on course but finally made rendezvous with the other groups o.k.

Mission #19

DATE: 9 May 1944
TARGET: MARQUISE RAILWAY C/D GUNS
CREW: Johnson, Seebalt, Eldridge, Moore, Sgts. Tracy, Wheeler, Griffiths.
POSITION: Led second box.
LENGTH: 2:00

Take off and join up was perfect and we started climbing to altitude. We were leading the second box and first box wandered all over south England killing time and getting altitude. It was only nine minutes from Dungeness to the target and we had to be on the bomb run over the English Channel. We were bombing by flights and the colonel wanted us to stay right together. The haze was quite bad and visibility was not good. We were almost over the coast and no target yet. Flak started coming up and we made a turn or two while hunting the target. Finally George spotted it and made a quick (15 second) run. The bombs hung up and had to be salvoed. We made a quick turn left and out over the channel. We were the only other flight out of six that dropped. The others didn't see the target at all or didn't see it time to bomb. George got an excellent hit.

Mission #20

DATE: 11 May 1944
TARGET: MALO LES BAINS C/D GUNS (Dunkerque)
CREW: Johnson, Seebalt, Eldridge, Moore
POSITION: Led second box.
LENGTH: 2:00

Take off was late and visibility was barely two miles. We joined up 15 minutes behind the first box and headed for Sheerness N.W. of London. The haze was so thick we could barely see ground looking straight down. As we came up to N. Foreland visibility picked up a little and we could see about two miles. We were about to turn around because of the bad visibility when we spotted the coast and Dunkerque. The run inland was just enough to get on the heading for the bomb run. Flak started about the time we leveled out for the run and the other flights took their interval to bomb. Flak was pretty thick and accurate on the bomb run and followed us on our breakaway, but we got out o.k. On the bombing run someone called out flak. Tom thought he said bombs away and started to turn off. He got leveled out again just as the bombs dropped but he had lost altitude and the bombs were 300 feet over. No ships lost but some battle damage.

Mission #21

DATE: 13 May 1944
TARGET: DUNKERQUE COASTAL DEFENSE GUNS
CREW: Hale, Steen, McConnell, Moore, Freeman, Sgts. Castoro, Calkins, Tippens
POSITION: Led group.
LENGTH: 2:00

This looked like the worst yet. Up to now they hadn't sent us right over the heavy flak area but here it was. Right down main street. Nothing to do but grit your teeth and drive into it. We figured our bomb run as short as possible and hoped they wouldn't get many shots at us. Take off and join up was without incident. We climbed NNW and banked to get altitude and went on course two minutes early, killing time in route to N. Freeland to let the second box catch up.

The "Duck" Freeman was on the Gee box and we made landfall a little left of course — rather we spotted Dunkerque just in time to go around it to the left. Visibility was only about four miles. We went in at Furness and started our turn to come around on our bomb run at 350 degrees. After we turned back towards Dunkerque, Mac and I picked up our reference point for the bomb run and swung onto the bomb run a little early. Mac was on the sight and had course killed, and so far nothing had happened. This time I told the crew to stay off the interphone during the bomb run and everything went fine except Mac's throat mike went out and I had to relay his conversation — which was short.

About ten seconds before bombs away it started coming up and man-o-man what a noise it made. They had us plotted exactly and flak burst all around us and splattered like hail on the ship. It seemed like someone would surely be hit and I think we all said a silent prayer. Bombs went away and Hale racked it over the right and got out of some of it but they followed in the turn and continued to fire. We bombed by flights and there were Marauders all over the sky. I heard Hale ask for a fire extinguisher and so Mac went back out of the nose. A check of the crew found everyone O.K. except Sgt. Tippens had a minor hit by flak but he was already up front sending a message to "Parade."

The smoke in the instrument panel proved to be harmless. The wheel and flap indicator was out but otherwise seemed to be OK. Hale maneuvered to pick up the other flights and get the formation back together. Sgt. Castoro looked the ship over and could find nothing seriously wrong. The right flap had a hole in it and several other holes could be seen at various places in the wings and fuselage. One hole looked like it might have hit the left tire.

The trip home was uneventful except for a sigh of relief to see the English coast again. We came over the field and started our landing procedure, making a wide pattern to check the wheels as best we could. They went down and locked as far as we could tell. We braced for a hard landing but all wheels had locked and we all got up and started to look out the hatch. We had no left brake so everyone got braced again. Steed pulled the air bottle as we left the runway and we stopped just short of the taxi strip and scrambled out like bees from a hive. I went out through the nose wheel door. Nothing happened except the #3 man came in with no right brake and went off the runway across from us.

Our ship had about 60 holes in it and was out for four days. Several cylinders were hit, and the wing tanks. All and all, it was rough but no ships were lost and no one hurt seriously.

Mission #22

Date: 20 May 1944
Target: CORNEILLES AIR FIELD
Crew: Johnson, Graves, Eldridge, Moore, Sgt. Castoro, Calkins, Tippens
Position: Led second box.
Length: 3:30

The percentages finally caught up with us today and we had to bring our bombs back. We led the second box and Major Smith led the group. The weather was not so good with medium clouds over the islands and visibility about four miles. We made bomber and fighter rendezvous o.k..... Landfall was o.k. and we stayed close because the 322nd was following us. We managed to see enough to pick up check points, especially the Seine River. As we turned at the I.P we couldn't see the airfield but picked it up soon enough and George took over.

I was checking switches and waiting for the indicator lights to go. It looked to me like we were past the release point and just then George looked up and unhooked the trigger — dry run! He had synchronized on the wrong A.P. and would have hit a French village. The airport had changed quite a bit since our photograph had been taken. When he saw the dispersal area, it was too late to get on the target. Flak started coming up about this time and we broke sharp right to avoid Paris.

We decided to make a second run and started around. Then we saw the other boxes going on back and hesitated to stay behind all alone, so we decided to make a pass at the secondary — Avereau Fayville — which was about 20 miles west. Visibility was so poor that we couldn't see much but finally spotted it just off to our right. We made a pass at it but couldn't get lined up in time, so went on to join the first box. The trip home was rather uneventful. Bandits were reported to be near us but we didn't see any. George felt badly about the whole affair but it happens to the best. We would have gone around if we could have got the radio conversation straight. Col. Vance was mumbling something to us from the first box and we didn't understand at the time.

Mission #23

DATE: 24 May 1944
TARGET: ACHIET AIR FIELD
CREW: Johnson, Hynes, Eldridge, Moore, Sgts. Castoro, Calkins, Tippens
POSITION: Led second box behind Norgard.
LENGTH: 3:20

Pre-briefing was early—at 0683—and we finally got out of the sack about 0625 and made it on time. We crept through the door to the War Room to peek at the ribbon on the map before going all the way in. Since it looked like a milk run from a distance, our morale went up 100 percent.We had a one hour delay after we got out to the ship and we went back to the mess hall with Hynes for another cup of coffee (his first). Take off and join up was difficult because of haze, but we got together and headed for north Foreland.

Bomber and fighter rendezvous was o.k., but visibility was almost nil. As usual we were leading the second box and Norgard and Offenburg with Col. Witty were leading the group. We started across the channel and visibility was still bad. We strained our eyes for the Belgium coast but didn't see it until almost on top of it. We came in at Nieport instead of Furness and headed generally east. We could see the ground most of the time by looking straight down. Some spots were covered with a thin layer of stratus clouds. I stuck my head up in the nose and looked straight down and called out highways, rivers, railroads, etc. to George. He did D.R. [dead reckoning] on the map and kept us plotted. Between us we knew where we were almost all of the time. Norgard got over within a mile of Ghent so we slipped over to the right of him. By now he was about 8 miles left of course and nearly to the first turning point. A few minutes later he turned south and took us down over Ath and Chieves airport. We left him and went around the airfield, as they usually throw up some flak. However, not a shot was fired and we joined back up with them as they came over Mons about 15 miles left of course.

Visibility was now six to eight miles and getting better. George and I started looking for the I.P. and when we were almost there got all the switches on and everything all ready to go. But when we started looking for the airfield there were a dozen of them around and for a few minutes we weren't sure what the score was. Soon we found ourselves and discovered that we were still SE of the target. We had gone farther south than we planned and so had a long bomb run. Visibility was unlimited and George took plenty of time on the run. As we came up on the target I could clearly see the revetments in the dispersal area, although there was no sign of activity. Bombs went away OK and this time I beat George leaning forward to see them hit. Ours and those of the first box hit almost at the same time. George really laid them in the area, his first bomb hitting the A.P. [aiming point]. We broke right from the target and since the first box was left we overshot the rally point and let them get ahead of us.

As we headed back north visibility became poor again and we went by our turning point and headed for Ghent again. About six miles SW of Ghent the first box made a right turn and so we left them and headed for the coast. George and I were working hard trying to pick up pin points. About ten miles short of Ostend we found one and turned sharp left and came out at Furness. The 322nd followed us out and we took off across the channel. We tried to tie in with another box for fighter protection but without much success and came on home landing ahead of the first box. They were really P.O.'d but we didn't let it worry us.

Mission #24

DATE: 28 May 1944
TARGET: AMIENS MARSHALLING YARDS
CREW: Johnson, Seebalt, Eldridge, Moore, Sgts. Castoro, Calkins, Tippens
POSITION: Led the group and the 391st.
LENGTH: 3:15

Anything would have been an anticlimax to the morning mission (flown by an earlier group), but since this was our first time at leading the group (and the 391st following), we were a little more excited than usual. The route in was long and a roundabout way. We had such a short time to get ready that there was no time to lose. Re-briefing was at 1600 and take off at 1730.

Take off was uneventful and our box joined OK, but we never picked up the 2nd box until we left the coast going out. The 391st was a little late and as a result the formation never looked very sharp. Graves, flying deputy to us, had to abort and the bomb sight in Aultman's ship went out, so number two flights had no sight.

We hit fighter rendezvous 20 seconds early and continued on course expecting them to pick us up. But just before landfall we got a bit concerned about it because up to then only four P-47s had shown up. There was some cloud cover just above us and it was a good day for fighters. To make it worse someone asked about them — in the clear — over the radio. Tom finally asked Tippens to contact Bomber Command and see what the score was. Their only reply was "We have nothing for you." Which we concluded meant go in without them.

Landfall was OK, and we went on down below the Seine, turned back East and were about half way to the I.P. when les Andleys threw a little flak at us. Nothing serious but we went around in an evasive turn. Beauvais shot at us too. At the I.P. George and I were busy trying to pinpoint ourselves and as visibility wasn't too good we couldn't make out Ameins. In about a minute we picked it up and started our bomb run. George had to change the sight for a thousand feet lower altitude because of clouds. Flak was reported at the target and we made evasive turns as long as possible. We took only a 35 second PDI [Pilot's Directional Indicator] run but they shot at us for about 15 or 20 seconds of the run. I guess everyone was sweating it out. The morning mission had upset us all a little but Tom held it straight and level and George laid them on the target. We broke sharp left and then right and were OK so far. George pulled the sight out so we could use the nose gun if necessary and then went back to transfer fuel. Our formation went to pieces and Jones dropped behind. Gradually they all came back together except Jones and he kept crisscrossing underneath us. We thought this was just because he was losing power. (It later developed that he had very little rudder control, no elevator trim control, holes in all fuel tanks, and no hydraulic pressure plus a wounded gunner. He did a beautiful job of landing at Manston with both engines cutting out on his base leg. No one was seriously hurt although the ship burned.)

Calkins reported a large hole in our left flap but otherwise we seemed OK. I sweated out the rest of the route home because we had to go between Lillie and St. Omar (an area of exceptionally heavy flak). Visibility was good, though, and we made it OK. There were two fighters with us and everyone was watching for enemy fighters, but none came. About five minutes from England, Jones was still having trouble and so Tippens sent in a position report on him to Bomber Command. We came on home and had to wait for four planes to make emergency landings before they would clear us. One, from another squadron, cracked up on the runway and two of the crew had been shot up a bit. Our landing, although we were set for a flat tire, was uneventful.

Jim Reynolds left the formation on a single engine at the target and was later shot down by light flak. His bombardier came back to the group after Paris was liberated.

Mission #25

DATE: 6 June 1944 (D-Day)
TARGET: GUN POSITIONS ALONG THE BEACH

CREW: Johnson, Williams, Eldridge, Moore, Sgts. Castoro, Calkins, Tippens.
POSITION: Deputy group led behind Norgard.
LENGTH: 3:45

The day before bombardiers, navigators and pilots of the flight leaders were briefed on the route and target. Times and everything pertaining to the mission were given except the day. About 2200 that night, a briefing was called for 0200 the following morning. Many suspected and a very few knew that this was *it.* We got up at 1230 after trying in vain to get a little sleep and ate breakfast. Two fried eggs, sausage, pancakes and coffee. Everyone was there. You might say the group hardly went to bed at all. Everyone had one eye on the sky to see what was going on, as they walked to the mess hall and then to the briefing room. There was a full moon doing its best to peek through a layer of cumulus clouds at about 6,000 feet. Those of us who knew this was the big day — and most of the men guessed it was — knew also that there would be no "red" procedure today. We would go come clouds or fair weather. We sat around the mess hall having an extra cup of coffee and saying a silent prayer that the weather would break. About 0140 we went to the briefing room. MPs had the place well-guarded and we were checked in one by one at the door. Once you were in, you stayed and went on the mission.

The briefing room was full as the group was putting up 54 airplanes on the mission. Throughout the room war correspondents were casually taking a few notes and visiting with the crews they were to fly with and in general getting their story together. The map with the route of the mission was still covered and when the screen was lifted, to say everyone was watching would be a gross understatement. We were going in at 6,000 feet and we knew they might shoot the hell out of us with everything from rifles to 105s.

En route, we soon could see the flashes of the naval guns in the distance lobbing shells onto the coast. The landing barges were coming in and the air was full of planes of all kinds. This was it! As we neared the enemy coast we kept wondering when it would come. Surely they would shoot at us. As we approached the coast and skirted the point we could make out the naval vessels and also the guns on the shore firing tracers and rocket shells. It seemed that every minute they would start on us. Our targets were right on the beach and we paralleled the beach on the bomb run. Bomb bay doors were open now and were on the run. It seemed an eternity but it was only a minute or less and bombs were away. Our gunners were cutting loose at most anything they could see. Tracers could be seen going in all directions. I think some of our own bullets came closer to us than the Jerries. We saw three ME 109s but they didn't bother us. Our bombs hit on the beach and near the target area. We turned left over the secondary target and then tried to climb up and right to go up on top to go home. But we ran into icing and had to go back down. To the right and left we could see rocket guns shooting at someone. I kept expecting them to hit us next. We turned right and across the peninsula and out be over the Isle of Guernsey.

Mission #26

DATE: 7 June 1944
TARGET: LA PRENELE C/D GUNS
CREW: Johnson, Lowery, Eldridge, Moore, Sgts. Castoro, Calkins, Tippens.
POSITION: Led 2nd box behind Bentley.
LENGTH: 2:40

By some miracle they let us sleep till 0600 this morning. The weather was still bad and we didn't have too much enthusiasm for a mission. Pre-briefing was simple. They just showed us the target and the route. We managed to get some breakfast but the coffee wasn't so good.

Take off and join up was not so exciting except the ceiling was only about 1,000 feet and we went up on top of the lower layer and found about three more above that one and came back down below and went on course at 1,000 feet. We were then eight minutes late. I was back on the Gee and George went up in the nose. We were following the first box and I checked our course with Gee. We left England still eight minutes late and found we could climb to 3,000 feet. Before hitting the target area we got to 6,000 feet. George was busy figuring data for all altitudes and I kept on the Gee. We turned into the target and by some hook or crook George saw what he thought was the target and after a 15 second run we dropped — or rather salvoed the bombs. A flight of the first box made a second run on the target and we circled out over the channel and waited for them. We came home at about 2,000 feet and landed OK.

George hit the wrong target. Hit another spot that looked like the primary one mile away.

Mission #27

DATE: 12 June 1944
TARGET: CONDÉ SUR NOIREAU BRIDGE
CREW: Johnson, Bailey, Eldridge, Moore, Sgts. Castoro, Schneider, Tippens
POSITION: Led 2nd box behind Maxwell.
LENGTH: 3:05

Pre-briefing was at 0400 and we were relieved to see that the weather was clearing up. Metro (weather) said no middle and no low clouds. At the last minute we found Calkins was still sick and we went for one of the new gunners. He got there just in time to climb into the ship. It was his first mission.

Join up and the trip to the target was uneventful except for a little uneasiness when we saw that the target might be covered with a low cloud. We made landfall north of Caen over our own beach head and went into the target. We got fouled up a little when I misjudged what the last box was going to do at the I.P. and found ourselves ahead of them and southeast of the target. At the last minute we swung right and behind the first box, and the target popped out from under a cloud. George had a short run but did OK. All six bombardiers used the wrong aiming point and all but one hit where they aimed. The Royal Australian Regiment had bombed about half of the town and the photographs we had were too old to be much help.

Coming back we got a fairly good look at our own ground troops. We now have three emergency landing strips on the beach head.

Mission #28

DATE: 13 June 1944
TARGET: ST. PIERE SUR DE ROAD JUNCTION
CREW: Hale, Deford, McConnell, Moore, Sgt. Castor, Tippens
POSITION: Led 2nd box.
LENGTH: 3:20

Sam Ackerman had gone on leave so I flew with Hale. Schifani wanted to lead a mission so we took the 2nd box. It was a rush job and not much time after briefing until time over target. It looked like a screwy route as landfall was so close to Le Havre, but we went as briefed and flew over our own troops north and east of Caen. We drew some fire from Caen but were out of range. Turning at Cramount we went to our I. P., a sharp bend in the river, and turned toward the target, and we were going to use it to pick up the target. There it was big as life and we followed it and there was a town that must be the target. The first box was heading for it too. About halfway down the run a big railroad running east stood out like a sore thumb and I discovered we were heading for the wrong target. We made a hard right turn and picked up the right one. I suggested that we go around again but Mac said he thought he could make it OK. It was a short run but we dropped and then circled three times waiting for Schifani. Mac hit about 500 feet right. Schifani never did drop. It was quite a sightseeing tour as we circled the countryside. Visibility was very good and we could see the whole country. Each time we passed the target we got a better look at our bomb hits. One bomb hit directly on the railroad northwest of town but otherwise it didn't look like much damage had been done. Our bombs hit in a very concentrated pattern in the edge of the village. There was a fire and lots of smoke.

Mission #29

DATE: 14 June 1944
TARGET: QUINSVILLE C/D GUNS
CREW: Johnson, Hynes, Eldridge, Moore, Sgts. Castoro, Calkins, Tippens
POSITION: Led 2nd box.
LENGTH: 2:45

At last after nearly three weeks we had our own ship, *B for Belts*, back. It had been in the depot for repairs — a new gas tank, wing span, and numerous small things such as hydraulic lines, etc. Its last trip was over Amiens and it took a beating.

Today we were 20 minutes behind the first box and so were on our own. This was one of the most interesting missions since D-Day. The targets were three gun positions that had been giving our troops and ships trouble since D-Day, and naval gun fire had failed to silence them. The ground troops were only a few miles west of the town here and at 1430 they were to withdraw and at 1440 the first box was to bomb. At 1500 we were to hit the target. We couldn't be late and the first box couldn't be early. If we hit the target it would mean a big help to the troops. Metro reported four to six tenths cloud at 5,000 feet over the target. We joined up and went directly to Selsy Hill, where it looked like we could go up to 8,000. We climbed to 9,000 and headed out across the channel three minutes early. As we neared the target area it was apparent that we would have to go down. At 3,000 feet we leveled off and started in for the Isle of St. Marouf, our I.P.

We were early but decided to go on in, as it was better to be early than late. The air was rough and it was difficult to do good sighting. On the bombing run Hynes called the ground station to see if it was OK to bomb. I was all set to cut the switches if we couldn't and at the last minute — after Tom poked him a few times — he said OK. He had the word but forgot to tell us. We dropped our two 2,000-pound bombs and broke away fast to avoid the concussion. Our flight went every direction and the concussion wasn't bad at all. The bombs looked good. P.I. showed five excellent hits. Ground troops took place.

Mission #30

DATE: 24 June 1944
TARGET: CHERBOURG (FORT de ROUGE)
CREW: Johnson, Webb, Eldridge, (1st Lt.) Moore, Sgt. Castoro, Calkins, Tippens
POSITION: Led 2nd box behind Maxwell.

The O.O. ([Operations Officer] Cahill) woke George and I at 0400 and we promptly went back to sleep, but George happened to wake up at 0430, which was the time of pre-briefing. We hurried and got there just as it was over. However, no one said anything and we got the "poop" and went to breakfast. It was a direct support mission on a fortified hill and CHQ [Command Headquarters] just south of Cherbourg. It had been firing at our boys on the ground and giving them plenty of trouble. Three groups of Marauders plus fighter-bombers were to attack between 0745 and 0800. Our group was the first to go in. Our own troops were only a mile or so short of the target, so it had to be a good hit. The flak situation might be rough although the AA gunners would probably be busy with other things — we hoped.

Briefing at 0515 was uneventful. Col. Vance warned us not to drop short no matter what happened. He said he hoped that if our attack was successful the troops might take Cherbourg today.

We took off on time, made a perfect join up with Maxwell and went on course immediately. The route went around to the west of London to avoid the area marked off for the defense against "buzz bombs." Lead navigator was on the ball and so George and I spent most of the time across the channel studying the target pictures and area. We were to go down to the Isle of St. Marouf, make a hard right turn, go up to Volones, our I.P., and make our run on 335 degrees. Bombing was by flights on converging headings. The area had been flooded and changed so much that we weren't sure of Volones but followed Maxwell and could soon see Cherbourg and lined up on the target area. There were some low clouds and, as it was early yet, quite a bit of mist on the ground. I finally spotted the target by reference to the dock and harbor and George saw it about the same time. We were 100 feet below Maxwell and just behind him.

It was a bright morning with the mist rising in light clouds from the ground. Below were the orchards and fields of Normandy. Ahead was the great port of Cherbourg, one of the finest in Europe. For some reason I didn't expect we would get any flak and none came up as we made a minute and 40 second run. Bombs away and we started evasive action and headed out to sea. A few bursts of flak came up at six o'clock but none close to us. The group behind us got a lot and one ship had a little trouble but finally came back into position. Our bombs hit OK and the whole target area was a mass of smoke and flames. It was a good show and the boys on the ground took the hill shortly after 0800.

Mission #31

DATE: 8 July 1944
TARGET: NOGENT le ROI BRIDGE
CREW: Johnson, Cahill, Eldridge, Moore, Sgts. Castoro, Calkins, Tippens
POSITION: Led the group.
TIME: 3:45

After a long wait — nearly three weeks — we finally get another mission. The group had a late one the night before and we figured they couldn't possibly have an early one, but they did. Woke us up at 0345 for pre-briefing at 0430. George and I went down early to get the details. It was a rail bridge over a small river between Chartes and Dreax. It didn't look too bad. Some flak was reported over most of the route but not a lot, and the target should be free of flak. At the last minute, someone came and said there was reported flak at the target. Rivers was making up the flight plan and we went to have some breakfast.

Briefing was S.O.P. [standard operating procedure] and we went out to the plane, K-9-B, for Bolts. Some had forgotten to wake up the crew chiefs so Castoro was checking over the plane. We started engines early so we could pre-flight them. Since this was Jack's first trip with us, I checked our timing carefully and at exactly 0655 we rolled down the runway and we were off into the wild blue.

Join up was nearly perfect and we went on course a minute early rather than late and make an extra turn. We climbed on course and got our equipment adjusted. It was a beautiful morning and visibility was good. We could see the whole of Southern England, and off between London and Dover we could see an almost solid black mass of barrage balloons — part of the defense against buzz bombs.

We went to N. Foreland and then across to Durgeness where we met our fighters. We were a minute early but as we approached Durgeness we could see squadrons of P-47s approaching from two o'clock, and soon they were all around the formation.

Visibility was so good we could see the French Coast, Pas de Calais area, and almost to Le Havre 70 miles away. I was so sleepy I almost took a nap going across the channel. As we approached the coast we could see Dieppe on our left and Le Havre on our right and up ahead like a huge, lazy snake lay the Seine River. We could see for miles and miles, which was a big help. We started our evasive action just before landfall and kept it up all the way in and out! Our flight plan wasn't working out so well, so George took three drift runs, and we found out wind was quite different than metro. We called the other flights and gave them the new wind.

As we approached the target area we could see a bank of cumulus clouds that looked like they might be over our target. Sure enough, they were. Just before we came abreast of Chartes we went over clouds and I had to D.R. around, and since there were occasional breaks we hoped to find a hole. It was a little close with Chartes on one side, Dreaux on the other and Paris only a short way on another. We saw a check point and the target, but not soon enough to make a run. So, around again. This time I thought we were approaching Dreaux instead of the target and closed the bomb bay doors on George. The third pass we got a run but we dropped a little early as George rolled the indices up searching for the target and they passed. Low clouds were bothering us considerably, and we hit 750 yards short but knocked out the rail line.

Someone called us — we thought it was Seebalt — and asked us to take them around again. So once more we made a tight 180 and back over the check point. I thought I was talking with Curt but discovered I had turned the wrong jack box and was still on the inter phone. Dreaux threw up a black cloud and so we turned left this time and headed for home. (Later we learned it was Churchill that called us and he was planning to drop on us, but we sure slipped him a "Quickie," as we had already dropped.)

Turning left, we cut off quite a little of the route home and tried to pick up the second box. We turned South awhile but finally headed home, as they were hunting targets of opportunity. Seabalt and Harrison dropped on an intersection on the way home. We zigzagged out of France and back to the U.K. As we approached Manston planes began to drop out like flies going in for gas. We came on home OK.

Mission #32

DATE: 19 July 1944
TARGET: LES PON de CE RAIL BRIDGE
CREW: Johnson, Cahill, Eldridge, Moore, Sgts. Smith, Hamilton
POSITION: Led second box.
TIME: 4:00

We were up early for briefing at 0500 and got as far as the end of briefing before an indefinite delay came through. It looked like a milk run and weather didn't look very bad, so we were anxious to get off, but no soap. We lay around until 1630 when they pre-briefed us again on the same target but with a slightly different route. We got the poop together and out to the ship. Everything was ready. Ondra had even changed the position of the PDI back where the gun sight had been. Not having flown a mission in so long it seemed a little strange to be checking equipment carefully and to have a bomb load—4 × 1,000 pounds. Col. Maxwell led the group and as we taxied out he started his take off. Exactly six minutes later we rolled down the runway and off into the blue. Join up was good and we went on course on time.

Shortly after leaving the field we had to climb through some broken cumulus clouds. They were quite thin but we sweated a little. The wing men stayed tight with us, and we came out right behind Maxwell. Our #2 flight, led by Joseph, was lost but he finally caught up at the I.P.

We topped the clouds at 9,000 feet just as we left Selsey Hill. It looked fairly good for the Continent, though, and as we headed out across the channel. The gunners test fired their guns and we kept an eagle eye out for landfall.

Landfall was good although visibility was bad. As we went inland it picked up and the clouds became scattered. Maxwell went well to the left and we followed them, although it was quite a bit off course. From here on into the target we could see for miles and we had a good look at the rolling orchards and hills of France. Not a sign of life was visible from 11,000 feet, except an occasional wisp of smoke.

We turned at the I.P. and went in trail with the other flights. We were to bomb 4th but as we went down the run we found ourselves overrunning the 1st and 2nd flights. Number 3 flight never did pull up in good position so we went on in. We could see the highway bridge which was west of our target, a long way out but for a few minutes it looked like some had beaten us to the rail bridge and knocked it out. But as we came closer we could see it plainly. George was taking a long run and there was no reason not to, although the town of Angers was almost underneath us there was no flak and it was just like dropping them on Mullett Key.

As we approached the point of release it looked like we might have to pull off to keep from having the bombs of the 2nd flight hit us. But just as we were about to pull away their bombs dropped and ours went also. The air was literally full of 1,000-pound bombs, dropping down to the target below. At first they seemed to almost follow the ship, then as they dropped away they took their own path and pointed their noses down.

As soon as George had taken a look I pushed him back and had a look at the target. All I could see was a huge cloud of black smoke over the bridge.

As I watched, another flight's bombs walked across the right approach. It looked like the bridge should be blown to bits.

On the way home we had good visibility to landfall. We passed by Le Mans and Laval and headed for the coast at Cabourg. As we approached the coast, clouds and haze reduced visibility to a few miles and I wasn't sure just where we were. I couldn't find a check point and had to rely on dead reckoning. We were following the first box quite closely. The tail gunner reported one ship leaving the formation and going on single engine. About three minutes inland flak started coming up at the first box. We stayed with them awhile in evasive action, then when they broke left we went right and pulled out of the area. The front line boys had turned some of the 88s up at us. Some of the bursts were uncomfortably close but it is amazing how we looked out and saw the black puffs — some close enough to the see the ugly red flash and to hear the "wump" of the explosion — and yet we felt no fear at the moment.

We pulled out and met the first box out in the bay. Going home we let down, attempting to get below the clouds. But when we hit England we found that it was mostly haze and we sneaked around London at 2,000 feet, being able to see less than two miles ahead. We landed without further incident and a quick check up showed only a few flak holes in some ships — none in ours. As we made our pattern we heard the plane that had gone on single engine over France call the tower for landing instructions. It sounded good to hear him coming in OK. One ship had left the first box at the Normandy coast, no doubt low on gas. Several ships stopped off in South England for fuel.

Mission #33

DATE: 25 July 1944
TARGET: ST. LO AREA
CREW: Johnson, Deford, Eldridge, Moore, Sgts. Tippens, Castoro, Calkins
POSITION: Led second box.
LENGTH: 3:00

This was another direct support mission for the boys in Normandy. Over 3,000 planes, including 1,500 heavies, three groups of Marauders and hundreds of fighters. We were to attack at 1210 and under no circumstances were we to attack after 1215. Apparently we were the last one because the ground troops were to move up immediately after 1215.

Briefing was at a decent hour and it looked like a good mission except that weather might be stinker. (At the time we little realized the importance of the mission or anticipate the fame that this day was to achieve. This was to be the first breakthrough for our troops and from this beginning, the battle of Normandy grew into the battle for France, and the race to Berlin was on.)

We took off and joined up on schedule and climbed to the base of medium stratus layer of clouds. Visibility was very limited and as we crossed the channel we were forced to go down to 9,500 feet. The air was very rough and formation flying was difficult. It was the first time I had seen rough air at that altitude. We had been warned emphatically to be sure we were past our own troops before dropping, and "Parade" called us en route and said there was considerable smoke over the target area. We were to drop our frag bombs just south of St. Lo–Pierres highway and about five miles west of St. Lo. George and I had it figured out so we could drop by dead reckoning from the coast and be sure we were past our own lines. However, we picked up the area OK and George put 75 percent of our bombs in the area (200-foot interval bombing by box) and would have done better except the low flight of the first box crowded us a little.

The air was full of airplanes going and coming. We must have met several hundred heavies coming back as we went out. Flak was meager over the target, and we made a hard right and back across our own lines and home.

Two days later the ground forces made a complete breakthrough.

One group of Marauders and one or two groups of heavies dropped on our own troops killing among others Gen. McNair.

Mission #34

DATE: 25 July 1944
TARGET: MAINTENON RAIL BRIDGE (near Chartes)
POSITION: Led the group.
LENGTH: 4:00

We had just hit the sack when they called pre-briefing. Since Hale was on leave, we took his place leading the group. We'd had our fun for the day on the morning mission and in the P.M. we were back on bridges again. It was right near the one we had made a pass at a week ago so we knew the country well. The weather looked bad and "cloudy." Gifford said it looked like a scrub to him.

But no delay, and we took off on schedule. Climbing on course we found that the ceiling was less than 8,000 over the channel, and since the field order specified not to attack less than 8,000, we had Tippens contact Bomber Command to see if we should go on in. But before he could complete the message we were at landfall and had crowded up to 8,500 under the layer of middle stratus. An A-20 group was coming out just as we came in and we almost met at that narrow path — the only safe entry to France — St. Caburg. The fighters met us, P-38s, here and we went on in. Visibility was good and the ceiling lifted to about 12,000 feet.

As we went on the bombing run George went to work and we settled down to sweat it out. No flak reported but one never knows. They went away and we started a big sharp right turn. George almost had the doors shut when someone yelled "Fighters!" No fooling, they were there and made one pass at us. I couldn't see them as I had backed out of George's way, but they said we could have touched them. Tippens and Cakins got in a good burst, especially Tippens, and we might have got some holes in him. The P-38s took over and that was the last we saw of Jerrie.

George hit over for some unexplainable reason and so did Curmode. Two flights did hit though and got the bridge. (We later discovered that Deford had pulled the throttles a little on the bombing run, which may have accounted for the miss.)

We came home in as tight a formation as you ever saw and got a little flak at landfall because I got too close to Trouville.

We were all pooped when we landed and decided one a day was enough.

Mission #35

DATE: 5 August 1944
TARGET: CANNERE RAIL BRIDGE (NE of Lemans)
CREW: Johnson, Col. Witty, Eldridge, Moore, Sgts. Tippens, Castoro, Calkins
POSITION: Led second box behind Maxwell.
LENGTH: 2:50

This looked like a milk run and everyone was in high spirits and good humor at pre-briefing and briefing. Lt. Col. Witty was riding co-pilot with us. We had been scheduled to go to Nantes early in the morning the day before and later on a bridge NE of Angers, but both were scrubbed. Metro report wasn't so good for this mission but we got off and to altitude over the channel OK. Witty made us hold a course through a thin cloud layer and we lost the first box and had to meet them at fighter rendezvous at Caborg. We made a big 360 turn off the coast; Tippens was on the Gee for us and did a good job, as the coast and channel had 10/10 cloud. Maxwell's radio was out and we couldn't contact him. But after our circle we located him or rather found they were in the vicinity and started on into target.

About this time "Parade" (Bomber Command) called us and said "Return to base." We were already inland about 10 miles and made our turn around Lisieuz, a small French village that had been blown off the map except for a beautiful cathedral on the South edge of town. There was one lone burst of flak way off to the west as we came back out. The first box went over the top of us as we were turning to come out and Maxwell's wing man finally conveyed the message to him that we were going home. (Learned later that the fighters were weathered in so they re-called the mission.)

Mission #36

DATE: 5 August 1944
TARGET: CANNERE RAIL BRIDGE
CREW: Johnson, Clay, Eldridge, Moore, Sgts. Tippens, Castoro, Calkins
POSITION: Led second box.
LENGTH: 4:00

Same mission as the morning except a different axis of attack and instructions to go as low as 4,000 feet to go in. This created considerable discussion, as we didn't like the idea of making landfall at that altitude. After talking with wing, we were finally told to use our judgment and by takeoff weather had cleared considerably. They didn't want us to go in from the west because they weren't sure where the German armor was.

Takeoff and join up was without incident. We climbed to 11,500 feet over the channel. Just as we left Selsey Hill going out a buzz bomb just missed the formation and fell in the channel underneath us. The concussion was surprisingly strong even at 8,000 feet. The plane bounced as much as when the bombs drop on the target.

The fighters met us at landfall and we went on in at altitude. There was a big thunderhead almost on course and we just skirted the edge of it. Our P-47 escort played tag around the clouds searching for any stray "bandits." As we approached the target area the clouds broke, but Maxwell had already gone down to 9,000 feet, putting us at 7,500. Visibility was stinker because of the haze. I was able to keep us located fairly close until shortly before the I.P., when I got confused, but George put me straight.

We turned on the bombing run and tried to pick up the target. I saw it and put George on it. Things didn't work out quite right, though, and we went around, as did all except one flight. (George's parachute caught on the secondary clutch and un-clutched it, disabling the Norden bombsite.) Next time we dropped and hit 475 feet left of the rail bridge but bracketed a road bridge. Hudgins and Schifani didn't drop and we took them around again and once more after that. All five flights hit good, but as we left the target, the bridge was still standing. Hudgins never did drop.

P.S. This was a party night.

Mission #37

DATE: 9 August 1944
TARGET: VERBERIE RAIL BRIDGE (near Compiegne)
CREW: Johnson, "Bitchin' Benney" Seth, Eldridge, Moore, Sgts. Tippens, Castoro, Calkins
POSITION: Led second box behind Maxwell.
LENGTH: 3:10

(Forgot to write this one up until 28 August, after flak leave.)

We sweated this one out because the flak situation was so uncertain. Worked out OK though and George got an excellent hit.

Mission #38

DATE: 28 August 1944
TARGET: HAM FUEL TANKS
CREW: Johnson, Allyn, Eldridge, Moore, Sgts. Tippens, Castoro, Calkins
LENGTH: 3:35

Mission was first called early in the morning. We were awakened at 0600 and had just started to taxi out when they called in a delay. It was raining when we left briefing and it was really a stinker. We lay around all day and at 1600 they called up again on the same target but with a little different route. The weather had cleared and a strong wind was blowing. We got off OK and joined up. I messed up the join up by missing the time to turn on the downwind leg. We got together, though, and headed for Claxton and then to Furness.

There was a layer of cumulus clouds right at landfall but we were able to see enough to make landfall OK. The clouds broke right at the coast and visibility was almost unlimited. We went on down between Lillie and Hazebrook. There was a strong wind from the Southwest and we made our bombing run downwind. Bombing was by flights on converging axes. We leveled out on our run and George took a drift run. The tanks were just west of a brewery and our pattern covered nearly 1,800 feet (28 × 100 GP's).

We took about a minute run and George did OK, hit the SW corner of the tanks. Two flights didn't drop and we made a circle while they went around again. Coming back everything worked OK. We could see some Royal Air Force Lancasters catching flak over St. Omar and Dunkerque. After landfall out we had to keep dodging them. Finally, I looked up and there we were almost to N. Foreland. We were getting down under the clouds and then turned north and came in at Claxton. After hitting the English Coast I handed the junk out of the nose and almost got lost. George kept telling me right where we were and we argued a bit and finally hit the field OK. They gave me a bad time after that one.

Mission #39

DATE: 5 September 1944
TARGET: BREST GUNS
CREW: Johnson, B. D. Stevens, Eldridge, Moore, Sgts. Tippens, Castoro, Calkins
POSITION: Led the group.
LENGTH: 4:10

This was a long one. Made four passes at the target because of cloud cover and finally dropped. Hit a little right. An uneventful trip except for the long haul and the tiresome trip over water. Coming home it was nearly dark and George was on the Gee box, but somehow wasn't doing much good as he kept trying to tell me we were where I knew we weren't. No coverage.

Mission #40

DATE: 11 September 1944
TARGET: METZ FORT
CREW: Johnson, "Wild Bill" Young, Eldridge, Moore, Sgts. Castoro, Calkins, Dzedzic
POSITION: Led group.
LENGTH: 3:45

Morning mission came back about 1230 from a target in the same area. Seabalt landed in France with a wounded man. They had K-9-B too. One ship landed with only one main and no one was hurt. Another couldn't get his nose wheel down and didn't do too good a job landing going off the runway and seriously injuring the co-pilot.

With this as a background we started working on the second mission. Takeoff and join up was OK except that our 360 turn was a minute early and we made a second turn to pick up the second box.

Our route was: Claxton, N. Foreland, and Gravelines, to I.P. It was quite a treat to fly down by St. Omer, Lille, etc., straight and level and see our own boys down there on the ground. We stayed at 8,000 until we were at Hirson, then went on up to 12,500. We took evasive action from the I.P. to the target even though our target was just over our own lines (1,500 yards).

As we went on the run, flak started coming up. It wasn't accurate but we could hear and feel it. George took a short run and we got the hell out of there. Someone didn't drop — it turned out to be Catlin — and we made a circle to wait for him. When we finally got started home everyone else was ahead of us. We finally put the nose down and got the formation in shape just as we came across the channel. Most flights hit fair to excellent.

Mission #41

Date: 19 September 1944
Target: DUREN M/Y GERMANY
Crew: Johnson, Col. Witty, Eldridge, Moore, Sgts. Tippens, Castoro, Calkins
Position: Led group.
Length: 3:30

Our first mission to Germany. No one thought we would get a mission today. The ceiling was only 1,000 to 1,500 feet and looked plenty thick. We could hear the heavies up on top and gave them the V for Victory. But about 1030 the Tonoy announced briefing. George and I went up to the War Room and took in the pre-briefing. It didn't look too bad but the route and bombing run took us over country where there was some quite heavy fighting and everyone expected there would be flak. The biggest problem was weather and to add to the confusion, there would be another group of gliders coming over our field about the time we took off.

No delay, and so we took off on schedule. We had to make our join up at 1,200 feet because of the ceiling. We got the group together fairly well, though, and headed out on course. No gliders in the area thank goodness. As we hit Claxton on the way out the ceiling went down to almost zero and we had to go on instruments. After leaving the English coast we started climbing by flights. We broke out at about 5,000 feet but there was another layer above us. Tippens was on Gee and kept us plotted all the way. We made a double drift just before landfall to let the rest of the formation catch up.

The clouds began to break up as we went inland and we were able to see Ghent; 20 minutes before the I.P. we had Tippens go back to his guns. Our heading kept us right on course and as we approached the German border visibility picked up so that we were able to see the ground fairly well. We started evasive action as we approached the front lines. We continued it as we came to the I.P. and headed down toward the target. We couldn't see the target but followed the river down and found the town of Julich. The target came into view then and George took over. He made about three more evasive turns and then on to the bomb run. It was a short one and it didn't even seem long before we could feel the bombs go away. We turned sharp right off the target and headed for the rally point.

Everyone dropped on the first pass and in a few minutes we were back over our own lines and headed home. The weather soon socked in again and we were barely able to see Brussels, which was right on course.

We let down to 5,000 feet going out and saw several other groups going in and some forts going home too. Tippens finally got a weather report from the base and we let down from Claxton to Braintres hoping there were no P-47s around the area. We broke out in the clear again and made our landing OK.

Everyone hit and everyone made it home OK. A swell job by everyone.

The following missions were flown out of Ponoise-Cormeilles in Northern France. This base was built by the French in 1937, and then seized by the Germans in 1940. It was liberated by the Americans in September of 1944. After extensive repairs (ironically much of the damage was inflicted by Marauders while the base was in German hands), the base became operational for the Ninth Air Force and was designated "A-59." Our 344th Bomb Group operated from this base from September 30 until early April, 1945. From this base, many of our missions extended into Germany. The airfield is still in use today for general civil aviation. A memorial to the Americans is on display at the base.

Mission #42

DATE: 6 October 1944
TARGET: ARNHAM BRIDGE
CREW: Johnson, Major Stahl, Eldridge, Moore, Sgts. Tippens, Castoro, Calkins
POSITION: Led group.
LENGTH: 3:25

This was our first mission (3rd for the group) from our new base in France (A-59). Briefing was up at group at the chateau and we also had breakfast up there. Weather looked snafu but we went ahead anyway and outside of being short flak suits and everything being generally mixed up, we got off on time. Taking off we just barely cleared the radio towers SE of the field. The haze was so thick that we were on instruments immediately. By some stroke of luck (Tom and I got our signals crossed up a little) join up was OK and we headed out on course through the haze.

About 10 minutes out Gee and I were checking our position, not too successfully either, when Tom called to see what our compass read. We found we had been flying about 10 degrees to the left because of the gyro precession.

Gee and I picked ourselves up at Monticier and corrected our heading. Tippens wasn't having too much success with the Gee at first. As we went NE visibility picked up and by the time we reached Cambrai we could see 10 or 15 miles.

Fighter rendezvous was at Louvain and we arrived 6 minutes early. We made a 360 and called the fighters, who said they would meet us over the target. Visibility continued good and we could see the I.P. and target area. Taking evasive action all the way, we headed into the target. Flak was "probable and expected" but as we got closer and closer none came up. George leveled out and started his run. I looked at the indices and they still had 20 seconds to go. I ducked a little deeper into the nose. No flak yet and bombs released.

Capt. Brady didn't drop and requested permission to go around. We made three 360s around the rally point while they made a second run. We had got just a little flak as we turned off the target, but when Brady headed in again they turned everything loose at him. One ship, flown by Moore, went down. Four chutes were reported.

Coming home was uneventful except Dick Hynes went off by himself and got shot at.

Mission #43

DATE: 19 November 1944
TARGET: NEIWEID BRIDGE
CREW: Johnson, Seavy, Eldridge, Moore, Sgts. Tippens, Castoro, Calkins.
POSITION: Led group.
LENGTH: 3:35

This was a "hurry up" job that got underway after the morning mission had landed. It was the first time since being on the Continent that there was even a possibility of two missions in one day. The morning mission had gone down almost to Switzerland to hit a bridge across the Rhine. They had fair weather but by the time we got around to go we had our usual variety of clouds from 2,000 feet on up with rain in between. (John Graves blew a tire on takeoff in the morning but did a good job of handling it and no one was hurt.) Several of our ships were "out" and several more had no gas because the re-fueling truck had been stolen in Paris the night before. We were flying *V-Victor*, a ship that we had not flown in before. It had only one Jack box in the nose and the armor plating was not moved back. The radio compass didn't work; we didn't have time to get all of our flying clothes and went out to the airplane only ten minutes before engine start time. We were given a fifteen minute delay but after that we were on our way.

Join up was snafued by the second box. A strong wind blew us about ten miles from the field and they didn't fly according to the regular join up pattern. But we came back to the field and picked them up OK. Going on course to Albert, at 2,500 feet we hit the low clouds and started an instrument ascent. We broke out at 6,500 feet and attempted to pick up the rest of the formation. Not all of the group got off the ground and we finally got 25 airplanes with us. At 9,000 feet and shortly after taking a heading eastward toward the front lines, we hit middle clouds and started to pick up ice. Tom let down through the stuff and we came out in the clear around 4,500 feet and in the vicinity of Charlieville. The weather looked somewhat better up ahead and we decided to go on up and have a look at it. We had two flights with us at this time.

Over the front lines at Bastogne we were able to get our altitude and Tom called Parade to see if we were to go on in. Our fighters had not shown up and most of the formation had turned back. They told us to make a 360 and stand by. When we made the turn one flight just made a 180 and went home. We heard back, "Proceed with the mission." (Later we learned that Dick Hynes was on duty at Parade). So with five airplane and no fighters we headed for the target, which was about forty miles over the lines.

Snow covered most of the ground here and I wasn't able to pinpoint our position exactly. But we were soon able to see the Rhine River and located the target area. About this time the flak started to come up and I gave the head set and mike to George. Tom was really racking it up in the turns but the flak stayed on us pretty well. Just before we went on the bomb run George said, "Our next turn will be to the right," and Tom thought he said "Turn right" and so turned. George had un-caged his sight and the gyro tumbled. Nothing to do but straight and level while he got it caged again. I was trying to make sense out of all the switches on the panel of this G model. I opened the doors accidently and decided it was too soon and closed them again. I thought I opened them again but found out later that I didn't. Just as the indices passed I hit the salvo switch and that was when the doors opened and the bombs released. The wing men had quite a time getting their bombs out. Most of them just salvoed as soon as they could.

We were getting flak all the way down the bomb run and as we turned off to the left we got even more of it. It seemed to be bursting too close for comfort. The red centers of the bursts were all too visible. One burst knocked two holes in the nose and about the same time the right wingman's prop went up to 2,700 rpms and I thought our engine was gone. Covy slid out in front of us and one of the ships went out of formation. Web Allyn had turned back before going on the bomb run.

Turning off the target, we had a heavy head wind and it seemed hours before we were clear of the flak. We finally got away from it though, and other ships came back into formation. As soon as we were over the front lines Tom dropped down under all the clouds, which took us down to 4,000 feet. We hit some rain and had to go as low as 2,000 feet to keep the ground in sight. Coming back to base was not very exciting except I felt like a heel for messing up the bomb run. Our bombs couldn't have been anywhere near the target unless George's sighting was way off. The bombs must have been a good two seconds late going away.

It was nearly dark when we arrived back at the field but we had no trouble finding it. When we landed we learned that all but two of the airplanes were accounted for. Web Allyn and another pilot by the name of Hegg were missing.

Next morning: Word has been received from Chiozza that two officers and two enlisted men from the crew are OK. Web and Sgt. Dowditch have been reported dead. No details, yet.

Still later: Web and Sgt. Bozich killed in action; others OK. Crew bailed out SW of Luxemburg near town of Chanley, Belgium. Web didn't get out in time and Sgt. Bozich "froze"—unable to find any trace of Bozich. Their ship received transfer system and started fire in bomb bay. Fubel put out the fire and they were able to get back over friendly territory.

Mission #44

DATE: 9 December 1944
TARGET: BAUWHOLDER WAREHOUSE AREA
CREW: Johnson, Ballinger, Eldridge, Moore, Sgts. Lott, Faulk, Harris
POSITION: Led group on PFF (Pathfinder Force).
LENGTH: 3:35

After two days of briefing and waiting out, we finally got a mission lined up. Tom decided to take this PFF, as we could fly one PFF mission per month. Pre-briefing was at 0715 and although the weather wasn't too good we took off as briefed. The airplanes were all iced up and it took a lot of work to get the frost and ice off. I had my intermediate flying suit on, as I planned to stay in the navigator's compartment. Also had my fleece lined boots on.

Join up was OK and although we had 15 minutes to kill, we headed out en route to avoid a snow flurry that was moving onto the field. At St. Quentin we made a 360 trying to get up on top of the middle clouds. We were already over 10/10 at 4,000 feet. Pathfinder ship took over the lead soon after this as we reached 14,000 feet. He dog legged back and forth trying to kill time and we ended up five minutes early at the target. The clouds built up to 14,000 feet and above and we picked our way through the tops of them. Pathfinder suggested going back several times but Tom would say, "Let's go a little further and see what it looks like."

I was on Gee and trying to keep us plotted. Reception was good and I would have dropped only about 10 seconds later than the PFF did had I been dropping on Gee. Just before the I.P. I called for a MSW fix [a navigational signal from the ground to the plane] and finally got an answer. "You are 20 miles south of Koblenz." It was about right but I am still not sure if it was ours or the Germans'.

Our bombing run was down a valley in the clouds and we were barely above this cloud layer at 12,200 feet. After an 11 minute bomb run straight and level we finally dropped and headed home. After the first turn we took the lead and had to climb back to 14,000 feet to get out over the clouds. As soon as we were back over friendly territory, Tom let down through the top clouds. It snowed and iced up and the windshield frosted over and everyone but me almost froze. I used Gee all the way and brought us in OK.

The 386th aborted but 391st hit the same target. On 15 December seven flights bombed on us. The 391st PFF ship dropped while in clouds and no one saw the bombs go. the 386th aborted. PFF for our box wanted to turn back but Tom wasn't about to turn back until we had crossed the bomb line and by that time we were surrounded by clouds and couldn't turn around without going to the target.

Mission #45

DATE: 24 December 1944
TARGET: KONZ KARTHAUS RAIL BRIDGE
CREW: Johnson, Ballinger, Eldridge, Moore, Sgts. (Reinhart's crew)
POSITION: Led group (maximum effort).
LENGTH: 3:30

The German "Breakthrough" was in its 8th day today and this was the second day of good weather since the start of the offensive on 16 December. The weather turned cold and the skies cleared. Yesterday the Luftwaffe came up in strength and our wing lost about 20 ships to fighters. Our group was the only one that didn't get jumped.

As a result of all this we were not a little apprehensive about the whole situation. However, pre-briefing was not until 0915 and we had time to eat and shave. The target was about five miles beyond the bomb line and was just south of Trier. The railroad was a supply line for the 7th German Army opposing our 10th Armored Division. Weather was CAVU [ceilings and visibility unlimited].

As we joined our box, the tower called and said to make another 360 to pick up the third box. At the last minute they had been ordered to put up maximum effort. We went on course after making two 360s. We were still five minutes early and dog legging to kill time. The weather was perfect except for a ground haze. I stayed on the Gee box and also looked out the window. It was the first time we had used this procedure on a visual mission.

At fighter rendezvous we could not contact any fighters. We were five minutes early and so made a 360. Still no fighters so we made another. Just as we had about decided we would have to give it up, the fighters appeared and we went on in. George took over from the I.P. He took a few evasive turns and used a 35 second run. At bombs away, I tried to give evasive action but the inter-phone was so bad that Tom couldn't read me. George took it and I went up in the cockpit where I could use sign language. We had a 60 mile an hour wind from the east and were soon back over our own lines. There was some flak on our left and low.

Back at Luxemburg, the rally point, we made a 360 to tighten up our formation. The third box, led by Seabaldt, didn't stay with us so we headed back to base.

Results were excellent, according to crew reports. We got the bridge next to the rail bridge but someone else got the rail bridge.

Mission #46

DATE: 22 February 1945
TARGET: HAMM, GERMANY, RAIL BRIDGE
CREW: Johnson, Covey, Eldridge, Linden, Moore, Sgts. (Cevey's crew)
POSITION: Led group.
LENGTH: 4:10

This mission was known through the U.S. Army Air Forces as "Clarion." It was a combined effort on the part of the 9th, 8th, and 15th Air Forces plus the 2nd, 19th, and 29th Tactical Air Command. Over 6,000 aircraft were sent against German rail lines in an attempt to completely demoralize the rail workers. Our targets were small but the group was to cut the rail line in several places. We had nine flights of five ships each on nine different targets. Reinhart led our high flight and was to bomb a marshalling yard just east of our target. He missed or rather aimed at the wrong target.

There was little indication when we went to bed that the mission would run. We had been briefed for nearly two months on the mission and had been grounded from operations all this time. Several of the crews that had been briefed had completed their tour by virtue of the additional credit on lead teams. Col. Witty and Florsheim were in England. Brammer called Tom about midnight and told him to be ready to fly. When the O.D. [officer of the day] came in and woke up George he said, "You've got the wrong man. They don't want me." The O.D. finally convinced him that this was it and we got ready and went up to eat. Form and John were eating and we tried to eat some pancakes but they didn't taste very good.

Up at pre-briefing the war room was filled. Capt. Murphy was briefing and it was a big job. The mission called for bombing at 8,000 feet and the going down and strafing the target. This was the first time since the fateful day nearly two years ago when 10 Marauders went in on the deck and none came back, that Marauders were briefed to strafe. No one knew what would happen! There was no heavy flak plotted to the target and only one three-gun light flak position. But, we couldn't be sure.

Just before briefing a two hour delay came in. This gave us time to get organized and ready. We went back to the area and ate again. Out at the airplane everyone was out to see us off. Jake Hilton was out — John, of course and all along the line as we taxied out men stood and watched. It wasn't an ordinary mission going out. Everyone knew it was something big and different. And there was a big question in everyone's mind as to how it would work out. I, for one, was glad to be started so I could keep busy.

Takeoff and join up was normal and we turned on course. The weather was beautiful. Visibility was unlimited except for a small patch of clouds over Paris. We had 45 minutes to fighter rendezvous at Longyen and there wasn't much to do except watch the check points go by. George came up in the nose and was setting up the sight. He didn't have a tachometer so had to use my stop watch. The inter-phone was quiet. The tail gunner called up to report the pins were pulled. The turret gunner had some trouble with his interphone and called to test it. Lindon called now and then to give me a fix and check with me. Mostly everyone was just ready for the job ahead.

We made fighter rendezvous two minutes late but picked up our escort OK. Going across the front lines south of Trier, we started our evasive action and from then on it was constant turning as we took evasive action all the way. Visibility was still excellent and the Mosselle and Saar River valleys were filled with fog and haze. They stood out like giant caterpillars on the ground. It made navigating easy. As we turned east and crossed the Rhine above Koblenz, we met two boxes of Marauders coming out. It was a narrow "alley" to go between the plotted flak and George and I were both watching every check point. We turned north toward our I.P. and started down to 8,000 feet.

(We came in at 12,000.) As we came up to the I.P. and George and I were trying to spot it in the distance we saw two small lakes and sure enough they were right at the I.P.

We reached our altitude OK and headed for the target. George got all ready and I got Tom started for the target area. We took very little evasive action on the run, putting our trust in S-2, which said no heavy flak. When George said PDI the target was about 10 miles off. He told us later that he had to use extended vision to pick up the target and he had the drift all killed when he got the extended vision rolled out. Bombs went away OK and we got ready for the fun — we hoped.

As we pulled over to the right George gave me the bomb sight and he got the nose gun going. I tried to get the bomb sight back out of the way but the gyro was spinning yet and I couldn't get rid of it. Tom started his left turn and descent. We couldn't get back over to the target because of the smoke and Tom started firing. Covey opened the co-pilot's window and fired his .45. Everybody was firing everything and hoping they were doing some good. We got down to about 500 feet and pulled out. It was a success so far and we were ready to go home. We headed back to the I.P. and started collecting airplanes. Four of us got together (four flights) but Clay called and said one of his flights hadn't bombed. We told him to bomb and not to strafe. He said he would strafe anyway so we said we are going home. Mueller took off ahead of us as we made the second 360. (He had the second box.)

At 11,000 feet we leveled out and headed home. Evasive action was the rule all the way home. Just past the Rhine we picked up the second box. They dog legged and came in behind us. Just as we crossed the bomb line out, there were two bursts of flak off to the right. It was a big relief to be back in friendly territory. Flak suits came off and we headed west and started down. As we crossed the Saar we could see the ground forces fighting for a bridgehead across the Saar.

It was more than a successful mission. It was a moral victory. Everyone had expected the worst and it had been nearly a milk run. Some light flak had come up at some of the formations but we were on our way home now. The waist gunner said he was sure that at least one of the spans of the bridge was down. We relaxed and enjoyed the ride home. About 10 miles from the field we called "Rightwing" and got an answer.

Back at the field everyone was out to sweat us in. They were lined up to count the ships as they came back. We taxied up to the hard stand and climbed out.

Up at group, Clay and Offenburg were P.O.'d because we left them, but we told them we gave them a chance to come out with us but couldn't wait all day. Offenburg got off course coming out and got flak at Trier. Clay lost his hydraulic system.

We got no photo coverage. Camera didn't work. Reinhart bombed the wrong target, one mile off. The group didn't lose a ship and none were badly damaged. Col. Witty got home just as the formation landed.

Tom's biggest worry: He didn't have his dog tags with him.

Mission #47

DATE: 19 March 1945
TARGET: VOKMARSEN RAIL BRIDGE
CREW: Johnson, Bert Hale, Eldridge, Melbye, Moore, Sgts. ?
POSITION: Led the group (had two boxes of twelve ships each).
LENGTH: 4:45

This was the first mission for us since the big strafing job in February. They got George up at 0400 for mission planning. Pre-briefing was at 0715. We had breakfast of fried eggs and cereal. Since the missions the last few days had been support of the Seventh and Third armies, we fully expected the same for today. However, they had us going up to this little old bridge way up in back of the Ruhr.

We talked the plans over and went down to briefing for a while. The weather was CAVU and we expected it to continue that way for several hours at least. Takeoff was on time and the join up was OK. We went on course six minutes early and met the fighters about four minutes early. They were P-38s and we had no trouble making contact with them. We made the check points all OK to the Rhine and Lacker Lake. As we started across the Rhine we started evasive action. We were doing all right, going in north of Neiwied and south of the Remegan bridge head, until we got across the autobahn and then flak started coming up at six o'clock. Tom kicked more rudders into the turns and it still was plenty accurate. We were making a fast ground speed and George and I were both trying to pin point our position exactly. The flak lasted for about three minutes and we escaped without serious damage. One ships in the other box lost an engine and had to turn back. Going on to the target pilotage was still difficult. Haze was cutting down visibility and a lot of smoke from the battle area was blowing on into the target area.

We located the I.P. and started toward the target. Visibility was worse as we headed into the sun and I couldn't see the target at all. George saw the area and started his run synchronizing on a tree short of the target. When he finally saw the target itself he wasn't able to get Tom onto it much before bombs away. We dropped on the first pass although George had only about

30 seconds after he actually saw the target. We hit right about 240 feet (George estimated 400 feet). We were the only flight to bomb on the first pass and we circled twice while the other flights dropped. We followed the last flight to bomb on its bomb run and saw his bombs hit. It looked like he got the bridge. We cut the rail lines to pieces and the place was a mess in general.

Coming back home we still had trouble doing good pilotage and got left of course about four miles. This time we stayed south of the bridge head and didn't see any flak fired at us. There was beaucoup flak around us. There were several other groups of Marauders as well as A-26s, 17s and Lancasters over the area. Two ships landed at Luxemburg for gas and five landed at A-68 for gas. We got home OK and only had one hole in the ship — in the rear bomb bay.

Mission #48

DATE: 23 March 1945
TARGET: DINSLAKEN COMMUNICATIONS CENTER
CREW: Johnson, Hathaway, Eldridge, Moore
POSITION: Led the group
LENGTH: 3:45

This was an early one. George went up to mission planning at 0400. Tom and I went up to pre-briefing at 0615. They had just given us a new target. It was right at the edge of the Ruhr Valley and we sweated a little until we saw it was also just over the bomb line and counter-battery fire would be in effect. Our release point was just over the Rhine. The weather was good and we got ready to go. We came back to the squadron and got our flying clothes and .45s.

Takeoff was normal except that when it came time to take off, the 497th was still taxiing across the runway. We delayed takeoff three minutes. Join up was OK and we went on course. At Weert we made a 360 to kill time and make our TOT [time over target] on time. Hathaway called the ground station and gave them the word that we were on time. After making the 360 I gave Tom a heading for the I.P. We flew a few minutes and George said we were right on course.

We could see the Rhine, and although a huge black smoke screen was billowing up just short of the target, we found the I.P. and headed for the target. George started evasive action. We argued about the check point that we had selected to go on the run over. I finally won the argument and George put Tom over it. We had interphone trouble and I gave my mike to George. We had trouble getting Tom to turn left at one time. We would tell him to take a certain heading and he would start turning the wrong way. We finally got together and went on the run. It was a good run and only a few bursts of flak came up. We got out and headed home. Results were superior for us and high for the flight.

These last two missions were flown out of Belgium. The Army Air Corps designated the field A-78. It is located in the southern part of the country and is still used, today, by F-16s. The base has two parallel runways running east-west.

Mission #49

DATE: 7 April 1945
TARGET: GOTTINGEN MARSHALLING YARDS
CREW: Johnson, Foster, Eldridge, Moore, Sgt. Morrison
POSITION: Led the group (first mission flown off A-78 by group).
LENGTH: 3:40

This target was exactly on the bomb line and was a high priority target. The rail yards were jammed with rolling stock pushed up in an attempt to stop the 1st and 3rd Armies' advance. We were briefed on this target yesterday but it was scrubbed. This was the third day on the loading list. (Peterman called us up to pre-briefing in the morning and they didn't even have a zero hour for the mission.)

Pre-briefing was at 1230 and just after briefing an hour delay came. It looked like a scrub but take off time came around and no word. We had to take off a minute late because everyone had to taxi across the runway. Join up was normal and we headed out on course 12 minutes early. There was about 6/10 stratus based at 5,500 feet and we climbed almost straight up through a hole—I mean there was a hole right on course and we went up through it—not straight up; hardly in a 26. Fighter rendezvous was at Koblenz at 8,000 feet but we had to fly at 9,000 to keep the second box out of the clouds. The fighters met us just as we started a 360 to kill time. We continued our turn and left fighter rendezvous one minute early. P-47s were the escort.

Gissen was the next turning point. There was about 8/10 cloud below us yet with large open spots. George and I were able to keep ourselves located fairly well and Morrison was getting good Gee fixes. As we approached the target area it looked like too many clouds. We went on to the I.P. and turned toward the target. The second box had called and said he would have to go up a thousand feet if he bombed, as he was too close to the clouds. We climbed up to 11,000.

We could see the town of Gottingen and the target area as we went up toward the target. There was a ridge of clouds right over the target and about the time George got on the sight he couldn't see anything but clouds. We turned short of the target and turned left. This wasn't in the plan but the 391st was still going around on the target (Their TOT was 20 minutes earlier than ours) and they were in the way to turn right.

We came around short of the I.P. a little and headed up the railroad to the target. We could line up on the target area but still couldn't see the AP. We decided to ride it out and hope for a chance to put the cross hairs on the target. The break came about ten seconds before bombs away. George got in one correction and just before the indices crossed he said, "I'm going to let 'em goes, Tom." Tom said OK, and we let 'em drop. The first box all dropped and the second box called and said they were going up and drop on the GEE target. We waited back at the I.P. for them. Coming out we zigzagged all over Germany trying to let the second box get into position. Everyone got into place, finally. We stayed up on top until we reached the vicinity of Malmedy, where we found a hole and let down.

Back at interrogation we discovered that Hale and Melbye had dropped on us and the third flight had dropped visually. The second box went up to the secondary and bombed on Gee.

Mission #50

DATE: 9 April 1945
TARGET: SAALFELD MARSHALLING YARDS
CREW: Johnson, Foster, Eldridge, Moore, Sgt. Morrison
POSITION: Led group.
LENGTH: 4:05

(Written at Palace Hotel, South Port, England, May 1)

This was the second mission of the day. While we were at pre-briefing the boys landed from the morning mission and they had bombed our target as a secondary target. Clouds covered their primary. They said the yards were full of trains and trucks so we kept the same target.

Takeoff and join up was normal and we headed for Frankfort, fighter rendezvous. We were just nicely on our way when the fighters called us and asked for our position. We talked back and forth and made the rendezvous as briefed over Frankfort. It was a long haul up to the target and we ground away at the miles.

Reaching enemy territory, we took evasive action and headed for the I.P.—a small village down in the hills southwest of the target. We were briefed to go in on a heading of north but there was such a heavy cloud of smoke over the target that we maneuvered in all directions trying to see around it. (We were the 5th group on the target.) George finally found the target through the smoke and we dropped on the first pass! He hit a little short and right. The other flights made two and three passes and we circled out in friendly territory for them.

Coming home the haze was terrific. When we got west of the Rhine I could just about see the ground looking straight down. I picked myself up at St. Vith (what remained of it) and took us in north of the field and made a left turn for runway 09.

Results: George apparently selected the wrong A.P. because of the change in the appearance of the target due to the previous bombing. Scored: Excellent.

Chapter 13

Author's Pilot's Log

PUBLISHED AND DISTRIBUTED

By

STEELE'S AID TO PILOTS

2227 W. WASHINGTON BLVD.

LOS ANGELES, CALIF.

Copyrighted 1943

by

C. Earl Steele

Printed in U. S. A.

By Smith Printing House, Los Angeles, Calif.

NAME CARL H. MOORE Lt. A.C. LIC. NO.

ADDRESS 344th Bomb Gp 494th Sqdn. PHONE

CITY STATE

IN EMERGENCY — PLEASE NOTIFY

NAME LEWIS C. MOORE

ADDRESS R.F.D. # 3 PHONE

CITY QUINCY STATE MICH

Aircraft are Designated as to Type   Airplanes as to Class

TYPE		CLASS	
a. — Airplane	....	a. — Single-engine, Land	= Se-L
b. — Autogiro	= Auto.	b. — Single-engine, Sea	= Se-S
c. — Glider	= Gli.	c. — Multi-engine, Land	= Me-L
d. — Lighter-than-air aircraft	= Ltaa	d. — Multi-engine, Sea	= Me-S
		e. — Unconventional	= Uncon.

LOG BOOKS: (20.67) The following rules shall govern pilot log-books:

GENERAL: Every certificated pilot and every person receiving flying instruction shall keep an accurate record of his flying time in a log-book in which the entries with respect to solo flying time have been certified to by him and the entries with respect to dual instruction have been certified to by his certificated instructor. Log-books shall be bound records and the entries shall be **accurate, legible, in ink or indelible pencil**, and so arranged as to facilitate easy reference thereto.

CONTENTS: The log-book shall contain the date of flight, the make and model of aircraft flown, its type, and, in the case of an airplane, its airplane class and horsepower, the aircraft identification mark, a statement of solo, dual instruction, instrument and night flying time, the duration of the flight, the points between which such flight was made, and, in addition, when any flight results in serious damage to the aircraft, a notation to this effect. Flying instruction time shall be logged in the same manner and, in addition, the instructor shall make complete entries in the log-book of his student showing the nature of each maneuver in which instruction was given and the time spent thereon. The instructor shall attest each such entry with his initials, pilot certificate number and pertinent rating. A log-book shall be presented for inspection, upon request and reasonable notice, to any authorized representative of the Authority or State or municipal officer enforcing local regulations or laws involving Federal compliance.

LOGGING INSTRUMENT FLIGHT TIME: (20.673) Instrument flight time may be logged as such only when the aircraft is flown solely by reference to instruments either under actual or properly simulated flight conditions. (Over-the-top flying shall not be logged as instrument flight time).

DATE 19 43	AIRCRAFT IDENT. MARK	MAKE - MODEL and HORSEPOWER OF AIRCRAFT	FROM	TO	CLASS OR TYPE			DURATION OF FLIGHT Total Time to Date
							Type of Mission	
12-4		AT-23						
12-4								
12-6								
12-8								
12-9								
12-11		B-26 C	Shreveport La ~~Lakeland, Fla~~	Lakeland Fla ~~Local XC~~			T	
12-12		✓	Lakeland Fla.	Local			T	
12-13		✓	✓	✓			T	
12-13		✓	✓	✓			T	
12-14		✓	✓	✓			T	
12-17		✓	✓	✓ ✓			Gp. Mission	
12-19		✓	✓	✓			✓	
12-20		B-26 C-26	Lakeland Fla.	Gp. Mission			T	

CARRY TOTALS FORWARD TO TOP OF NEXT PAGE

SOLO FLIGHT TIME			LINK	DUAL INSTRUCTION as instructor or Student			REMARKS: Each maneuver and the time spent thereon, attested to by the Instructor is to be entered in this column for all instruction received. Any serious damage to the aircraft MUST be entered here also.
Day	Night	Instrument					
		Bomb Trainer					
		1:00					
	✓	Nite	Celestial		Allyn & Graves		Landed at Mobile to leave Goodner
✓							Air to water Gunnery
	✓	✓	✓				
✓							Bombing & Gunnery
✓							"
✓							
✓							
✓							
							PILOT'S SIGNATURE

DATE 19 44	AIRCRAFT IDENT. MARK	MAKE - MODEL and HORSEPOWER OF AIRCRAFT	FROM	TO	CLASS OR TYPE			DURATION OF FLIGHT Total Time to Date
							Type of Mission	355:35
1-4		B-26 B50	Hunter Field Savannah Ga.	Local			Cal	2:00
1-7		✓	✓	✓			✓	3:00
1-10	42-95977	✓	✓	✓			✓	1:30
1-12	✓	✓	✓	✓			✓	1:30
1-12	✓	✓	✓	W. Palm Beach, Fla Morrison Field			Ferry	3:45
1-20	✓	✓	Morrison Field	Porto RICA BORINQUEN FIELD			✓	5:20
1-21	✓	✓	BORINQUEN FIELD	TRINIDAD WALLER FIELD			✓	4:10
1-21	✓	✓	Waller FIELD	British GUIANA Atkinson Field			✓	2:00
1-22	✓	✓	Atkinson Field	Belem, Brazil			✓	4:30
1-23	✓	✓	Belem, Brazil	Natal, Brazil			✓	5:15
1-26	✓	✓	Natal, Brazil	Ascension Island			✓	8:15
1-27	✓	✓	Ascension Island	Liberia. AFRICA. Roberts Field			✓	5:15
1-28	✓	✓	Roberts Field	Senegal, Fr. W. AFRICA DAKAR, RUFISQUE Fld.			✓	4:45
1-29	✓	✓	DAKAR,	TINDOUF, Algeria			✓	5:30
1-31	—	Doug- C-47	TINDOUF	FR. MORROCCO MARRAKECH	Passenger		✓	(2:00)
CARRY TOTALS FORWARD TO TOP OF NEXT PAGE								412:20 58:45

SOLO FLIGHT TIME			LINK	DUAL INSTRUCTION		as instructor or Student	REMARKS: Each maneuver and the time spent thereon, attested to by the Instructor is to be entered in this column for all instruction received. Any serious damage to the aircraft MUST be entered here also.
Day	Night	Instrument					
							Sighted Sub – were called into Waller for Details
							Lost R. Eng. 200 mi. out of Tindouf. Held Alt. of 6000' on single engine after throwing out 1 [illegible]
							gun, Pot-Pot – Life Raft. etc.
							PILOT'S SIGNATURE

DATE 19 44	AIRCRAFT IDENT. MARK	MAKE - MODEL and HORSEPOWER OF AIRCRAFT	FROM	TO	CLASS OR TYPE			DURATION OF FLIGHT Total Time to Date	
							TYPE of MISSION	412:20	
2-9	42-107573	B-26 C-45	MARRAKECH	Local			Test	2:45	
2-14	42-95964	B-26 B-50	✓	✓			Fuel Test	4:10	
2-17	42-107573	B-26 C-45	✓	St. MAWGAN England.			Ferry	9:10	
2-19	✓	✓	St MAWGAN &	Return			✓	2:30	
2-20	✓	✓	✓	Stansted, Eng AAB #169			✓	2:30	
2-24	42-95941	B-26 B-50	AAB #169	LOCAL			T	2:30	
2-25	✓	✓	✓	✓			T	2:30	
2-29	42-95916	✓	✓	✓			T	3:45	445:10
3-1	42-[illegible]	B-26 B-50	✓	✓			T	2:30	447:40
3-2	✓	✓	✓	✓			T	2:55	450:35
3-3	42-107573	B-26 C-45	✓	✓			T	2:35	453:10
2-6							T	(1:30)	
2-11							T	(1:30)	
3-4			AAB # 169	Local			T	2:00	45[illegible]
CARRY TOTALS FORWARD TO TOP OF NEXT PAGE								455:10	5[illegible]

SOLO FLIGHT TIME			LINK	DUAL INSTRUCTION	as instructor or Student		REMARKS: Each maneuver and the time spent thereon, attested to by the Instructor is to be entered in this column for all instruction received. Any serious damage to the aircraft MUST be entered here also.
Day	Night	Instrument					
							Weather closed in - returned to St. M.
							PILOT'S SIGNATURE

DATE 19 44	AIRCRAFT IDENT. MARK	MAKE - MODEL and HORSEPOWER OF AIRCRAFT	FROM	TO	CLASS OR TYPE			DURATION OF FLIGHT	Total Time to Date
							Type of Mission		455:10
MARCH-5	7573	Martin B-26C-45	Stanstead, Eng.	8 mi N.W. DIEPPE	ME-L		Diversion	2:50	458:00
3-8	42-95876	B-26 B-50	"	LOCAL			T	:30	458:30
3-9	42-95912	✓	Station #169	"			T	3:00	461:30
3-11	42-107573	B-26 C-45	✓	✓			✓	1:15	462:45
3-13	✓	✓	✓	✓			✓	2:00	464:45
3-14	42-95890	B-26 B-50	✓	✓			✓	2:30	467:15
3-19	42-107573	B-26 C-45	✓	Hazebrouck Noball East of St. OMER		1	Combat	2:45	470:00
3-20	✓	✓ ✓	✓	CREIL R.R. YARDS		2	C	3:45	473:45
3-22	42-95941	B-26 B-50	✓	Local Test Hop			Test	:20	474:05
3-22	42-107573	B-26 C-45	✓	344 Boreham & Return			T	1:00	475:05
3-24	42-95892	B-26 B 50	✓	Scrubbed			C T	1:15	476:20
3-25	42-107573	B-26 C-45	✓	Hirson Rail yards and return		3	C	3:40	480:00
3-26	✓	✓ ✓	✓	IJmoden E Boat Pens & Return		4	C	3:35	483:35
4-4	921	B-26 B-50	✓	Local			Local	1:30	485:05
4-4	890	✓	✓	✓			✓	2:00	487:05
CARRY TOTALS FORWARD TO TOP OF NEXT PAGE									487:05

SOLO FLIGHT TIME			LINK	DUAL INSTRUCTION as instructor or Student			REMARKS: Each maneuver and the time spent thereon, attested to by the Instructor is to be entered in this column for all instruction received. Any serious damage to the aircraft MUST be entered here also.
Day	Night	Instrument					

~~Nav~~ ~~Nav Bomb~~

Sorry—no combat time—
Diversion Mission—1st. Combat Mission—

495th Ship Norguard, Johnson, Curmode, Offenberger Practice Bombing Mission—ceiling [illegible]

Practice Bombing at Red Grave—3 bombs at 1500' with D-8—Capt Johnson, Curmode.

—Dry Runs on Targets—Johnson, Graves, Curmode, McConnell

willms

Practice Bombing and Gunnery—Johnson, willms, Curmode, Horsin

1st Combat Mission—No Flak No fighters—ON Loading list 11 Consecutive Days Johnson, Graves, Curmode, Tippins, calkins, Castoro—

2nd—Same Flak. Johnson, Willms, Curmode, Tippens, Vellecca, Calkins, Castoro

Test hop—L. Engine cutting out. Johnson, Graves, Guay, Trippin.

Andre, Salinger, Johnston

Mission Scrubbed after take-off Seebolt, Webb, Ross.

Johnson, willms, Curmode, Tippens, calkins, Castoro, Campbell.—Bombs dropped on Target McConnell did a good job. 322nd Gp lost 2 ships from flak at Montdidier.

Johnson, willms, curmode, Tippens, calkins, Castoro. Bombs dropped Short and ~~a little~~ to Right.

Seebolt, Graves,—GEE equipment out—Mission N. G.

Johnson, Graves, DIGBY, Bowers—Nite Local—

PILOT'S SIGNATURE

DATE 19 44	AIRCRAFT IDENT. MARK	MAKE - MODEL and HORSEPOWER OF AIRCRAFT	FROM	TO	CLASS OR TYPE			DURATION OF FLIGHT	Total Time to Date
									487:05
4-5	42-95890	B-26 B50	Station #169	Channel & Return			Recon	2:15	489:20
4-5	42-107573	B-26 C-45	✓	Local			T	1:30	490:50
4-6	870	B-26	✓	✓			T	1:35	492:25
4-8	42-107573	B-26 C-45	✓	"Belgium" and Return		Mission #5	C	2:55	495:20
4-9	42-95890	B-26 B50	✓	Local			T	:30	495:50
4-9	✓	✓	✓	✓			T	2:00	497:50
4-11	✓	✓	✓	RAIL YARDS at MONTIGNIES-Sur-Sambre.		6th	C	3:20	501:10
4-13	892	✓	✓	Le Havre & Return		7th	C	2:45	503:55
4-13	921	✓	✓	Local			T	2:00	505:55
4-15	573	✓ C-45	✓	✓			T	1:30	507:25
4-16	K9T	✓ B-50	✓	-✓			T	1:25	508:50
4-17	573	✓ C-45	✓	Charl-le-Roi Rail yards		8th	C	3:00	511:50
4-20	890	✓ B-50	✓	Gun Position Near La Havre		9th	C	3:10	515:00
✓	✓	✓	✓	NO BALL N.W. St. OMER [illegible]		10th	C	2:30	517:30
4-21	K9T	✓	✓	Local			T	:45	518:15
CARRY TOTALS FORWARD TO TOP OF NEXT PAGE								518:15	

SOLO FLIGHT TIME			LINK	DUAL INSTRUCTION as instructor or Student			REMARKS: Each maneuver and the time spent thereon, attested to by the Instructor is to be entered in this column for all instruction received. Any serious damage to the aircraft MUST be entered here also.
Day	Night	Instrument					
	1:00						Johnson — Graves, Dierk, Bailey — Weather Recon. for Early Morning Mission — Some fun
✓							Johnson — Willms, — Tippins — ANDRA. —
✓							Major Maxwell, — Sarby, Mullier — Ackerman — "GEE" Training Mission —
✓							Johnson, Mus. Smith. Curmode. Target was R.R. at Haslett. — Hit frontal weather near Brussells and turned North and back out. Heavy flak at Courtrai — SNAFU
✓							Graves, Retzer-Rivers — "Gee" flight — Blew fuse and returned.
	2:00.						
✓							Hale, Aultman, Ackerman, McConnell — Rail yards — Bombed thru Broken Clouds — Operated GEE Box all the way
✓							Seebolt, Sandstrom, Eldridge — Target covered with clouds — All Bombs returned.
✓							Hartnett, Willms. McCullum, Sgt Lasky GEE Training and Transition.
✓							Johnson, Webb, Eldridge — PDI Runs
✓							Allen, Johnston, Cook — Flew Co-pilot — Tried a take-off and landing — Fun
✓							Johnson, Sandstrom, Eldridge — Perfect weather — good results. Left formation on return because of L. Eng
✓							Johnson, Smith, Eldridge — followed Pathfinder — Miss Target about a mile. Lead 2nd Box
✓		✓	✓	✓			Lead 2nd Box — Poor Vsby. — Gee. did a good job. 1st Box didn't Drop. Harvey Johnson went down. 8 Flak Holes
✓							Hynes, Amberry — Local formation for new Crews
							PILOT'S SIGNATURE

DATE 19 44	AIRCRAFT IDENT. MARK	MAKE - MODEL and HORSEPOWER OF AIRCRAFT	FROM	TO	CLASS OR TYPE			DURATION OF FLIGHT Total Time to Date	
									518:15
4-22	42-110573	B-26 C-45	Station 769 England	No Ball 8 mi East Bercks-Sur-Mer		11th	C	2:15	520:30
4-22	✓	✓	✓	No Ball 3 mi SW St Pol France		12th	C	2:35	523:05
4-25	890	✓ B-50	✓	NO-BALL Cherburg		13A	C	3:10	526:15
4-27	✓	✓	✓	CAMBRAI Marshalling Yards		14th	C	3:00	529:15
4-28	✓	✓	✓	Local			T	1:45	531:00
4-29	573	✓ B-45	✓	To Hastings and Return			T	1:50	532:50
4-30	✓	✓	✓	No-BALL North of Hisden. Near Fruges	OK [illegible]	15th	C	2:30	535:20
5-2	K9S	✓	✓	Rail yards at VALenciennes		16th	C	3:00	538:20
5-3	573	✓ ✓	✓	Local			T	2:00	540:20
5-5	✓	✓	✓	Boreham, wethersfield East Hadley & Return			A	2:15	542:35
5-7	890	B-26 B 50	✓	Rail Yards at Mezieres Charleville		17th	C	3:35	546:10
5-7	K-9C	✓	✓	Local			T	1:00	547:10
5-8	K9B	✓ C45	✓	✓			T	1:45	548:55
5-9	K9S	✓ ✓	✓	Round House CALAIS		18th	C	2:00	550:55
5-9	✓	✓ ✓	✓	288 mm. Rail Guns N.E. Boulogne		19th	C	2:00	552:55
CARRY TOTALS FORWARD TO TOP OF NEXT PAGE									552:55

SOLO FLIGHT TIME: Day	Night	Instrument / Link / Dual Instruction as instructor or Student / REMARKS: Each maneuver and the time spent thereon, attested to by the Instructor is to be entered in this column for all instruction received. Any serious damage to the aircraft MUST be entered here also.
✓		Sandstrum, Johnson, Eldridge, Diery (And that's all!!!) Flew lead in #2 Flight 1st Box. Hale lead. No flak. Good Results.
✓		Seebolt, Peters, Eldridge — Carried K-20 camera and took pictures. Allen injured by flak.
✓		Johnson, Col. VANCE, Eldridge. — Hit target on 2nd pass at target. No flak No fighters — Excellent results (Baker on "GEE"
✓		Johnson, Graves, Eldridge — A long ride and lots of navigation.. No flak No fighters — Geo. loved them in —
✓		Johnson, Graves, Schnubel, Curmode, Eldridge — Practice Bombing on East Hatley Range — Not much excitement. —
✓		Johnson, Seebolt, Rivers, Eldridge — At last minute our Box was made #1 and we took off — Got to 10,500 over SE England and were re-called because of weather
✓		Johnson. Seebolt, Eldridge, Rivers — All bombs in Target Area. But no hits, 1st Box hit a small village short of Target.
✓		HALE, Graves, Mcconnell, Rivers. — Bombed by Flights and lead the Group. All Good Hits
✓		Johnson, Graves, Eldridge, Curmode, — Practice PDI Checked Tom out on GEE Box.
✓		HALE, Johnson, Tippens — Delivered invitations to DANCE — Had Dinner At Boreham — Some ride — Buzzed the field —
✓		Johnson, Seebolt (?) [Day after the party]. Eldridge. Nearly 1½ hrs over enemy territory. A Long Haul — Bombed By flights — followed Norgaard and wandered all over France. Good results
	✓	Sandstrum, Seavy — Nite formation
✓		Johnson, HALE, Eldridge, Mcconnell, Rivers — Practice Bombing on East Hatley Range
✓		HALE, Maj. Smith, ~~Eldridge~~ Mcconnell — A Big show — over 200 P-47's dive bombing Flak guns. 3 groups of Marauders — we had Malfunction and salvoed. Bombs went over 300'
✓		Johnson, Seebolt, Eldridge — Climbed up to 13,500 and Bombed by flights. We were only flight that dropped. No one else saw the target. — Bombs hit good.
		PILOT'S SIGNATURE

Jack Cahill to our ship

DATE 19 44	AIRCRAFT IDENT. MARK	MAKE - MODEL and HORSEPOWER OF AIRCRAFT	FROM	TO	CLASS OR TYPE			DURATION OF FLIGHT	Total Time to Date
				Cormeilles					552:55
5-11	K-9-A	B-26 · B 50	Station 169	Gun position Dunkerque		20th	C	2:00	554:55
5-13	K-9-S	✓ ✓	✓	Ditto only in Town center of		21st	C	2:00	556:55
5-15	K-9-J	✓ C	✓	Local			T	:50	557:45
5-19	K-9-S	✓ B-50	✓	Leconfield - North of Hull near Humber River & Return			T	2:20	560 05
5-20	K-9-B	✓ C-45	✓	Airfield at Cormeilles (NW Paris		22nd	C	3:30	563:35
5-21	K-9-V	✓ ✓	✓	Kemble RAF Field and return			T	1:15	564:50
5-22	K-9-B	✓ ✓	✓	Rodgrave Bombing Range & return			T	2:00	566:50
5-24	K-9-B	✓ ✓	✓	Air Port at Aichet, France		23rd	C	2:30 3:20	572:40
5-26	K-9-V	✓ ✓	✓	Local			T	2:00	574:40
5-27	K-9-A	✓ B 50	✓	✓			T	2:15	576:55
5-27	K-9-J	· ✓	✓	✓			T	2:15	579 10
5-28	K-9-B	✓ C-45	✓	Engine shed at AMEINS		24th	C	3:15	582:25
5-28	K-9-V	✓ ✓	✓	Maston and Return			A	1:10	583 35
5-30	K-9-U	AT 23	✓	Tempsford & Return			A	1:10	584:45
6-4	K-9-K	B-26	✓	Kemble Cirencester			A	1:00	585:30
CARRY TOTALS FORWARD TO TOP OF NEXT PAGE									585 38

SOLO FLIGHT TIME			LINK	DUAL INSTRUCTION as instructor or Student	REMARKS: Each maneuver and the time spent thereon, attested to by the Instructor is to be entered in this column for all instruction received. Any serious damage to the aircraft MUST be entered here also.
Day	Night	Instrument			
✓		Johnson, Seebalt. Eldridge.			Bombed by flight and hit fairly good. Bomb run was a little SNAFU and flak was Rough—Vsby was v. BAD
✓		HALE, Steen, McConnell, Freeman			Poor Vsby. Caught Hell on Bomb Run. 150 holes in ship. No Left Brake—Tippens wounded Slightly. Bombs O.K.
✓		Johnson, WREN,			— Test Hop.
✓		Johnson, Graves, Eldridge, Selinger, Retzer, Castora, Tippins, Calkins.			— Took Retzer up on his day off. Landed at RAF Field with Halifaxes. Good Show and big Time. —
✓		Johnson, Graves, Eldridge.			Didn't drop bombs. — Geo. held them rather than hit a village — Made a pass at 2nd [illegible] — Evreux — but Vsby so bad that couldn't get a good run. —
✓		HALE, Peters, Brown, C.L., Thompson			— Business Run to Hospital — Staged around all Afternoon — Landed just before dark —
✓		HALE, Johnson, Eldridge, Tippens.			— Practice Bombing at 2000' — Had 2 Bombs each and HALE dropped 2 more dive Bombing — Good Show — P.M. Flight added
✓		Johnson, Hynes, Eldridge, Tippens, Calkins, Castora.			— Poor Vsby except at Target. — Excellant Bombing — Another Cook's Tour — Left Box at Ghent.
✓		Johnson, Eldridge, Sgt Gaynor			— Practice bombs on Red Grove. I dropped 5 — Geo 4 Tom — 1 Dive Bombing. Geo Flew RB — I flew back and helped Tom land???
✓		Sandstrom, Eldridge, Seelinger. Fedowitz.			Altitude test for Fedowitz — went to 18,500 — used oxygen — could have gone higher
✓		Johnson, Eldridge, Kolberg — Wren — perkins			— Practice Bombing low Alt. with D-8 sight — Did some D.R. Navi. and read platter wrong coming home —
✓		Johnson, Seebult, Eldridge — Tippens. Castora, Calkins			— A good job. I we led the Group and also 391st [illegible] Jones — crash landed at Manston — A long haul — good weather
	✓	Allyn, Sanders, Seelinger, wren, Graham			— Took Doc down to find the correct story on Jones and his crew — They were all coming O.K. — Ship wrecked.
✓		Johnson, Kolberg, Goodwin			— Took Willy up to his girls friends home where he starts 7 day leave —
✓		HALE, Johnson,			—
					PILOT'S SIGNATURE

DATE 19 44	AIRCRAFT IDENT. MARK	MAKE - MODEL and HORSEPOWER OF AIRCRAFT	FROM	TO	CLASS OR TYPE			DURATION OF FLIGHT Total Time to Date
								585:30
6-5	K-9-K	B-26 B-50	Cirenchester	Station 169			A	1:20
6-6	K-9-S	✓	Station 169	Beach road & return	*	25th	C	3:45
6-7	K-9-A	✓	✓	Cherburg Pen. — Gun Position.		26th	C	2:40
6-8	—	—	✓					
6-12	K-9-A	✓	✓	Bridges at Conde' Sur N.		27th	C	3:05
6-13	K-9-S	✓	✓	Road Junction St Pierre (S. of Caen)		28th	C	3:20
6-14	K-9-B	✓ C-45	✓	Gun Position on Coast East of Volunes		29th	C	2:45
6-21	K-9-B	✓ C-45	✓	Local			T	1:45
6-24	✓	✓	✓	Gun Position on Hill S. Cherbourg		30th	C	2:30
6-24	K-9-W	AT-23	✓	Aberdeen, Scotland		87:50	A	2:00
6-25	✓	✓	Aberdeen	Station 169			A	2:05
6-26	✓	✓	Station 169	Ireland Toome - Field			A	1:45
6-26	✓	✓	Toome	Aberdeen Scotland Dyce Field			A	1:30
6-28	✓	✓	Aberdeen	Station 169			A	2:05
6-30	K-9-S	B-26	Station 169	Local			T	1:15 617:35
CARRY TOTALS FORWARD TO TOP OF NEXT PAGE								617:35

SOLO FLIGHT TIME			LINK	DUAL INSTRUCTION as instructor or Student			REMARKS: Each maneuver and the time spent thereon, attested to by the Instructor is to be entered in this column for all instruction received. Any serious damage to the aircraft MUST be entered here also.
Day	Night	Instrument					
		CP Time					
✓							Hale - Johnson - Got rained in and had to stay overnite
2:15	1:30						D-DAY Major Johnson, Willms, Eldridge, Castoro, Calkins, Tippens. Flew #4 to Norgard who lead 9th Air Force.
✓							Major Johnson, Lowery, Eldridge. Castoro, Calkins, Tippens. - Led 2nd Box. I worked GEE and Geo. did Pilotage. Bad weather - Alt. 6000. Missed -
			1:00				Basic Problems.
✓							Johnson, Bailey, Eldridge - Castoro, Calkins, Tippens. Led 2nd Box. Bombed by Flights - All 6 Bombardiers used wrong A.P. hit the town the.
✓							Maj. HALE, Deford, McConnell, Castoro, Tippens - Led 2nd Box. Schianni Led 1st Box. Circled Target 3 Times waiting for Schianni. Hit 500' right.
✓	(Direct Support of Ground Troops)						Johnson, Hynes, Eldridge, Castoro, Tippins, Calkins - Led 2nd Box. 1st Mission with "B" since it went to Depot. Alt. 3000'. Geo hit 150' left but knocked out [illegible]
✓							Johnson, Eldridge, Marine - Ceiling 1000'. went up to Holbeach Bombing range - dropped 10 bombs - no sight - flew home - Geo. flew up.
✓							Johnson, Webb, Eldridge. Castoro, Calkins, Tippens. Led 2nd Box behind Col. Maxwell. Direct Support of Ground Troops. Hill was taken soon after. Good hits
✓							Johnson, Graves, Eldridge: Went up to get Ashley Smith and crew. Back from week leave. Geo. Flew up. I flew most of way back - weather not good.
✓		1:00					Return Trip. low ceiling coming home.
✓							Kolberg. Schnabel - Took Sandy to Ireland for 4 day leave. - Bad weather over Eng.
✓							Same - Taking enlisted men to Aberdeen. what a trip. followed rivers at tree top level - finally made it.
✓							Kolberg, Schnabel, Ashberry and enlisted men. - Not quite so bad - but more minimum Alt. and rain
✓		1:00					HALE, wolf - Joy ride -
							PILOT'S SIGNATURE

DATE 1944	AIRCRAFT IDENT. MARK	MAKE - MODEL and HORSEPOWER OF AIRCRAFT	FROM	TO	CLASS OR TYPE			DURATION OF FLIGHT Total Time to Date
								617:35
7-4	K-9G	B-26-C	Station 169	Chittenden and return			A	1:00
7-5	Y-5-Y	B-26 F	"	Aberdeen			A	2:10
7-5	✓	✓	Aberdeen	Station 169			A	2:30
7-8	K-9-B	B-26 B-50	Station 169	Nogent Le R. Bridges N. of Chartres		34th	C	3:45
7-10	K-9-U AT-23	AT23	"	Aberdeen			A	2:00
7-10	✓	✓	Aberdeen	Station 169			A	2:15
7-14	K-9-B	B-26 C-45	Station 169	Toome N. Ireland			A	2:00
7-15	✓	✓	Toome	Hixon Field England			A	1:35
7-15	✓	✓	RAF Hixon Field	Burtonwood E. Liverpool			A	0:30
7-15	✓	✓	Burtonwood	Station 169			A	1:00
7-17	✓	✓	Station 169	Local			T	1:30
7-19	✓	✓	✓	R.R. Bridge S.E. ANGERS, FRANCE		32nd	C	4:00
7-20	K-9-S	✓ B-50	✓	Local			Test	:45
7-20	✓	✓	✓	Zeale			T	1:20
7-20	✓	✓	Zeale	North Pickingham			T	1:20
CARRY TOTALS FORWARD TO TOP OF NEXT PAGE								643:15

SOLO FLIGHT TIME			LINK	DUAL INSTRUCTION as instructor or Student / REMARKS: Each maneuver and the time spent thereon, attested to by the Instructor is to be entered in this column for all instruction received. Any serious damage to the aircraft MUST be entered here also.
Day	Night	Instrument		
		C.P. Time		
✓		:30		Kolberg, Me. – Pick up Sandstrom who was returning from Ireland.
✓				Johnson and crew from 495th. Not a bad ride up except haze and clouds kept us on instruments most of time
:30	2:00			Johnson, & Sullivan's crew. Had trouble with left engine—finally got started about 2230 and made a nice trip of it.
				Johnson, Cahill, Eldridge, Castoro, Tippens, Calkins. Clouds over target. Made 3 passes and dropped – Made one more for another flight. Hit short—
				Allyn, Fubel, Willms, Eldridge plus crew – up to Scotland for weeks leave.
				Carrington, Eldridge, Carney, Thomas. – plus crew. — Bringing them back from leave.
				Johnson, Cahill, McConnell, Ott, ONDRA, Calkins, Castoro, Tippens. Went up to look up Replacements – Ceiling 0 at Toome —
				Same crew — (They left for Toome this morn) Replacements were down at Stone – so went down to see them.
				Took two men up on way home.
				Back home again.
				Cahill, Stevens, Cladder, Le Boeuf. GEE Trainer and PDI Runs —
	Le Ponts de Ce			Johnson, Cahill, Eldridge, Smith, Hamilton. – Led II Box. Geo. Laid 'em in on the bridge. —
				GRAVES, OREN. Went to 10,000' –
				Willms, Sullivan, Stevens, Eldridge, Allyn. – Took Web over to Flak House – GEE Trainer – PDI
				" " Took Steve and Sally up to see Friends —
				PILOT'S SIGNATURE

DATE 19 44	AIRCRAFT IDENT. MARK	MAKE - MODEL and HORSEPOWER OF AIRCRAFT	FROM	TO	CLASS OR TYPE			DURATION OF FLIGHT Total Time to Date
								645:15
7-20	K-9-S	B-26 B-50	North Pickingham	Station 169			T	:35
7-22	K-9-A	✓	Station 169	Redgrave & Return Bombing Range			T	2:15
7-23	✓	✓	✓	Toome			T	2:00
7-23	✓	✓	Toome	Station 169			T	2:00
7-25	K-9-B	B-26 C45	Station 169	Troops west of St Lo		33rd	C	3:00
7-25	✓	✓	✓	Rail Bridge at Maintenon Fr.		34th	C	4:00
7-30	✓	✓	✓	Local			T	1:30
8-2	K-9-S	✓ B-50	✓	✓			T	1:30
8-3	K-9-S	✓	✓	✓			T	1:40
8-5	K-9-B	✓ C-45	✓	Lisieux France — and return		35th	C	2:50
8-5	K-9-B	✓	✓	Bridge 10 mi NE Le Mans —		36th	C	4:00
8-7	K-9-R	✓	✓	Homesley South west of Portsmouth			A	1:00
8-7	✓	✓	Homesley South	Station 169 to Wethersfield			A	1:15
8-8	✓	✓	Wethersfield	Station 169			A	:30
8-9	K-9-B	✓	Station 169	Rail Bridge S.W. of Campiegne		37th	C	3:10
CARRY TOTALS FORWARD TO TOP OF NEXT PAGE								676:15

SOLO FLIGHT TIME			LINK	DUAL INSTRUCTION as instructor or Student	REMARKS: Each maneuver and the time spent thereon, attested to by the Instructor is to be entered in this column for all instruction received. Any serious damage to the aircraft MUST be entered here also.
Day	Night	Instrument			
		C.P.			
✓				Same crew – More PDI runs and GEE Time	
✓		:30		Johnson, Eldridge, Peters — Dropped 16 Bombs – Good results. Checked out Peters on the GEE Box.	
✓				Johnson, Kolberg, Eldridge, Nassr — up to check on replacement —	
✓		1:00		Same as above —	
✓		C		Johnson, Deford, Eldridge – Castoro, Calkins, Tippens — Followed Col. Maxwell. Direct Support – Frag. Bombs. Hit slightly left	
✓		C		Same crew – Bridge N.E. of Chartres. We hit over – 2 Flights hit it.	
✓		T		Johnson, Eldridge – (Willms) Instrument check for Willms	
✓		T		Allyn, Reed, Chiscizza, Cook – Practice mission for Webber crew – Tom flew lead flight we flew #2 —	
✓		T		Deford, Rizzo, Sugarman – Practice bombing – O.K.	
✓		C		Johnson, Lt. Col. Witty, Eldridge – Castoro, Tippens & Calkins. Led Box II Mission recalled at landfall – lack of fighter escort —	
✓		C		Johnson, Clay, Eldridge – Castoro, Tippins, Calkins – Finally made it. Geo. Dropped on 2nd pass – hit 300' left. Bridge still standing	
✓				Ashberry, Wilson, Sgt Dunn, Cpl – ?. Went down to 100 ft over Kolbergs ship	
	✓			Same crew – Our field was closed in and we landed at first open field – Col Hale told us to bail out if necessary – But we didn't	
✓				Came back home as soon as fog lifted next morning	
✓		G		Johnson, Seth, Eldridge – Castoro, Calkins, Tippens. A good show. No flak altho we "sweated." Geo took a long run and hit north end of bri[illegible]	
					PILOT'S SIGNATURE

DATE 1944	AIRCRAFT IDENT. MARK	MAKE - MODEL and HORSEPOWER OF AIRCRAFT	FROM	TO	CLASS OR TYPE			DURATION OF FLIGHT Total Time to Date	
									676:15
8-18	Bonnys Honey	B-26	169	Norwich			T	:30	676:45
8-18	K-9-C	✓	Norwich	169			T	:30	677:15
8-19	K-9-B	" ✓	Station 169	Local			T	1:45	679:00
8-24	K-9-Y	B-26 G-5	"	"			T	1:30	680:30
8-25	✓	✓	✓	✓			T	1:00	681:30
8-25	K-9-B	B-26-C45	✓	✓			T	:45	683:15
8-27	✓	✓	✓	✓			T	1:00	
8-27	K-9-F	B-26 F	✓	✓			T	:30	
8-27	K-9-S	B-26 B	✓	✓			T	1:00	
8-29	K-9-B	✓ C-45	✓	HAM. France & Return	38th		C	2:50	
8-30	✓	✓	✓	Local			T	3:00	
9-5	K-9-B	✓	✓	Brest Gun Position & Return	39th		C	4:10	
9-6	✓	✓	✓	Local			T	1:45	
9-11	K-9-W	✓	✓	Metz France & Return	40		C	3:45	
9-18	K-9-BII	B-26 G.	✓	Local			T	0:45	

CARRY TOTALS FORWARD TO TOP OF NEXT PAGE

SOLO FLIGHT TIME			LINK	DUAL INSTRUCTION as instructor or Student			REMARKS: Each maneuver and the time spent thereon, attested to by the Instructor is to be entered in this column for all instruction received. Any serious damage to the aircraft MUST be entered here also.
Day	Night	Instrument					
		C.P. TIME					
✓		~~:30~~	Col. HALE, 2nd & crew from 495th. went up to pick up K-9-C. for Depot.				
✓		:30	Return Trip				
✓		:30	Johnson, Eldridge, LeBoef — Practice Bombing —				
✓			HALE, Eldridge — AFCE Training — not to good.				
✓		:30	Johnson & ME — Just for fun — ½ Landing				
✓		:15	" " " " " 1 Landing —				
✓			Johnson, Eldridge, ONDRA, MARINI Local Refresher flight				
✓		:15	" " Glass, Swartz — Test Hop ½ P.P. Landing				
✓		:30	HALE, Johnson, Eldridge, — F.T.D.				
✓			Johnson, Allyn, Eldridge				
✓		:30	Johnson, Eldridge				
✓			Johnson, Stephens, Eldridge Castore, Calkins, Tippens. No Flak — Made 3 passes — Quite a bit of cloud — Good hit.				
✓		:30	" Eldridge, ONDRA — Calibrated ASI & Swung Compass				
✓			Johnson, Young, Eldridge, Calkins, Castore. Mission				
✓		:30	" Eldridge, ONDRA — Test Hop on new ship				
							PILOT'S SIGNATURE

DATE 1944	AIRCRAFT IDENT. MARK	MAKE - MODEL and HORSEPOWER OF AIRCRAFT	FROM	TO	CLASS OR TYPE			DURATION OF FLIGHT Total Time to Date
9-18	K-9-A	B-26 B 50	Station 169	Duren Germany & return		41	C	3:30
(9-9)								
9-24	K-9-8II	B-26 G 5					T	3:20
9-25	K-9-8II	B-26 B50	Station A-59	Local			T	1:15
9-27	✓	✓	✓	✓			T	1:15
10-6	K-9-A	B-26 B-50	✓	Arnhem, Holland & Return		42nd	C	3:25
10-6	K-9-8II	B-26 G 10					T	3:45
10-13		✓					T	2:00
10-18		✓					T	1:00
10-21		✓					T	1:25
10-22		✓					T	1:20 729:55
11-15	K-9-T	B-26 C 45	✓	Local			T	2:00
11-19	K-9-K	B-26 G 5	✓	Neuwied Bridge (near Koblentz) & Return		43	C	3:35
11-26	K-9TII	B-26 G	Station A-59	Local nite			T	1:30
~~[illegible]~~							~~C~~	~~3:35~~

CARRY TOTALS FORWARD TO TOP OF NEXT PAGE

SOLO FLIGHT TIME			LINK	DUAL INSTRUCTION as instructor or Student			REMARKS: Each maneuver and the time spent thereon, attested to by the Instructor is to be entered in this column for all instruction received. Any serious damage to the aircraft MUST be entered here also.
Day	Night	Instrument					
✓							Tippens worked GEE. Ascent & descent thru overcast. Johnson, Col. Whitty, Eldridge — Geo. hit the chokepoint — 320 flak
			1:00				
✓							
✓							Johnson, Maj. Shoal, Capt Herried, McConnell — PDI —
✓							
✓							Pathfinder ?
✓							
✓							
✓							
✓							
✓							
✓							Johnson, Eldridge, Moone, Tippens — Local "familiarization"
✓							Johnson, Spaog, Eldridge, Moore, Tippens, Cystero, Collins. Got E.a. 65 for E.M. Target with 5 ships, I forgot to open doors — hit Germany ... I got sick.
	✓						Graves, Cahill, Eldridge, Moore, Sgt Goodwin
✓							
							PILOT'S SIGNATURE

DATE 19 44	AIRCRAFT IDENT. MARK	MAKE - MODEL and HORSEPOWER OF AIRCRAFT	FROM	TO	CLASS OR TYPE			DURATION OF FLIGHT Total Time to Date
Dec 1	K-9-B	B-26 G-10	Station A-59	Local			T	1:50
12-4			"				T	:40
12-8			"				T	2:10
12-9			"	Baumholder Supply Depot		44	C	3:35
12-12			"				T	2:00
12-12			"				T	1:00
12-13			"				T	2:00
12-13			"				T	2:30
12-24			"	Konz-Karthaus RR Bridge		45	C	3:30
1945								—
1-5			"				T	:50
1-23			"				T	3:36
1-24			"				T	1:00
1-26			"				T	2:40
CARRY TOTALS FORWARD TO TOP OF NEXT PAGE								

SOLO FLIGHT TIME			LINK	DUAL INSTRUCTION as instructor or Student			REMARKS: Each maneuver and the time spent thereon, attested to by the Instructor is to be entered in this column for all instruction received. Any serious damage to the aircraft MUST be entered here also.
Day	Night	Instrument					
		Co-Pilot					
✓		1:50					Johnson, Eldridge, Ondra, Boky, PDI and GEE. Almost got a "Frog" & his truck on landing
							PILOT'S SIGNATURE

DATE 19 45	AIRCRAFT IDENT. MARK	MAKE - MODEL and HORSEPOWER OF AIRCRAFT	FROM	TO	CLASS OR TYPE			DURATION OF FLIGHT Total Time to Date
2-21	B-26G-10		A-59				T	2:10
2-21	"		"				T	1:50
2-21	"		"				T	1:10
2-22	"		"	operation clarion		44	C	4:10
2-25	"		"				T	1:20
3-11	B-26G45		"				T	:30
3-14	" G5		"				T	2:30
3-15	B-26G1		"				T	1:55
3-15	B-26G5		"				T	2:00
3-17	"		"				T	1:20
3-17	"		"				T	1:45
3-18	B-26G5		"				T	2:35
3-19	B-26G1		"	Volksmarsen RR Bridg (?)		47	C	4:45
3-23	"		"	Dinslaken communication (?)		48	C	3:45
3-24	B-26G5		"				T	2:00
			CARRY TOTALS FORWARD TO TOP OF NEXT PAGE					

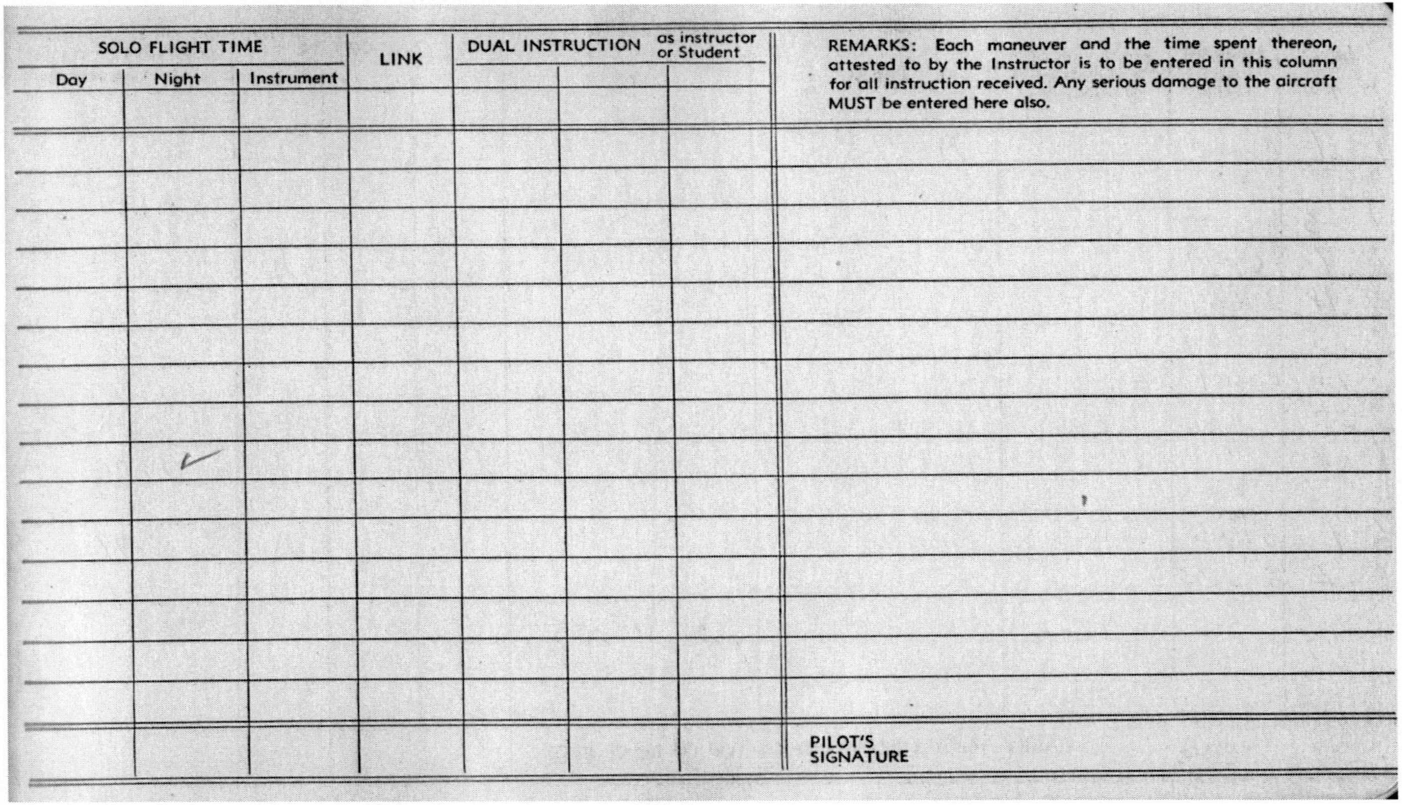

SOLO FLIGHT TIME			LINK	DUAL INSTRUCTION as instructor or Student		REMARKS: Each maneuver and the time spent thereon, attested to by the Instructor is to be entered in this column for all instruction received. Any serious damage to the aircraft MUST be entered here also.
Day	Night	Instrument				
	✓					
						PILOT'S SIGNATURE

DATE 19 45	AIRCRAFT IDENT. MARK	MAKE - MODEL and HORSEPOWER OF AIRCRAFT	FROM	TO	CLASS OR TYPE			DURATION OF FLIGHT Total Time to Date
								617:35
4-7	B-26G1		A-78			49	C	4:00
4-9	"		"	Sallfield marshall yds		50	C	4:05
4-23	B-26C45		"				T	1:25
5-9	C-47		"				A	2:00
5-11	B-26G1		"				T	2:00
5-25	B-26C45		"				T	3:00
5-28	B-26G1		"				T	1:00
5-28	"		"				T	1:30
5-28	"		"				T	1:00
6-1	B-26G5		"				A	3:40
6-2	B-26G25		"				A	1:45
								823:45
				(more)				
CARRY TOTALS FORWARD TO TOP OF NEXT PAGE								

SOLO FLIGHT TIME			LINK	DUAL INSTRUCTION as instructor or Student			REMARKS: Each maneuver and the time spent thereon, attested to by the Instructor is to be entered in this column for all instruction received. Any serious damage to the aircraft MUST be entered here also.
Day	Night	Instrument					
							PILOT'S SIGNATURE

DATE 19 45 Sept	AIRCRAFT IDENT. MARK	MAKE - MODEL and HORSEPOWER OF AIRCRAFT	FROM Santa Ana	TO	CLASS OR TYPE			DURATION OF FLIGHT Total Time to Date
4		B-17G	Douglas Plant, Calif	Local				1:18
5		"	"	"				1:35
6		"	"	"				1:15
10		C54G	"	"				:45
10		"	"	"				:50
11		"	"	"	Test			1:10
12		"	"	"		flights		1:30
12		"	"	"				1:10
13		"	"	"				1:05
14		"	"	"				1:55
14		"	"	"				2:05
14		"	"	"				:35
					(more)			

CARRY TOTALS FORWARD TO TOP OF NEXT PAGE

SOLO FLIGHT TIME			LINK	DUAL INSTRUCTION as instructor or Student			REMARKS: Each maneuver and the time spent thereon, attested to by the Instructor is to be entered in this column for all instruction received. Any serious damage to the aircraft MUST be entered here also.
Day	Night	Instrument					
							PILOT'S SIGNATURE

DATE 19 45 — Oct	AIRCRAFT IDENT. MARK	MAKE - MODEL and HORSEPOWER OF AIRCRAFT	FROM Santa Ana AAB Calif	TO	CLASS OR TYPE			DURATION OF FLIGHT Total Time to Date
1		AT-11	SAAB	Local				2:20
2		AT-6A	"	"				2:00
				END				
CARRY TOTALS FORWARD TO TOP OF NEXT PAGE								843:10

SOLO FLIGHT TIME			LINK	DUAL INSTRUCTION	as instructor or Student		REMARKS: Each maneuver and the time spent thereon, attested to by the Instructor is to be entered in this column for all instruction received. Any serious damage to the aircraft MUST be entered here also.
Day	Night	Instrument					
							PILOT'S SIGNATURE

AERONAUTICAL PRODUCTS

Published or Manufactured by

STEELE'S "AID TO PILOTS"
2227 W. Washington Blvd.
Los Angeles, California

No. 100—"Aid To Pilots"

A text or reference book.
Covers all C.A.A Pilot Regulations
100% up-to-date—all late changes and Amendments.

No. 200—Pilot Log Book

Size 4"x6½"—120 pages—Fine ledger paper.
Handmade Fabrikoid cover, Gold stamped.

No. 202—Pilot Log Book

Size 4"x6½"—120 pages—Fine ledger paper.
Paper cover—refill for "Pilot Kit."

No. 203—Senior Pilot Log

Size 5"x8"—144 pages—Fine ledger paper.
Handmade Fabrikoid cover, Gold stamped.
An excellent Log for either Military Pilot or Instructor.

No. 300—"Pilot Kit"

Discontinued for the "Duration."

No. 400—Compass Course Protractor

Very accurate. Available either round or square.

Other Pilot and Student supplies also available.

NOTICE

In cooperation with our Government, the **"Aeronautical Radio Facilities" will not** be published for the **Duration.**

Chapter 14

Martin B-26 Marauder Cutaway

The Martin B-26 Marauder
1. Bombardier's Station
2. Carburetor Air Intake
3. Pilot's Escape Hatch (open)
4. Pratt and Whitney R-2800 Engine
5. Co-pilot's Seat
6. Pilot's Seat
7. Navigator's Seat
8. Radio Operator's Seat
9. Life Raft
10. Navigator's Hatch
11. Forward Bomb Bay
12. Martin Mareng (Self-sealing) Fuel Cells
13. Aft Bomb Bay
14. Armor Plate
15. Martin .50-caliber Deck Turret
16. Twin .50-caliber Tail Turret
17. Armor Plate Bulkhead
18. Remote Feed Ammunition Track
19. Camera Mount
20. .50-caliber Waist Guns
21. Slotted Flap
22. Aileron Trim Tab
23. Landing Lights
24. Hinged Leading Edge
25. Firewall
26. Bomb Bay Doors
27. 47" Main Wheel
28. Catwalk Through Bomb Bay
29. Radio Equipment
30. Oxygen Supply
31. Package Guns
32. Main Entrance Wheel
33. Armor Plate
34. 36" Nose Wheel
35. Bomb Sight Window
36. Fixed .50-caliber Gun
37. .50-caliber Flexible Nose Gun

Chapter 15

Leading Particulars

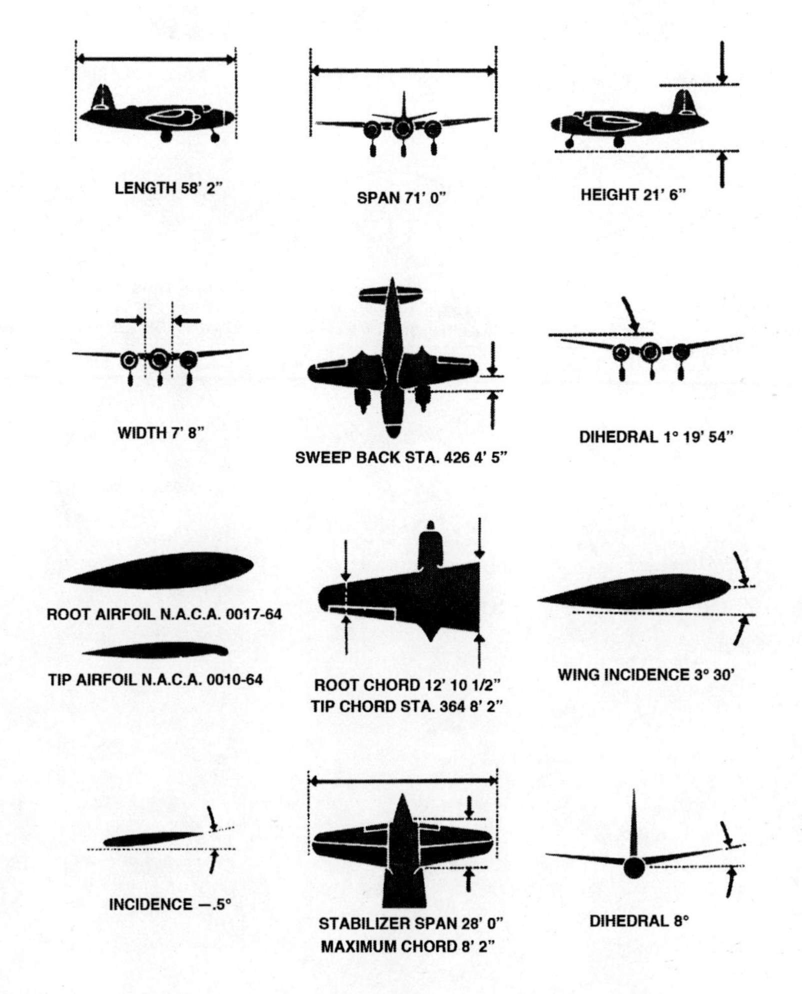

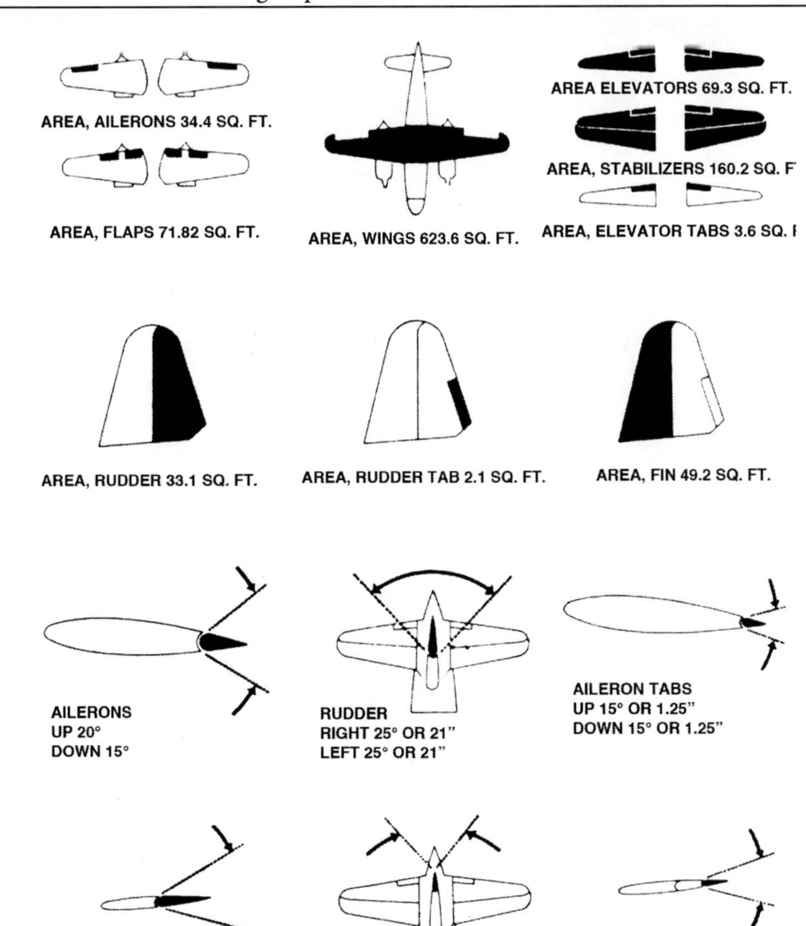
AREA, AILERONS 34.4 SQ. FT.
AREA, FLAPS 71.82 SQ. FT.
AREA, WINGS 623.6 SQ. FT.
AREA ELEVATORS 69.3 SQ. FT.
AREA, STABILIZERS 160.2 SQ. F
AREA, ELEVATOR TABS 3.6 SQ.
AREA, RUDDER 33.1 SQ. FT.
AREA, RUDDER TAB 2.1 SQ. FT.
AREA, FIN 49.2 SQ. FT.
AILERONS
UP 20°
DOWN 15°
RUDDER
RIGHT 25° OR 21"
LEFT 25° OR 21"
AILERON TABS
UP 15° OR 1.25"
DOWN 15° OR 1.25"
ELEVATORS
UP 20° OR 12.5"
DOWN 12° OR 7.5"
RUDDER TAB
RIGHT 15° OR 1.5"
LEFT 15° OR 1.5"
ELEVATOR TAB
UP 15°
DOWN 35°

Chapter 16

Marauder Specifications

Type	Medium Bomber (B26, B26A, B26B, B26C, B26F and G)	
Span	65 ft. (B26 through B26B4) 71 ft. (all later models)	
Length	58 ft. 6 in.	
Height	11 ft. 2 in.	
Wing Area	658 sq. ft.	
Gross Weight	37,000 lbs.	
Empty Weight	21,547 lbs. (short-wing)	24,000 lbs. (long-wing)
Wing Loading		48.6 lbs. per sq. ft.
Power Loading		8 lbs. per hp.
High Speed	323 mph (short-wing)	300-plus mph (long-wing)
Cruising Speed	258 mph	230 mph
Landing Speed		115 mph (without flaps)
Climbing Rate		1,500 ft. per min. (first minute)
Service Ceiling	15,000 ft.	15,000 ft.
Engine Type	Two Pratt and Whitney R-2800, 18-cyl.	
Engine Power	2,000 hp. each	
Fuselage or Hull	Al. alloy, monocoque; built around strong keel. Inside diameter is 67 inches, almost perfectly stream-lined.	
Wings	Full cantilever; break flush at fuselage (no center section).	
Armament	11 or 12 .50-caliber machine guns; deck and tail turrets. Bomb capacity: 4,000-plus pounds	
Range	1,000-plus miles	
Special Features	Self-sealing fuel tanks (Mareng cell); armor plate; Martin electric deck turret; wide use of plastics; emergency air brakes; auxiliary jet-like exhaust for added speed.	
Production Features	Broken down into 600 minor assemblies and 30 major assemblies, the Marauder called for many revolutionary innovations in manufacturing: spot welding for secondary structures; stretch press for making large, curved pieces of skin for the fuselage; more castings, forgings than in any comparable plane; fewer detail parts and rivets used. First test flown: Nov. 25, 1940, by William (Ken) Ebel.	

Chapter 17

Specific Engine Flight Charts

AIRPLANE MODELS *B-26B1 – B-26C								ENGINE MODELS R-2800-43		

*Use as preliminary data for B-26B1

CONDITION	FUEL PRESSURE (LB/SQ. IN)	OIL PRESSURE (LB./SQ. IN)	OIL TEMP		COOLANT TEMP		
			C	F	C	F	
DESIRED	14-16	75-85	50 to 70	120 to 160			
MAXIMUM	16	90					
MINIMUM	12	60					
IDLING	7	25					

MAX. PERMISSIBLE DIVING RPM: 2880		
CONDITION	ALLOWABLE OIL CONSUMPTION	
MAX. CONT.	33 U.S. QT/HR	55 IMP. PT/HR
MAX. CRUISE	21 U.S. QT/HR	35 IMP. PT/HR
MIN. SPECIFIC	13 U.S. QT/HR	22 IMP. PT/HR
OIL GRADE: (S) 1120		

SUPERCHARGER TYPE: Single Stage Two Speed Impeller

FUEL GRADE: 100 OCTANE

OPERATING CONDITION	RPM	MANIFOLD PRESSURE (BOOST)	HORSE-POWER	CRITICAL ALTITUDE		BLOWER	USE LOW BLOWER BELOW	MIXTURE CONTROL POSITION	FUEL FLOW (GAL HR ENG)		MAXIMUM CYL TEMP		MAXIMUM DURATION (MINUTES)
				with ram 31,000#	no ram				U.S.	Imp	C	F	
TAKE-OFF	2700	51.5	1920	—	—	Low	Do Not Use High Blower	A. R.	270	225	260	500	5
WAR EMERGENCY													
MILITARY	2700	49.5 43.2	1920 1490	3,200 14,300	1,200 13,400	Low High	10,000	A. R.	270 213	225 178	260	500	5
MAXIMUM CONTINUOUS	2400 2400	39.5 40.2	1550 1360	7,100 14,600	5,600 13,650	Low High	10,600	A. R.	190 170	160 140	260	500	No Limit
MAXIMUM CRUISE	2100 2100	32.0 31.7	960 960	14,600 19,000	13,600 18,400	Low High	14,600	A. L.	76 84	63 72	232	450	No Limit
MINIMUM SPECIFIC CONSUMPTION	1900 2100 2100	31.7 24.7 26.2	800 800 800	13,600 19,000 23,200	12,800 17,700 23,200	Low Low High	19,000	A. L.	41 62 65	51 52 54	232 232 232	450 450 450	No Limit

REMARKS:
1. Manifold Pressures Listed Are Maximum.
2. Fuel and Oil Consumption for One Engine Only.
3. All Powers Are for Operating Mixtures.

Adapted from Spec. AN-H-8, Dec. 18, 1942

Chapter 18

Flight Operation Instruction Chart

ALTERNATE CRUISING CONDITIONS

(NO WIND)

I (MAX. CONT. POWER) RANGE IN AIR MILES				FUEL	II RANGE IN AIR MILES		III RANGE IN AIR MILES		IV RANGE IN AIR MILES	
STATUTE		NAUTICAL		U.S. GALS.	STATUTE	NAUTICAL	STATUTE	NAUTICAL	STATUTE	NAUTICAL
AT S.L.	AT 12,000	AT S.L.	AT 12,000							
				1992	*Allow 105 Gallons to Take-Off and Climb to 5000'*					
1130	1270	990	1100	1890	1680	1460	1960	1700	2100	1820
1020	1150	810	1000	1700	1510	1310	1760	1530	1890	1640
900	1010	780	880	1500	1330	1150	1550	1350	1670	1450
780	880	680	760	1300	1160	1010	1350	1170	1440	1250
660	740	570	640	1100	980	850	1140	990	1220	1060
540	610	470	530	900	800	690	930	810	1000	870
420	470	370	410	700	620	540	720	620	780	680
300	340	260	290	500	440	390	520	450	550	480
180	200	150	170	300	270	230	310	270	330	290

I OPERATING DATA							II OPERATING DATA						III OPERATING DATA						IV OPERATING DATA					
R.P.M.	I.A.S. MPH	I.A.S. KNOTS	M.P. IN Hg	U.S. GPH	IMP GPH	DENSITY ALT. IN FEET	R.P.M.	I.A.S. MPH	I.A.S. KNOTS	M.P. IN Hg	U.S. GPH	IMP GPH	R.P.M.	I.A.S. MPH	I.A.S. KNOTS	M.P. IN Hg	U.S. GPH	IMP GPH	R.P.M.	I.A.S. MPH	I.A.S. KNOTS	M.P. IN Hg	U.S. GPH	IMP GPH
						30000																		
						25000																		
						20000																		
2400	212	184	40	330	276	15000	2200	195	169	36	247	206												
2400	221	192	41	340	284	12000	2150	202	175	37	247	206	2100	178	154	29.4	187	156						
2400	236	205	37	338	282	9000	2210	214	186	33	249	208	2100	194	169	31.3	195	162	2100	185	161	30.6	180	150
2400	248	205	40	378	315	6000	2200	217	188	34	246	205	2100	198	172	32.3	195	162	2100	191	166	31.6	175	146
2400	253	206	41	378	315	3000	2150	217	188	35	231	193	2100	199	173	33.0	180	150	*2100*	*196*	*170*	*33*	*158*	*132*
2400	257	208	42.0	378	315	S.L.	2130	220	191	37	225	187	2100	203	176	34.0	172	143	*2100*	*197*	*171*	*32*	*154*	*128*

Chapter 19

Summary of Estimated Performance, Model 179

These tables are based on a facsimile of Air Corps Circular Proposal 39-640. Some numbers were unclear on the copy so may not be entirely reliable.

BID NO.	UNITS	1	2	3	4	5
PERFORMANCE						
1 HIGH SPEED AT NORMAL RATED CRIT. ALT. + 2000 FT RAM	M.P.H.	*315*	*313*	*320*	*335*	*355*
HP/*N* g/(V_T/V_c)		1350/.824/.915	1350/.824/.911	1350/.858/.864	1290/.822/.892	1500/.792/.923
2 HIGH SPEED AT MILITARY RATED CRIT. ALT. + 2000 FT RAM	M.P.H.	*317*	*315*	*323*	*338*	*368*
HP/*N* g/(V_T/V_c)		1450/.794/.970	1450/.795/.970	1480/.835/.918	1380/.788/.954	1700/.790/.990
3 HIGH SPEED AT 15000 FT	M.P.H.	*315*	*313*	*320*	*314*	*324*
HP/*N* g/(V_T/V_c)		1380/.824/.918	1380/.824/.911	1380/.858/.896	1350/.819/.969	1500/.807/.968
4 SPEED AT 75% HP	M.P.H.	*295*	*293*	*298*	*317*	*314*
HP/*N* g/ALT		1125/.846/15000	1125/.846/15000	1125/.872/15000	1125/.827/24000	1125/.808/25000
5 OPERATING SPEED AT 15000 FT	M.P.H.	*227*	*275*	*254*	*250*	*244*
HP/RPM/*N* g		850/1550/.868	960/2090/.850	780/1860/.878	800/1900/.844	800/1900/.825
6 RANGE AT OPERATING SPEED – 1/2 FUEL OVERLOAD	MI ST	*1800*	*1800*	*1800*	*1520*	*1768*
7 FUEL FOR 3000 ST MILE RANGE AT ECONOMICAL SPEED	LBS	*7200*	*7310*	*7370*	*7825*	*8000*
8 SERVICE CEILING	FT	*26500*	*26000*	*26400*	*31100*	*34700*
9 SERVICE CEILING (SINGLE ENGINE)	FT	*13900*	*12600*	*12000*	*12000*	*13750*
10 TAKE OFF & LANDING OVER 50 FT OBSTACLE	FT	*2000*	*2200*	*2480*	*2360*	*2500*
TAKE OFF DISTANCE / LANDING DISTANCE	FT	2000/1980	2200/2050	2480/1990	2360/1900	2500/1930
CHARACTERISTICS						
WING AREA / ASPECT RATIO	SQ FT/–	600/7.05	600/7.05	600/7.05	*650*/7.05	*650*/7.05
TAIL AREA / EXPOSED WING AREA	SQ FT	200/503.5	200/503.5	200/503.5	200/550	200/550
FUSELAGE AREA / ROOT CHORD	SQ FT/FT	46.1/14	46.1/14	46.1/14	46.1/14.5	46.1/14.5
NACELLE AREA / AV WING THICKNESS RATIO	SQ FT/%	35.2/15	35.2/15	35.2/15	35.2/15	35.2/15
FULL SCALE C_D/L		.0231/.0597	.0231/.0597	.0231/.0597	.0221/.0597	.0221/.0597
PERCENT COOLING HP – HIGH SPEED / CLIMB	%	0/4	0/4	0/4	4/6	6/8

BID NO.	UNITS	1	2	3	4	5
ENGINE		WAC – 2600				
ENGINE TYPE		1 STAGE 2 SPEED	1 STAGE 2 SPEED	1 STAGE 2 SPEED	2 STAGE 2 SPEED	TURBO
ENGINE NOSE (SHORT, LONG)		SHORT	LONG	LONG	LONG	SHORT
ENGINE SPEC. NO. AND DATE		B-656-3/6-6-39	B-655-1/6-6-39	B-655-1/6-6-39	B-655-1/6-10-39	B-657-4/6-10-39
TAKE OFF HP/RPM		1700/2600	1700/2600	1700/2600	1700/2600	1700/2600
NORMAL RATING – ENG. CRIT. ALT./HP/RPM		13000/1360/2400	13000/1350/2400	13000/1350/2400	22000/1290/2400	25000/1500/2400
MILITARY RATING – ENG. CRIT. ALT./HP/RPM		12000/1450/2800	12000/1460/2800	12000/1480/2800	21500/1300/2800	25000/1700/2800
ENGINE WEIGHT / PROPELLER WEIGHT		2000/594	2105/594	2105/476	2210/476	1985/476
PROPELLER GEAR RATIO		2:1	2:1	2:1	2:1	2:1
PROPELLER DIA / NO. BLADES / σ (.7 RADIUS)		13.5/4/.127	13.5/4/.127	12.5/4/.117	12.5/4/.117	12.5/4/.117
PROPELLER DESIGNATION		C-5436-814Cc2	C-5436-814Cc2	C-5425-714Cc2	C-5423-714Cc2	C-5425-714Cc2
PROPELLER SPEC. NO.		P-39	P-39	P-36	P-36	P-36
WEIGHTS						
NORMAL GROSS WEIGHT	LBS.	24700	25581	24840	25140	25630
WEIGHT EMPTY	LBS.	18174	18464	18132	18767	18784
USEFUL LOAD	LBS.	6526	7117	6708	6373	6846
FUEL/OIL	LBS.	2250/254	2780/315	2412/274	2110/241	2535/289
USEFUL LOAD LESS FUEL AND OIL	LBS.	4022	4022	4022	4022	4022

BID NO.	UNITS	6	7	8	9	10	11
PERFORMANCE							
1 HIGH SPEED AT NORMAL RATED CRIT. ALT. + 2000 FT RAM	M.P.H.	*322*	*349*	*354*	*327*	*355*	*366*
HP/*N* g/(V_T/V_C)		1450/.824/.915	1460/.811/.914	1500/.793/.923	1490/.859/.969	1980/.786/.957	1625/.769/.970
2 HIGH SPEED AT MILITARY RATED CRIT. ALT. + 2000 FT RAM	M.P.H.	*324*	*355*	*380*	*335*	*368*	*392*
HP/*N* g/(V_T/V_C)		1500/.793/.980	1600/.783/.979	1850/.794/1.000	1600/.822/.956	1800/.769/1.000	2000/.743/1.082
3 HIGH SPEED AT 15000 FT	M.P.H.	*322*	*329*	*324*	*327*	*336*	*334*
HP/*N* g/(V_T/V_C)		1480/.824/.915	1540/.824/.968	1800/.807/.864	1450/.989/.867	1625/.803/.871	1625/.790/.870
4 SPEED AT 75% HP	M.P.H.	*292*	*323*	*312*	*296*	*327*	*325*
HP/*N* g/ALT		1125/.846/15000	1200/.830/23600	1125/.807/26000	1125/.872/15000	1290/.820/23800	1220/.801/28000
5 OPERATING SPEED AT 15000 FT	M.P.H.	*269*	*255*	*252*	*260*	*250*	*260*
HP/RPM/*N* g		925/2080/.854	860/1790/.838	980/1790/.820	980/1980/.879	830/1790/.836	910/1880/.819
6 RANGE AT OPERATING SPEED – 1/2 FUEL OVERLOAD	MI ST	*1800*	*1670*	*1660*	*1620*	*1800*	*1800*
7 FUEL FOR 3000 ST MILE RANGE AT ECONOMICAL SPEED	LBS	*7690*	*8780*	*8875*	*7775*	*8990*	*8460*
8 SERVICE CEILING	FT	*27100*	*31900*	*33900*	*27200*	*31800*	*33600*
9 SERVICE CEILING (SINGLE ENGINE)	FT	*13840*	*14000*	*12500*	*12000*	*15000*	*14200*
10 TAKE OFF & LANDING OVER 50 FT OBSTACLE	FT	*2100*	*2500*	*2500*	*2320*	*2500*	*2500*
TAKE OFF DISTANCE / LANDING DISTANCE	FT	2100/2080	2500/1970	2500/1970	2320/2070	2500/2120	2500/2120
CHARACTERISTICS							
WING AREA / ASPECT RATIO	SQ FT/–	600/7.05	*650* /7.05	*650* /7.05	600/7.05	600/7.05	600/7.05
TAIL AREA / EXPOSED WING AREA	SQ FT	200/503.5	200/550	200/550	200/503.5	200/503.5	200/503.5
FUSELAGE AREA / ROOT CHORD	SQ FT/FT	46.1/14	46.1/14.5	46.1/14.5	46.1/14	46.1/14	46.1/14
NACELLE AREA / AV WING THICKNESS RATIO	SQ FT/%	31.7/15	31.7/15	31.7/15	31.7/15	31.7/15	31.7/15
FULL SCALE C_D/L		.0231/.0597	.0221/.0597	.0221/.0597	.0231/.0597	.0231/.0597	.0231/.0597
PERCENT COOLING HP – HIGH SPEED / CLIMB	%	0/4	4/6	6/8	0/4	4/6	6/8

BID NO.	UNITS	6	7	8	9	10	11
ENGINE		P & W – 2800					
ENGINE TYPE		1 STAGE 2 SPEED	2 STAGE 2 SPEED	TURBO	1 STAGE 2 SPEED	2 STAGE 2 SPEED	TURBO
ENGINE NOSE (SHORT, LONG)		SHORT	SHORT	SHORT	LONG	SHORT	SHORT
ENGINE SPEC. NO. AND DATE		A-8019/5-15-39	A-8020/5-15-39	A-8021/5-15-39	A-8024/5-15-39	A-8025/5-15-39	A-8026/5-15-39
TAKE OFF HP/RPM		1850/2600	1850/2600	1850/2600	2000/2700	2000/2700	2000/2700
NORMAL RATING – ENG. CRIT. ALT./HP/RPM		13000/1450/2400	21500/1480/2400	25000/1500/2400	13000/1450/2400	21500/1560/2580	25000/1425/2660
MILITARY RATING – ENG. CRIT. ALT./HP/RPM		14000/1500/2800	21000/1600/2800	25000/1860/2800	13800/1800/2700	19600/1800/2700	25000/2000/2700
ENGINE WEIGHT / PROPELLER WEIGHT		2265/594	2375/476	2210/476	2505/476	2496/476	2320/476
PROPELLER GEAR RATIO		2:1	2:1	2:1	2:1	2:1	2:1
PROPELLER DIA / NO. BLADES / σ (.7 RADIUS)		13.5/4/.127	12.5/4/.117	12.5/4/.117	12.5/4/.117	12.5/4/.117	12.5/4/.117
PROPELLER DESIGNATION		C-5435-814Cc2	C-5425-714Cc2	C-5425-714Cc2	C-5425-714Cc2	C-5425-714Cc2	C-5425-714Cc2
PROPELLER SPEC. NO.		P-39	P-36	P-36	P-36	P-36	P-36
WEIGHTS							
NORMAL GROSS WEIGHT	LBS.	26087	26140	26140	25830	26538	26540
WEIGHT EMPTY	LBS.	18958	19285	19421	19164	19366	19480
USEFUL LOAD	LBS.	7129	6855	6719	6666	7172	7060
FUEL/OIL	LBS.	2790/317	2546/287	2422/275	2374/270	2829/323	2727/311
USEFUL LOAD LESS FUEL AND OIL	LBS.	4022	4022	4022	4022	4022	4022

BID NO.	UNITS	12	13	14	15
PERFORMANCE					
1 HIGH SPEED AT NORMAL RATED CRIT. ALT. + 2000 FT RAM	M.P.H.	*360*	*365*	*402*	*401*
HP/*N* g/(V_T/V_C)		1800/.845/.869	1725/.822/.883	2000/.798/.930	2000/.798/.930
2 HIGH SPEED AT MILITARY RATED CRIT. ALT. + 2000 FT RAM	M.P.H.	*365*	*377*	*414*	*413*
HP/*N* g/(V_T/V_C)		1900/.915/.926	1890/.794/.942	2200/.789/.980	2200/.796/.990
3 HIGH SPEED AT 15000 FT	M.P.H.	*352*	*345*	*365*	*364*
HP/*N* g/(V_T/V_C)		1800/.846/.849	1886/.839/.847	2000/.810/.964	2000/.810/.944
4 SPEED AT 75% HP	M.P.H.	*338*	*350*	*360*	*359*
HP/*N* g/ALT		1500/.869/17980	1800/.862/20200	1800/.826/28000	1800/.829/18000
5 OPERATING SPEED AT 15000 FT	M.P.H.	*300*	*295*	*263*	*292*
HP/RPM/*N* g		1190/2090/.880	1150/2000/.880	990/1725/.894	1170/2020/.823
6 RANGE AT OPERATING SPEED – 1/2 FUEL OVERLOAD	MI ST	*1800*	*1800*	*1800*	*1800*
7 FUEL FOR 3000 ST MILE RANGE AT ECONOMICAL SPEED	LBS	*8560*	*8870*	*9270*	*9295*
8 SERVICE CEILING	FT	*30200*	*31000*	*36800*	*36300*
9 SERVICE CEILING (SINGLE ENGINE)	FT	*16500*	*14400*	*17800*	*17080*
10 TAKE OFF & LANDING OVER 50 FT OBSTACLE	FT	*2390*	*2500*	*2500*	*2630*
TAKE OFF DISTANCE / LANDING DISTANCE	FT	2390/2170	2500/2200	2500/2200	2630/2240
CHARACTERISTICS					
WING AREA / ASPECT RATIO	SQ FT/–	600/7.05	600/7.05	600/7.05	600/7.05
TAIL AREA / EXPOSED WING AREA	SQ FT	200/503.5	200/503.5	200/503.5	200/503.5
FUSELAGE AREA / ROOT CHORD	SQ FT/FT	46.1/14	46.1/14	46.1/14	46.1/14
NACELLE AREA / AV WING THICKNESS RATIO	SQ FT/%	35.2/15	35.2/15	35.2/15	35.2/15
FULL SCALE CD./L		.0231/.0597	.0231/.0597	.0231/.0597	.0231/.0597
PERCENT COOLING HP – HIGH SPEED / CLIMB	%	3/6	4/6	6/8	6/8

BID NO.	UNITS	12	13	14	15
ENGINE		WAC – 3350			
ENGINE TYPE		1 STAGE 2 SPEED	2 STAGE 2 SPEED	TURBO	TURBO
ENGINE NOSE (SHORT, LONG)		SHORT	SHORT	SHORT	SHORT
ENGINE SPEC. NO. AND DATE		B-665/6-17-39	B-6695/6-17-39	B-670-1/6-17-39	B-670-1/6-17-39
TAKE OFF HP/RPM		2200/2600	2200/2600	2200/2600	2200/2600
NORMAL RATING – ENG. CRIT. ALT./HP/RPM		15600/1800/2400	16200/1725/2400	25000/2000/2400	25000/2000/2400
MILITARY RATING – ENG. CRIT. ALT./HP/RPM		18000/1200/2800	20000/1860/2800	25000/2200/2800	25000/2200/2800
ENGINE WEIGHT / PROPELLER WEIGHT		2500/604	2630/604	2480/604	2480/604
PROPELLER GEAR RATIO		16:7	16:7	16:7	16:7
PROPELLER DIA / NO. BLADES / σ (.7 RADIUS)		13.5/4/.127	13.5/4/.127	13.5/4/.127	13.5/4/.127
PROPELLER DESIGNATION		C-6435-814Cc3	C-6435-814Cc3	C-6435-814Cc3	C-6435-814Cc3
PROPELLER SPEC. NO.		P-41	P-41	P-41	P-41
WEIGHTS					
NORMAL GROSS WEIGHT	LBS.	27261	27225	27725	28232
WEIGHT EMPTY	LBS.	19664	20231	20554	20635
USEFUL LOAD	LBS.	7597	7494	7171	7597
FUEL/OIL	LBS.	3210/365	3118/354	2827/322	3210/365
USEFUL LOAD LESS FUEL AND OIL	LBS.	4022	4022	4022	4022

Chapter 20

Pilot's Operating Instructions

Flying Characteristics

a. TAXYING.—Taxying is greatly facilitated by the tricycle landing gear. Below 35 mph the airplane is directionally controlled by gentle use of engines and brakes. With practice, taxi turns can be made with slow engines and no brakes, permitting the airplane to roll out of turns on course without effort. The nose wheel swivels 40° each way, providing a minimum turning radius of 8½ feet. Do not attempt to pivot the airplane on one wheel as this will damage or break the nose wheel strut.

b. TAKE-OFF.—The airplane will accelerate rapidly during the take-off run. Wing flaps are lowered to increase lift and thus shorten the run necessary for take-off. A setting of 30° will give the best lift-drag ratio. A setting greater than 30° results in a large increase in drag with a correspondingly small increase in lift. In order to provide the final impetus for take-off, the nose wheel should be raised from the runway as soon as the airplane is well under way.

c. CLIMB.—The best climbing speed at full rated power will vary between 165 mph at 5,000 feet and 156 mph at 20,000 feet altitude with normal gross weight. Use lower blower and check cowl flaps and oil cooler shutters for proper adjustment.

d. DIVES.—Maximum diving speed is 353 mph with any load up to 35,767 lbs., normal overload. It is important to observe this limiting speed at high altitudes. Dives should preferably be executed with power on since the propeller governor controls will keep the engines within operating limits. If the engines are kept at a minimum of 10% power, any tendency to cut out when full power is applied will be eliminated. Fuel is supplied to the engines in diving attitude by forward outlets in the fuel tanks.

e. STABILITY.—With the C.G. as far aft as 26% MAC, longitudinal stability is satisfactory and there is adequate directional and lateral stability for turns. With the C.G. aft of 26% MAC, the airplane is not longitudinally stable. The airplane will no longer tend to fly itself, and the controls must be attended constantly.

f. STALLS.—With normal gross weight the airplane stalls at 113–123 mph clean, and at 97–107 mph with wing flaps and landing gear down. With a normal overload of 35,767 lbs. The stalling speed is increased about 10 mph. Stalls at high power occur suddenly and are accompanied by a drop of one wing. Power-off stalls are preceded by a buffeting of the tail surface, a warning which decreases as the power is increased. In steep turns, stalls will occur at must high speeds, the stalling speed in a 60° bank being 160 mph. Use of power in a steep turn will reduce stall speed slightly but also tends to stall the lower wing tip and roll the airplane over. For this reason, steep turns should not be executed at speeds below 200 mph.

g. LANDING.—Execute turns during the approach at a minimum speed of 150 mph. For a power-off landing, glide in at 135 mph, holding nose well down and permitting a rapid rate of descent in order to maintain control. Make a conventional landing holding the nose wheel off the ground for a considerable part of the run. Do not apply brakes until after the nose wheel has settled on the runway. Landings may be completed successfully at a somewhat slower speed with power-on.

SAFETY PRECAUTIONS

a. **GENERAL.**

(1) ALL ACROBATIC MANEUVERS ARE PROHIBITED.

(2) COWL FLAPS should be OPEN for all ground operations except for warm-up in extremely cold weather.

(3) Avoid SIDE SLIPS. The fuel system will not supply adequate fuel to the engines when the airplane is in a side slip.

(4) Shut off HEAT CONTROL HANDLES when going into combat.

(5) Never start engines in AUTO RICH.

b. **HYDRAULIC.**

(1) During flight return LANDING GEAR, WING FLAP, COWL FLAP and OIL COOLER SHUTTER control levers to NEUTRAL after using.

(2) Leave LANDING GEAR control lever DOWN when gear is down in flight or on the ground.

c. **ELECTRIC.**

(1) Always connect OUTSIDE POWER SOURCE for starting.

(2) PROPELLER TOGGLE SWITCHES must be set to AUTO. CONSTANT SPEED for STARTING, WARM-UP, TAKE-OFF and LANDING.

UNLOCK CONTROLS AND CHECK FORMS 1 AND 1A.

(1) Pitot Tube Covers removed.
(2) Fuel Tanks checked visually.
(3) Fuel Tank Caps secured.

(4) Fuel Tank Valves turned ON. (Fwd. Bomb Bay, each side of door.)

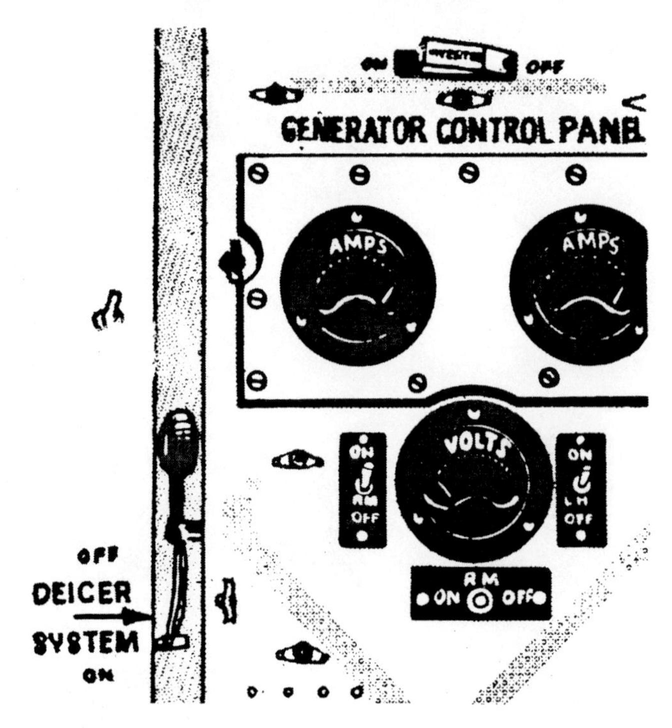

(5) Generators turned ON.

(6) Main Inverter Cut-off Switch turned ON.

(7) De-Icer Lever set to OFF position. (Navigator's Compartment).

(8) Bomb Bay Door Selector Handle shifted to CLOSED position. (Bombardier's Comp.).

(9) Check Flight Controls and Trim Tabs, having Co-pilot observe movement of surfaces.

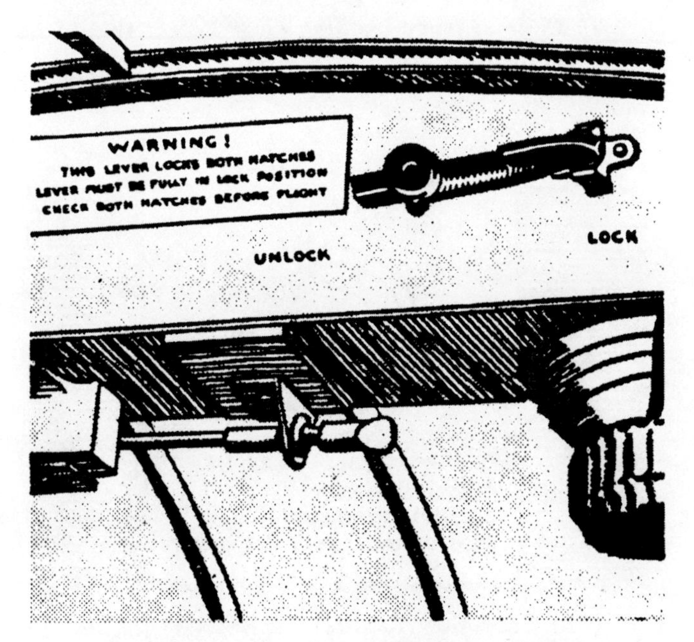

(10) Close and lock Overhead Hatches.

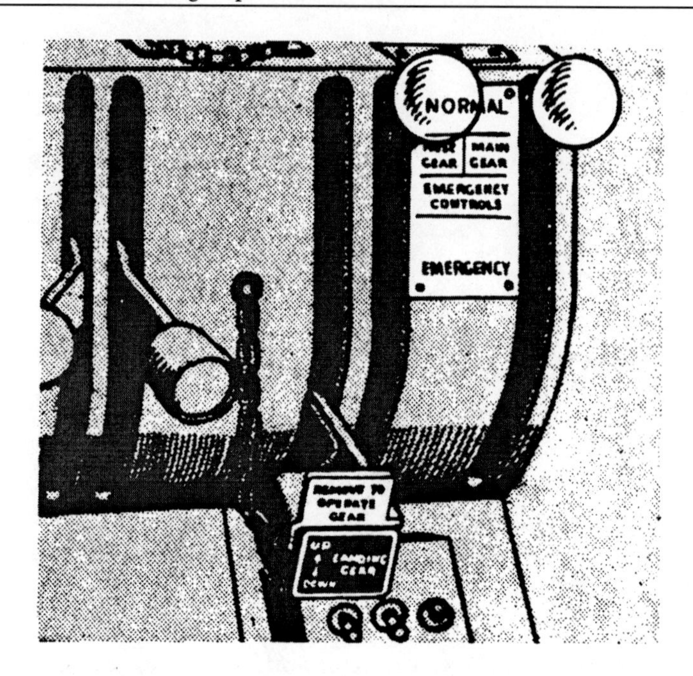

(11) Landing Gear Lever should be DOWN with safety lock installed.

(12) Emergency Landing Gear Levers should be in NORMAL position.

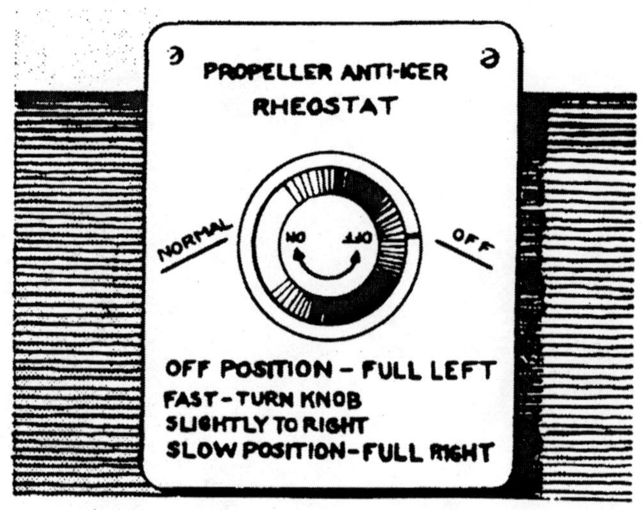

(13) Propeller Anti-Icer Rheostat should be turned OFF.

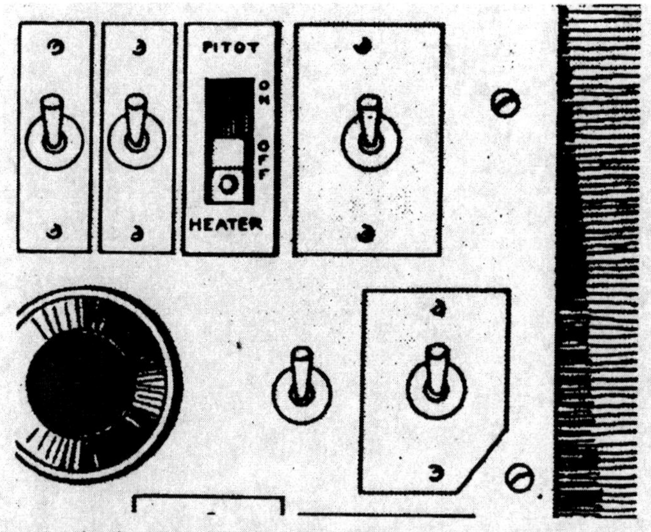

(14) Pitot Heater should be turned OFF.

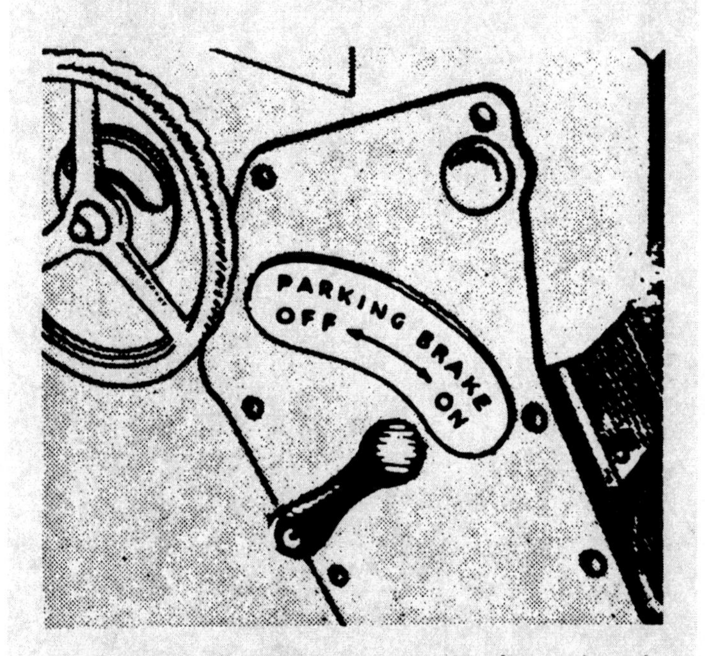

(15) Set Brakes for parking by depressing the brake pedals equally and fully. Pedals are locked in place by pulling Parking Brake Lever ON. Hydraulic pressure should read 850 to 1050 lb/sq in.

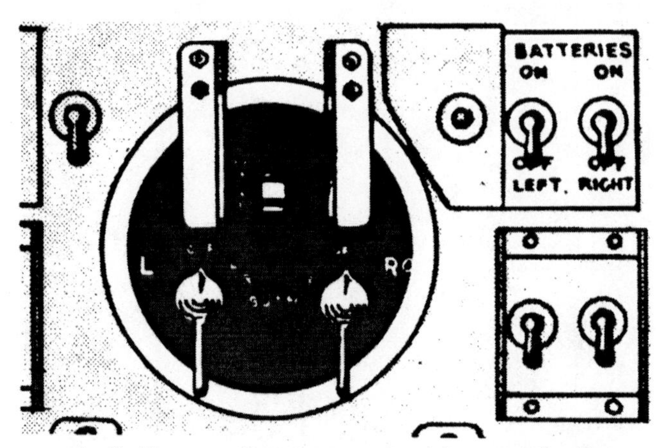

(16) Turn off Master, Ignition and Battery Switches.

(17) Have engines pulled through by hand 4 or 5 revolutions.

(18) Have Outside Power Source or Auxiliary Power Plant connected to outlet in Left Nacelle.

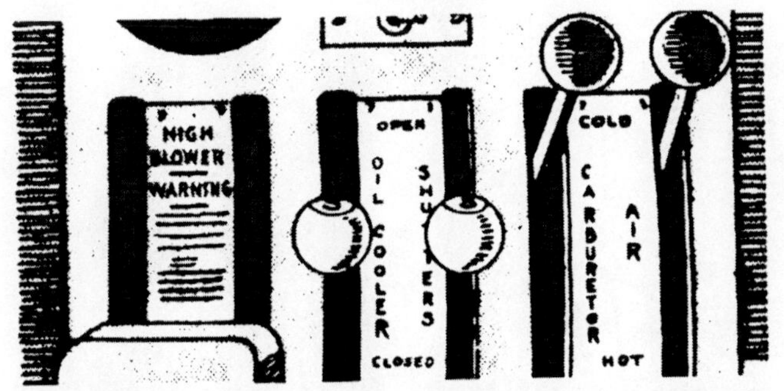

(19) Set Blowers LOW with Safety Cover in place.

(20) Adjust Oil Cooler Shutters to suit outside temperature.

(21) Set Carburetor Air Control Levers to COLD position.

(22) Pull Mixture Control Levers back to IDLE CUT-OFF.

(23) Push Propeller Governor Control Levers full forward to INC. RPM.

(24) Set Propeller Toggle Switches to AUTO CONSTANT SPEED after checking INC. and DEC. RPM settings and FEATHER switches.

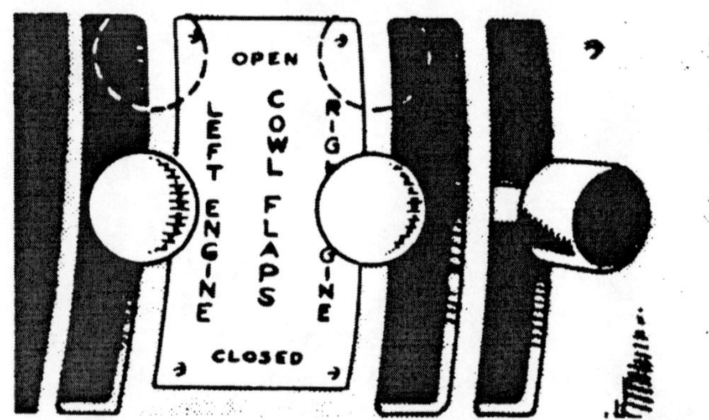

(25) Pull Cowl Flap Control Levers up to OPEN, allow flaps to extend fully, then return lever to NEUTRAL. Cowl Flaps must be fully open during all ground operation.

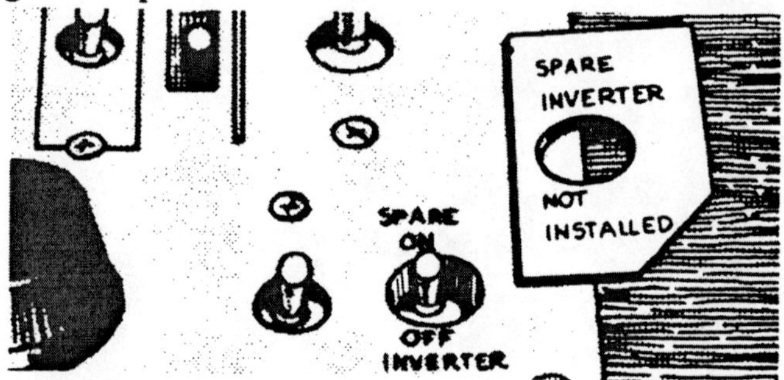

(26) Pull Inverter Selector Switch AFT (SPARE-OFF) to start Main Inverter.

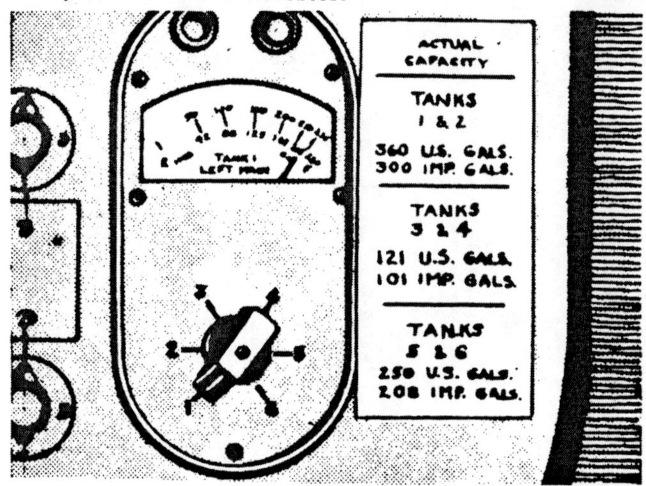

(27) Check Fuel Gauge operation at each setting.

f. STARTING ENGINES

STARTING PROCEDURE IS GIVEN FOR THE LEFT ENGINE. IN PRACTICE, ENGINES MAY BE STARTED IN THE ORDER DESIRED.

TO START COLD ENGINES IT IS NECESSARY TO PRIME LONGER AND TO REPEAT THE ENERGIZE AND MESH PROCEDURE UNTIL RESULTS ARE OBTAINED.

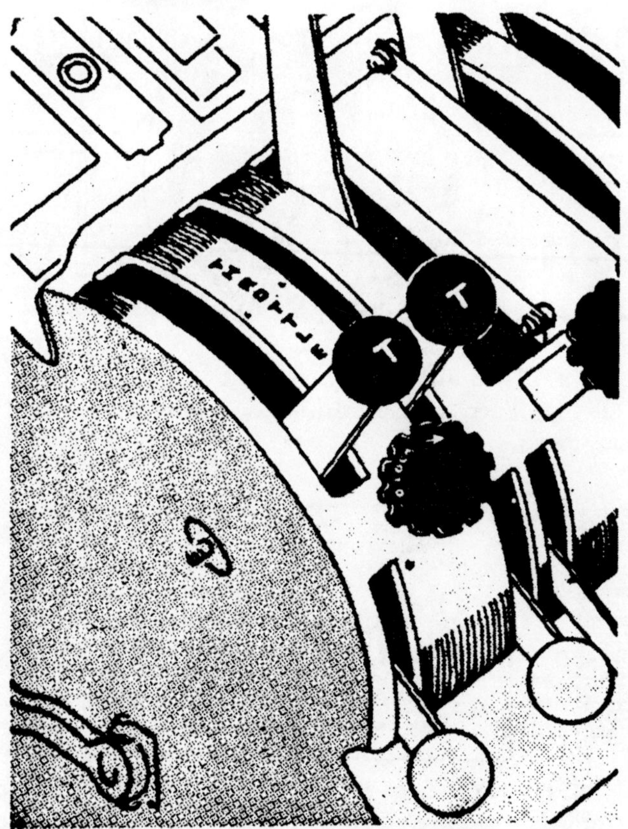

(1) Set throttles approx. 3/4 inch open for starting.

(2) See that propellers are clear, ground crew notified and fire guard posted.

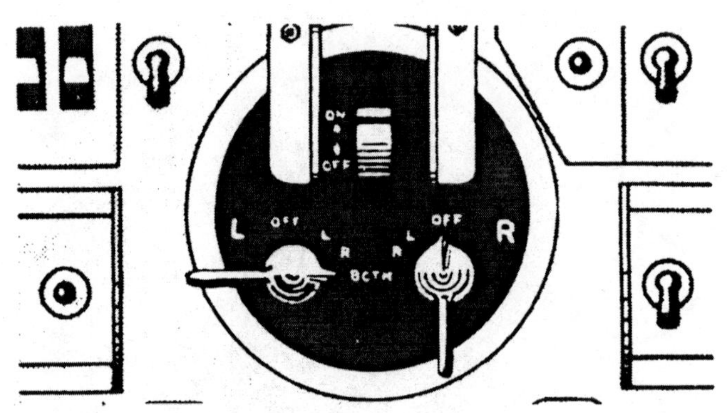

(3) Turn Master Switch ON.

(4) Turn Left Ignition Switch ON to BOTH magnetos.

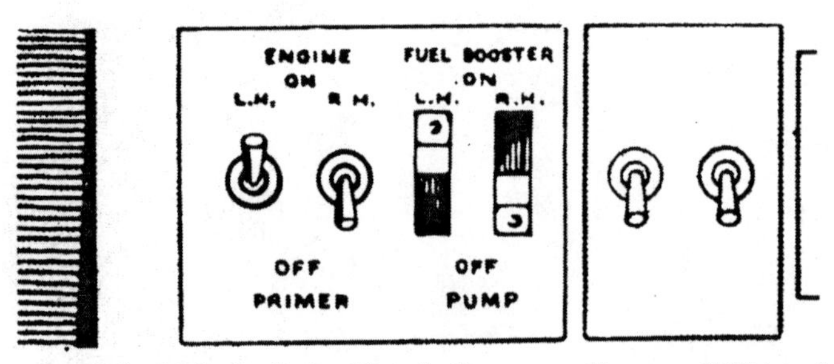

(5) Switch Left Hand Booster Pump ON and Prime left engine. Priming time will vary from no prime for hot engines to approx. 10 seconds for cold engines.

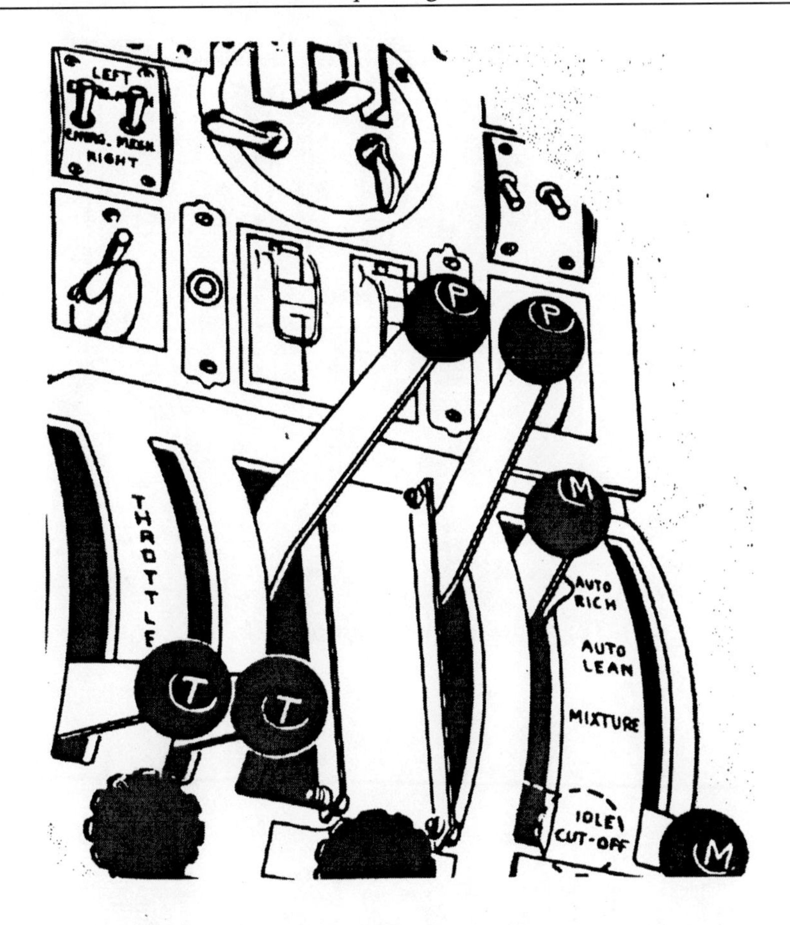

(6) Hold Energizer Switch to LEFT position until the inertia flywheel reaches maximum rpm (approx. 30 seconds), then engage the starter by holding the Mesh switch to LEFT position. Allow engine to turn over a couple of revolutions, then shift Mixture Lever to AUTO RICH for a slow count of three, returning to IDLE CUT-OFF for a slow count of five. Again advance to AUTO RICH and the engine should begin to fire. It may be necessary to return to IDLE CUT-OFF for a few seconds until the engine picks up. Manipulate the Throttle carefully to keep the engine down to 800 rpm for the first 30 seconds. If there is an indicated oil pressure, continue warm-up at 1000 rmp. Repeat procedure to start the right hand engine.

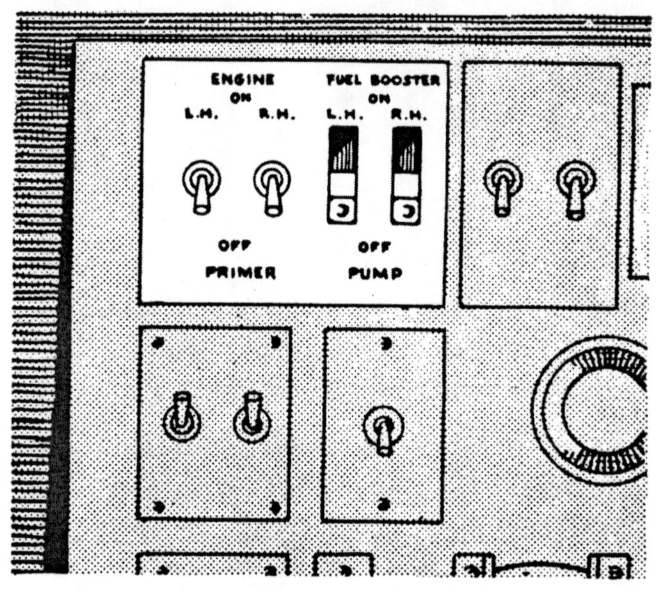

(7) Turn Fuel Booster Pumps OFF.

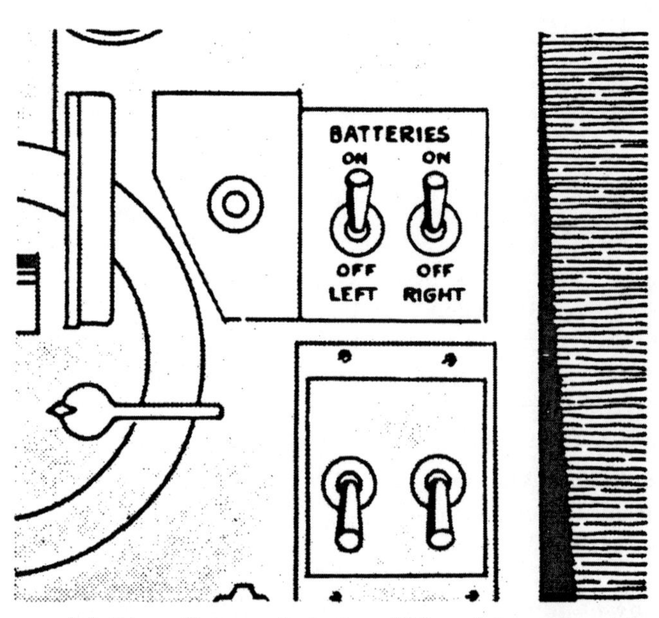

(8) Turn Battery Switches ON and have Outside Power Source disconnected.

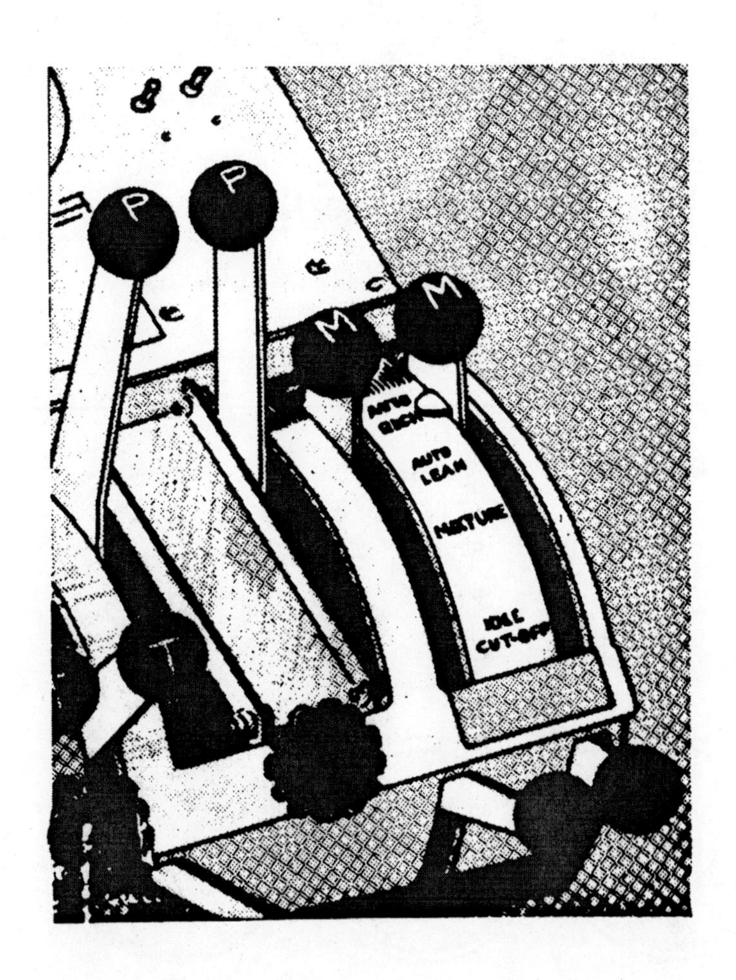

(1) Leave Mixture Levers in AUTO RICH.

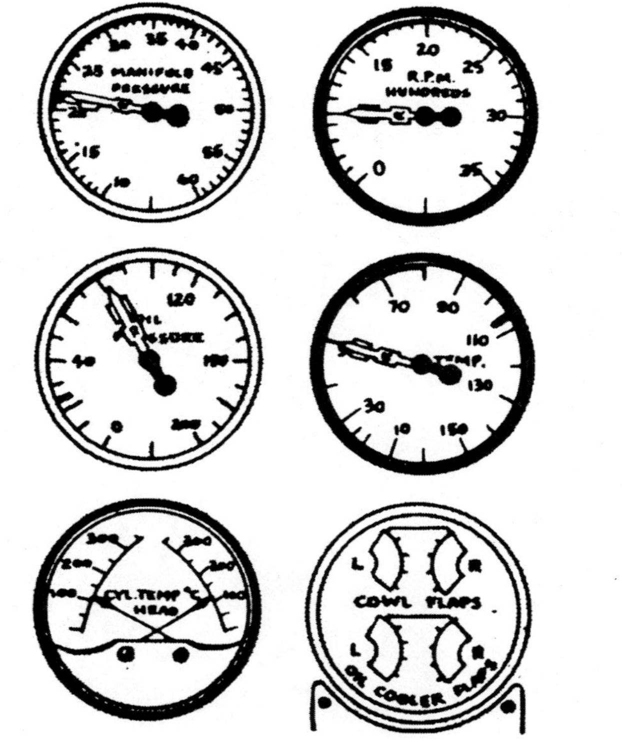

(2) Run engines under 800-1000 rpm until Cylinder Head Temperature reaches 120°C and Oil Temperature reaches 50°C.

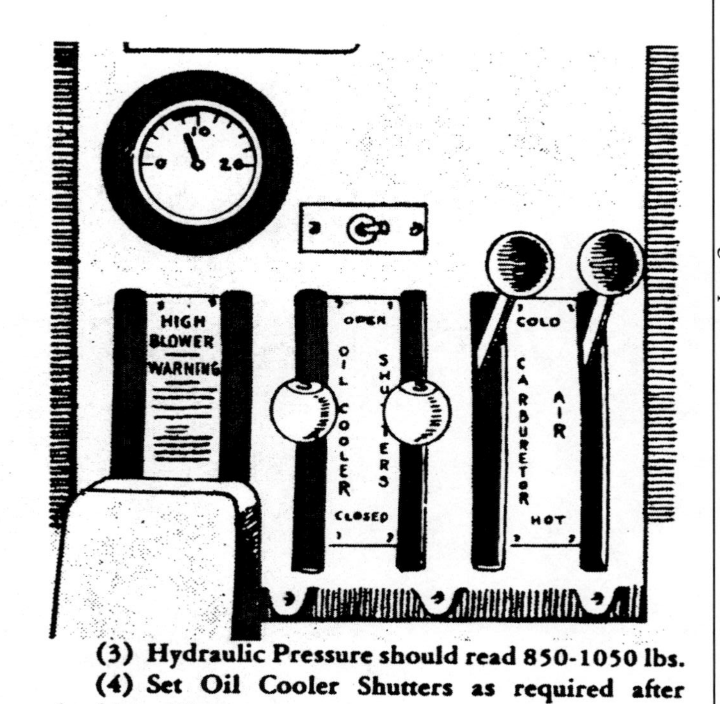

(3) Hydraulic Pressure should read 850-1050 lbs.

(4) Set Oil Cooler Shutters as required after checking oil temperature.

(5) Carburetor Air Control Levers remain in COLD position.

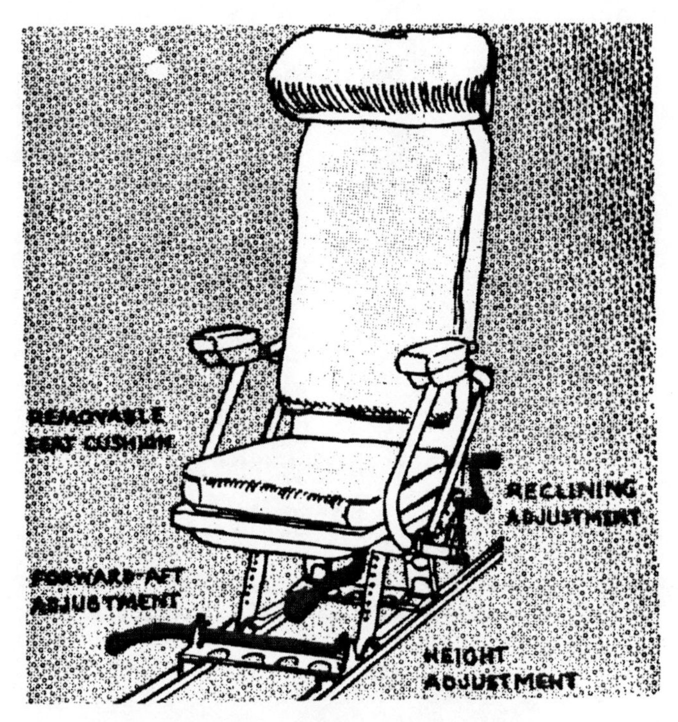

(6) Adjust Seat and fasten Safety Belt.

(7) Adjust radio and obtain taxy clearance.

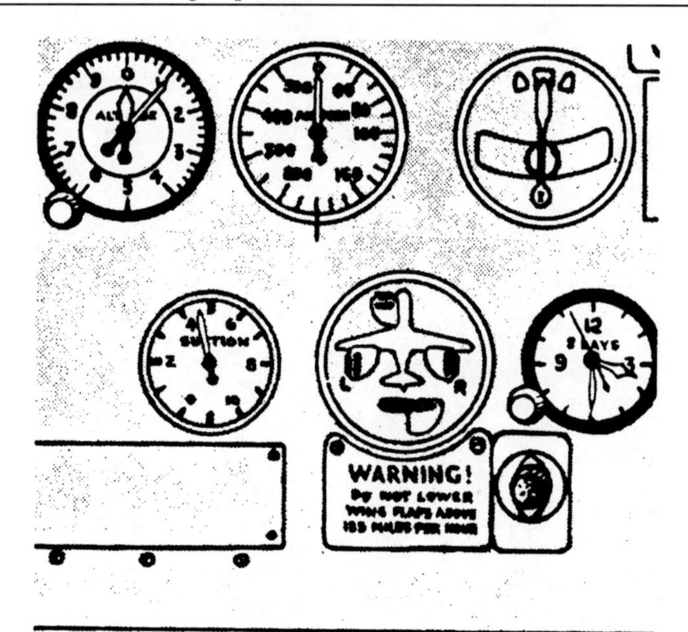

(8) Set altimeter to station pressure and check time, resetting clock if necessary.

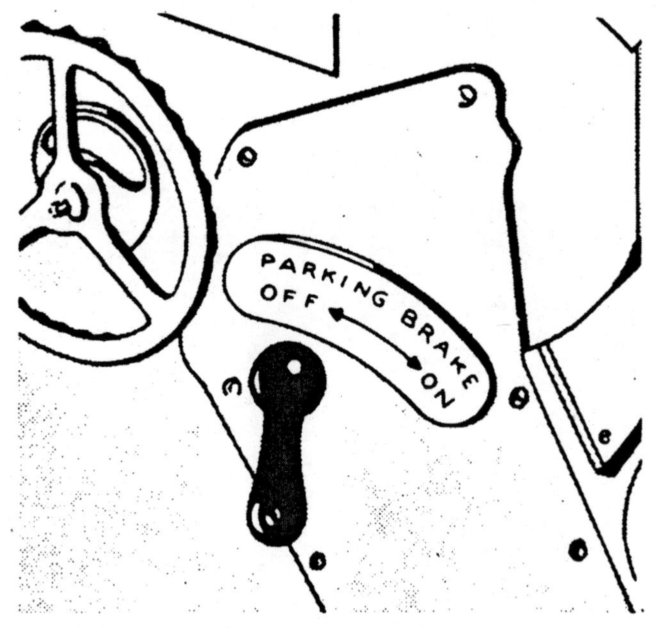

(9) Release parking brake by depressing pedals past lock position.

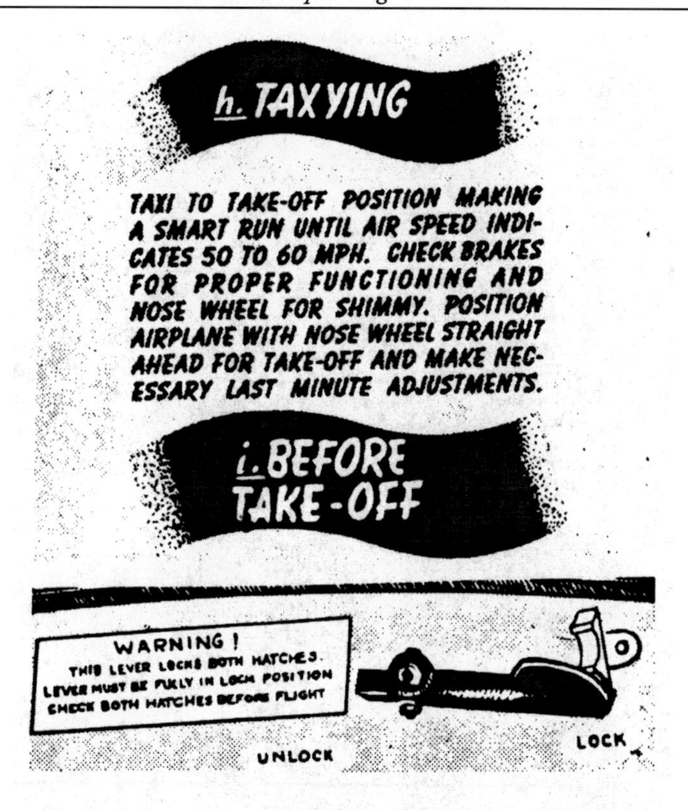

h. TAXYING

TAXI TO TAKE-OFF POSITION MAKING A SMART RUN UNTIL AIR SPEED INDICATES 50 TO 60 MPH. CHECK BRAKES FOR PROPER FUNCTIONING AND NOSE WHEEL FOR SHIMMY. POSITION AIRPLANE WITH NOSE WHEEL STRAIGHT AHEAD FOR TAKE-OFF AND MAKE NECESSARY LAST MINUTE ADJUSTMENTS.

i. BEFORE TAKE-OFF

(1) Check Overhead Hatches and Side Windows to make sure that pins are in place.

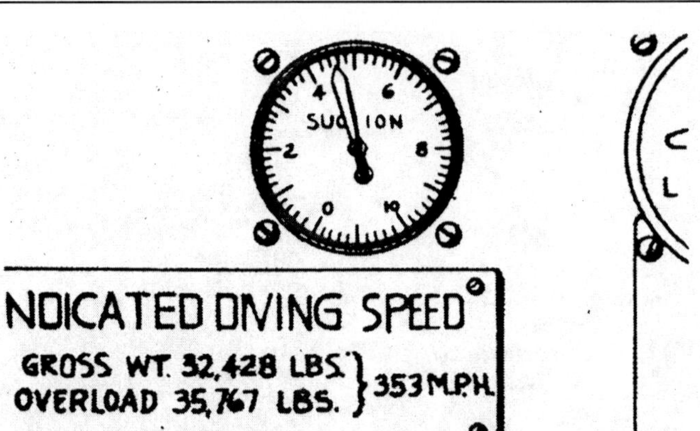

(2) Suction Gauge should read 4 in. to 5 in. Hg.

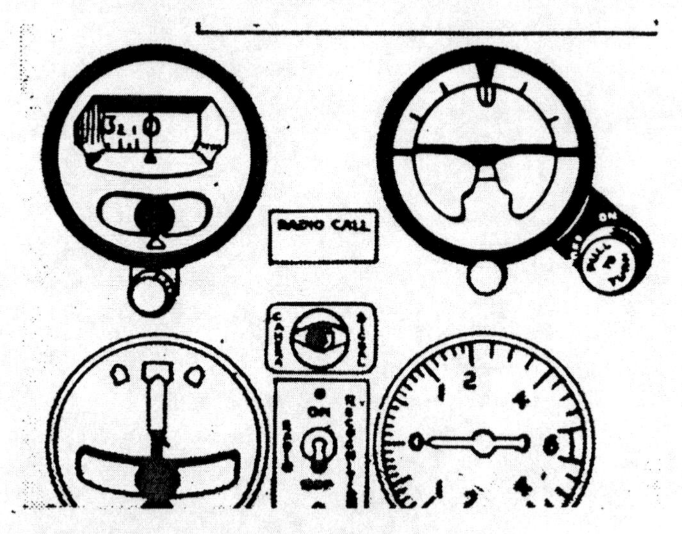

(3) Set and uncage Gyros.

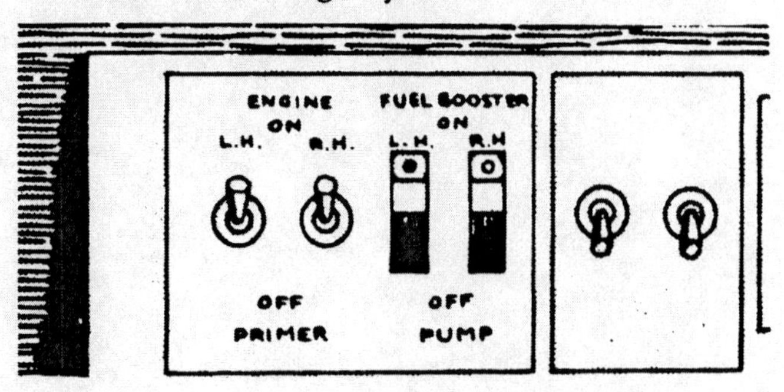

(4) Turn Fuel Booster Pumps ON.

(5) Set Trim Tabs for take-off:
Tail Heavy 5° (for normal loads).

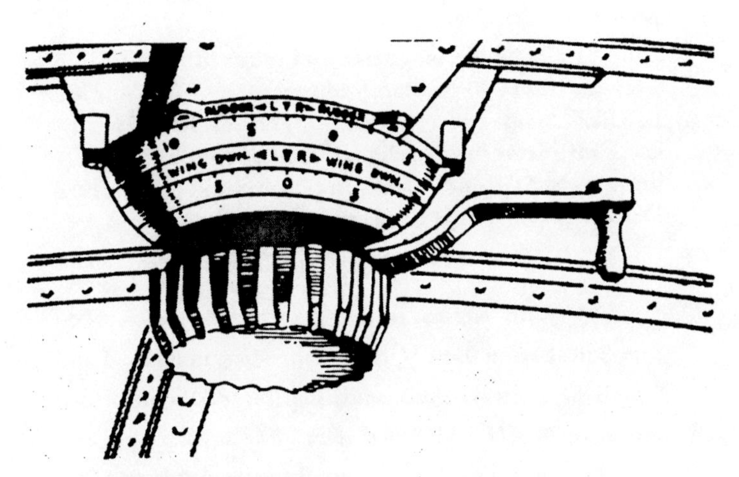

Right Rudder 2°—3°;
Aileron 0°.

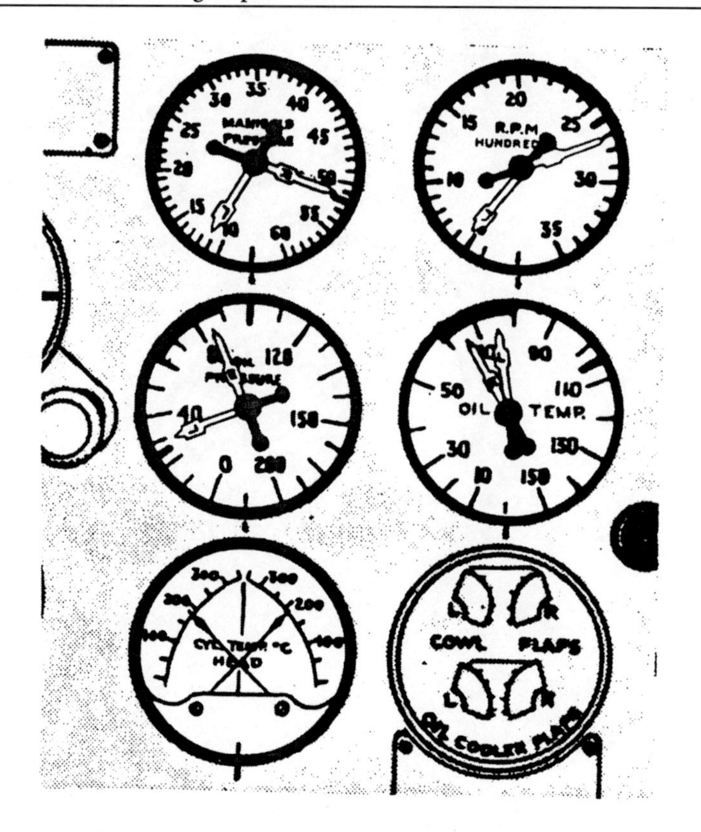

(6) Check operation of Propeller Governor Levers in INC. and DEC. RPM settings at 25 in. manifold pressure.

(7) Check the magnetos and plugs of each engine individually at 30 in. manifold pressure. When engine reaches 2100 rpm, switch to FIXED PITCH and check magnetos for a maximum drop of 75 rpm. Advance throttles to 51½-inch manifold pressure and check to see that full 2700 rpm is obtained.

(8) Remove safety lock from Landing gear lever.

(9) With engines running at not less than 1000 rpm, lower wing flaps ¼ to ½ depending upon load and length of runway. Push wing flap lever DOWN, then return to NEUTRAL when indicator shows proper setting. Release brakes and advance throttles slowly to 51½-inch manifold pressure.

(10) **MAXIMUMS FOR TAKE-OFF.**

Manifold Pressure...51.5 in. Hg.
Propeller Governor..2700 rpm (5 min.)
Fuel Pressure........Max. 17 lb.—Min. 15 lb.
Oil Pressure........Max. 90 lb.—Min. 60 lb.
Oil Temperature....Max. 80°—Min. 60°
Cyl. Head Temp.....Max. 260°—Min. 150°

WHILE THE AIRPLANE IS GAINING MOMENTUM FOR TAKE-OFF MAINTAIN CONTROL BY NORMAL USE OF THE THROTTLES AND RUDDER—AS THE NOSE WHEEL STRAIGHTENS OUT, OPEN THROTTLES SMOOTHLY TO MAXIMUM TAKE-OFF RPM.—HOLD CONTROL COLUMN BACK UNTIL NOSE WHEEL LIFTS CLEAR OF THE GROUND THEN EASE FORWARD TO NEUTRAL.

(1) Pull Landing Gear Lever UP to retract gear. When indicator shows full retraction, return lever to NEUTRAL.

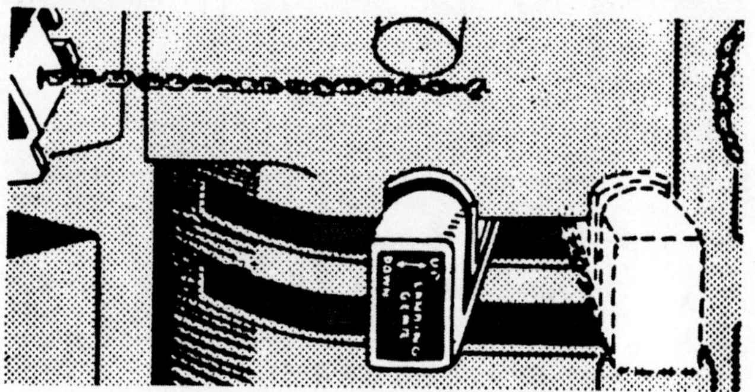

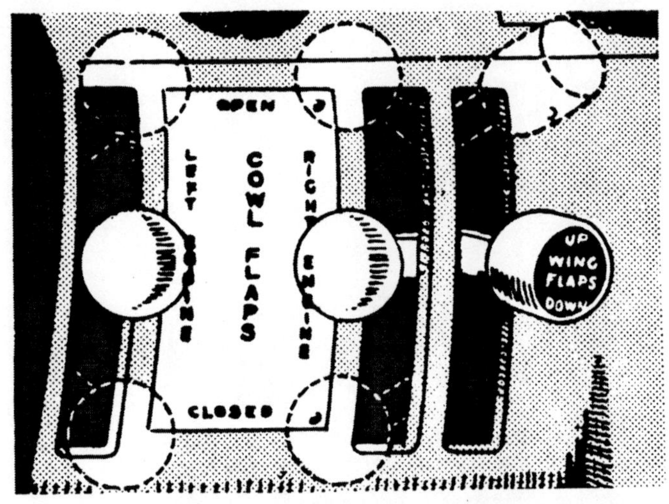

(2) Pull Wing Flap Lever UP to retract wing flaps. When indicator shows full retraction, return lever to NEUTRAL. Do not retract flaps until 500 feet altitude is obtained, with air speed not over 165 mph. Wing flaps should be retracted before reaching 165 mph.

(3) Set Cowl Flaps as dictated by cylinder head temperature, then return levers to NEUTRAL.

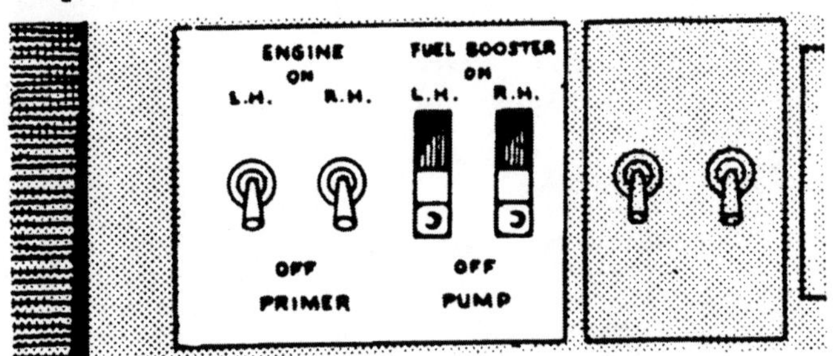

(4) Switch Fuel Booster Pumps OFF.

(5) Consult ALLOWABLE ENGINE FLIGHT CHART in APPENDIX II.

(6) ATTEMPT NO ACROBATICS.

ATTEMPT TO FLY STRAIGHT IN THE FINAL APPROACH BEFORE LOWERING LANDING GEAR OR WING FLAPS. NECESSARY TURNS SHOULD BE EXECUTED WITH A BANK OF 15 DEGREES OR LESS—CHECK CG WITH THE LOAD ADJUSTER AND CALL THE CREW TO STATIONS.

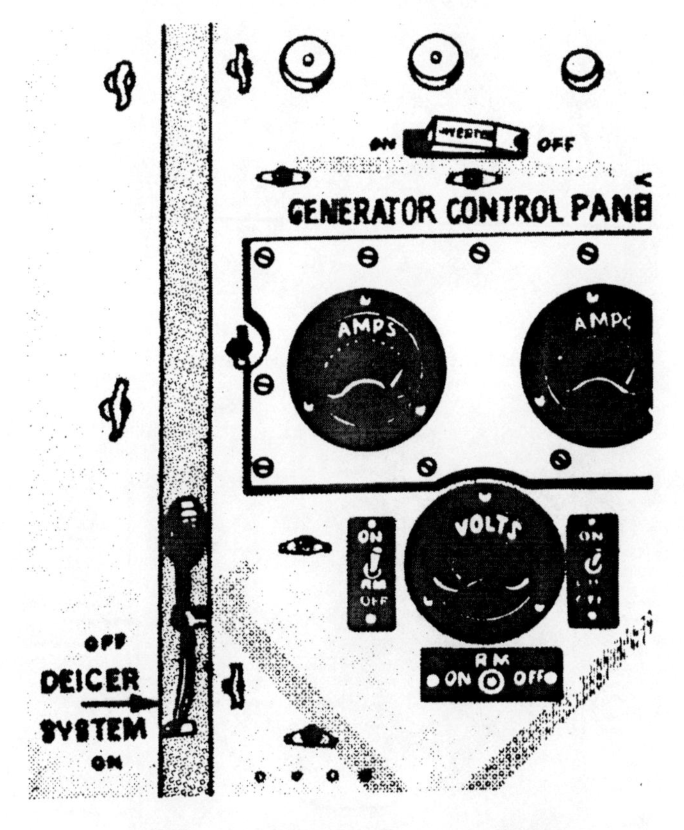

(1) Have Wing De-icers turned OFF.

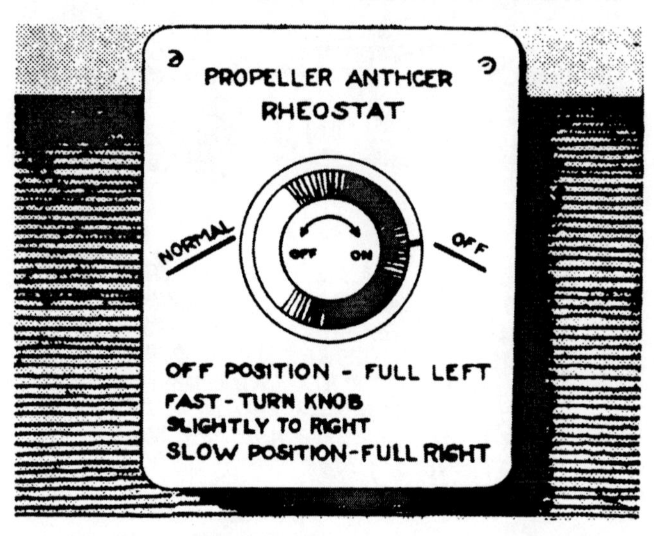

(2) Turn Propeller Anti-icer Rheostat OFF.

(3) Set Altimeter to station pressure.

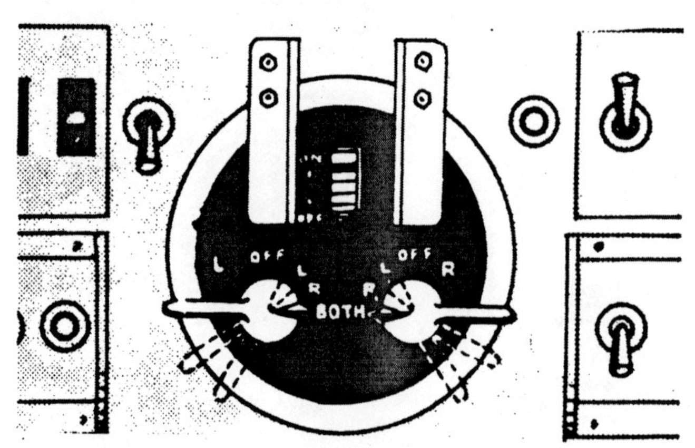

(4) Check right and left Magnetos at low power.

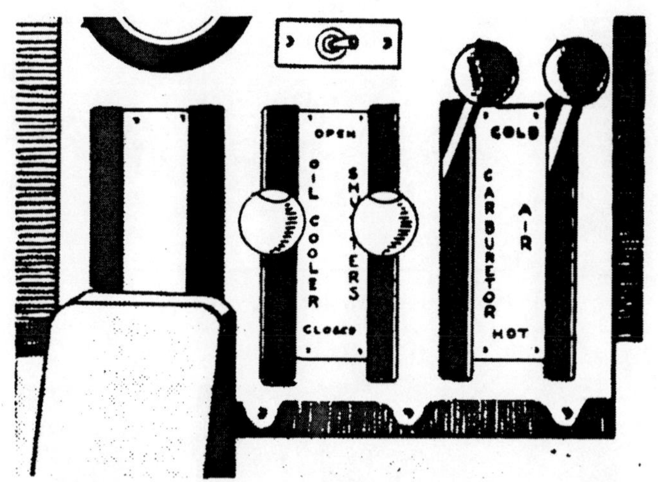

(5) Set Blowers LOW with safety cover in place.

(6) Adjust Oil Cooler Shutters to suit oil temperature.

(7) Set Carburetor Air Control Levers to COLD.

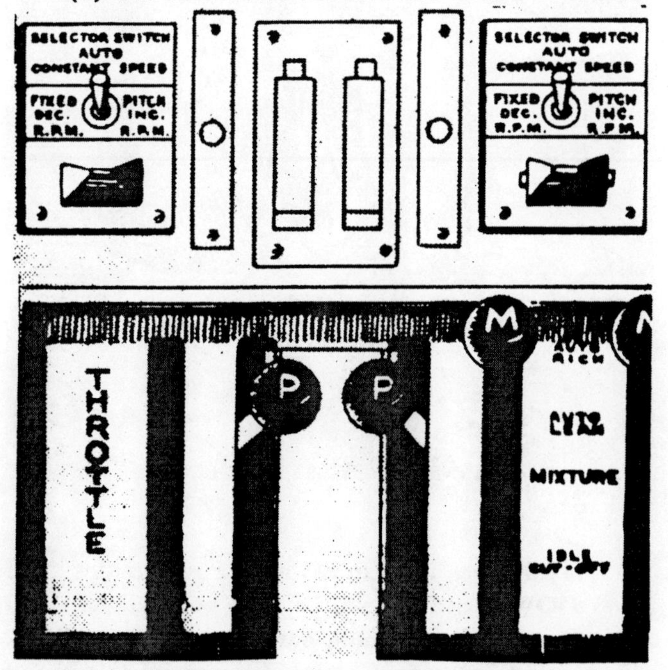

(8) Push Mixture Control Levers forward to AUTO RICH.

(9) Set Propeller Toggle Switches to AUTO CONSTANT SPEED and Governor Levers to 2250 rpm.

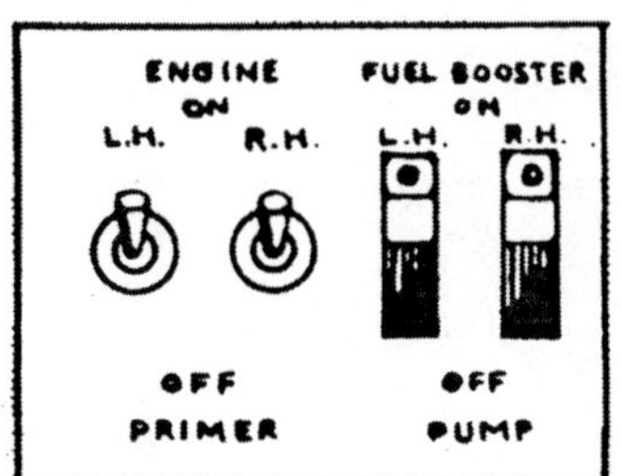

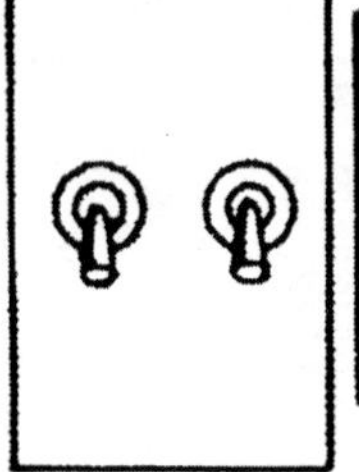

(10) Turn Fuel Booster Pumps ON.

(11) Reduce speed to 185 mph. Push Landing Gear Lever DOWN and leave in DOWN position. As throttles are retarded, a warning horn will sound until lock pins snap into position. Check Indicator for DOWN and LOCKED position. Check wheels visually.

(12) Lower Wing Flaps as desired, then return lever to NEUTRAL. Do not exceed 165 mph with flaps down.

m. LANDING

APPROACH THE FIELD, KEEPING THE NOSE WELL DOWN AND MAINTAINING AN AIR SPEED OF APPROX. 135 MPH.—MAKE A MODIFIED CONVENTIONAL LANDING ON THE MAIN WHEELS, LETTING THE AIRPLANE GRADUALLY SETTLE FORWARD ON THE NOSE WHEEL BEFORE APPLYING THE BRAKES.

n. AFTER LANDING

(1) Leave Cowl Flaps OPEN.

(2) Leave Landing Gear Lever DOWN and install safety lock.

(3) Retract Wing Flaps.

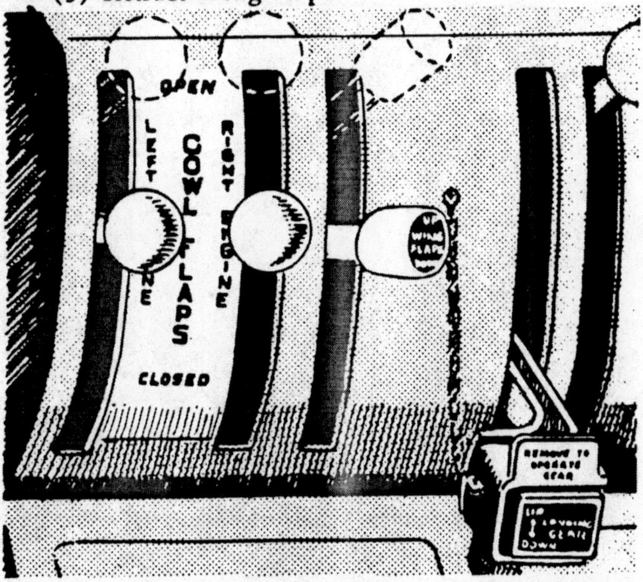

CAUTION: Before retracting flaps be sure landing gear lever safety lock is installed.

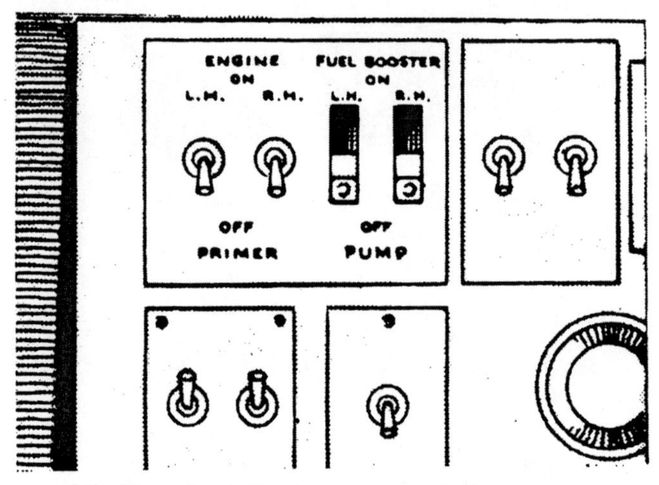

(4) Turn Fuel Booster Pumps OFF.

(5) Push Propeller Governor Levers forward to INC. RPM.

(6) The oil should be diluted if a cold weather start is anticipated. Allow engines to cool until cylinder head temperature falls below 50°C. With engines turning over approx. 800 rpm hold oil dilution switches ON for three minutes or longer depending upon weather conditions.

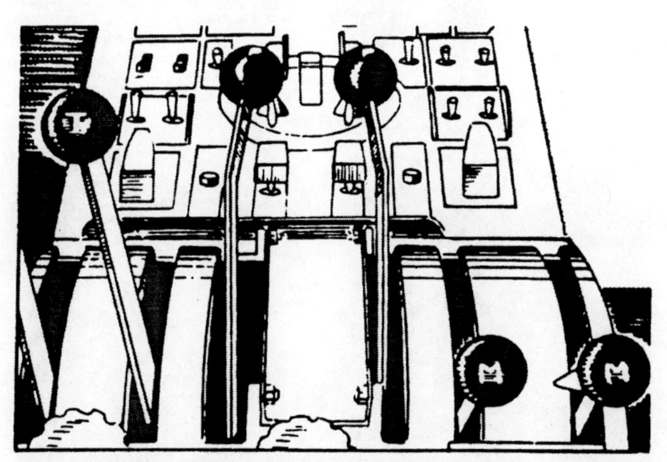

(7) Stop engines by pulling Mixture Levers back to IDLE CUT-OFF. When engines stop turn Ignition Switches OFF.

(8) Turn OFF Master, Battery and all other electrical switches used during flight.

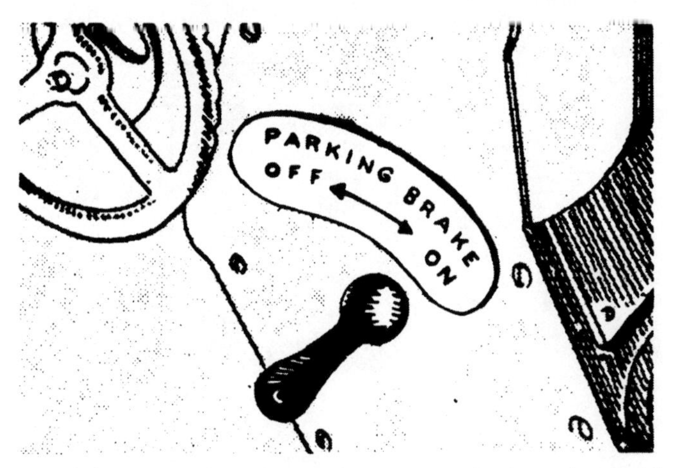

(9) Set brakes for parking. Block the wheels if brakes are hot from excessive use.

(10) Complete Forms 1 and 1A and lock controls.

Chapter 21

Marauder Serial Numbers

SHOWN IN MODEL SEQUENCE

Serial numbers	Model
40-1361 to 1561 (201)	B-26-MA
41-7345 to 7365 (21)	B-26A-MA
41-7368	B-26A-MA
41-7431	B-26A-MA
41-7477 to 7483 (7)	B-26A-MA
41-7366 to 7367 (2)	B-26A-1-MA
41-7369 to 7430 (62)	B-26A-1-MA
41-7432 to 7476 (45)	B-26A-1-MA
41-17544 to 17624 (81)	B-26B-MA
41-17626 to 17851 (226)	B-26B-MA
41-17852 to 17946 (95)	B-26B-2-MA
41-17625	B-26B-3-MA
41-17947 to 17973 (27)	B-26B-3-MA
41-17974 to 18184 (211)	B-26B-4-MA
41-18185 to 18334 (150)	B-26-10-MA*
41-31573 to 31672 (100)	B-26-15-MA
41-31672 to 31772 (100)	B-26-20-MA
41-31773 to 31872 (100)	B-26-25-MA
41-31873 to 31972 (100)	B-26-30-MA
41-31973 to 32072 (100)	B-26-35-MA
42-43260 to 43357 (98)	B-26-40-MA
42-43360 to 43361 (2)	B-26-40-MA

**This and all subsequent models had 71 foot wing spans; earlier models had 65 feet. MA following model indicates plan manufactured at Baltimore plant; MO designates Omaha plant.*

Serial numbers	Model
42-43459	B-26-40-MA
42-95738 to 95828 (91)	B-26-45-MA
42-95829 to 96028 (200)	B-26-50-MA
42-96029 to 96228 (200)	B-26-55-MA
41-34673 to 34680 (8)	B-26C-5-MO
41-34682 to 34686 (5)	B-26C-5-MO
41-34688	B-26C-5-MO
41-34694	B-26C-5-MO
41-34696 to 34701 (6)	B-26C-5-MO
41-34743 to 34776 (34)	B-26C-5-MO
41-34788 to 34847 (60)	B-26C-5-MO
41-34681	B-26C-6-MO
41-34687	B-26C-6-MO
41-34689 to 34693 (5)	B-26C-6-MO
41-34695	B-26C-6-MO
41-34702 to 34742 (41)	B-26C-6-MO
41-34777 to 34787 (11)	B-26C-6-MO
41-34848 to 34907 (60)	B-26C-10-MO
41-34908 to 34997 (90)	B-26C-15-MO
41-34998 to 35172 (175)	B-26C-20-MO
41-35173 to 35370 (198)	B-26C-25-MO
41-35372	B-26C-25-MO
41-35374 to 35515 (142)	B-26C-30-MO
41-35517 to 35538 (22)	B-26C-30-MO
41-35540	B-26C-30-MO
41-35548 to 35551 (4)	B-26C-30-MO
41-35553 to 35560 (8)	B-26C-30-MO
42-107497 to 107830 (334)	B-26C-45-MO
42-107831 to 107855 (25)	B-26C-45-MO
42-96229 to 96328 (100)	B-26F-1-MA
42-96329 to 96428 (100)	B-26F-2-MA
42-96429 to 96528 (100)	B-26F-6-MA
43-34115 to 34214 (100)	B-26G-1-MA
43-34215 to 34414 (200)	B-26G-5-MA
43-34415 to 34464 (50)	B-26G-10-MA
43-34540 to 34614 (75)	B-26G-10-MA
43-34465 to 34539 (75)	B-26G-11-MA
44-67805 to 67944 (140)	B-26G-15-MA
44-67970 to 67989 (20)	B-26G-20-MA

Serial numbers	Model
44-68065 to 68104 (40)	B-26G-20-MA
44-67990 to 68064 (75)	B-26G-21-MA
44-68105 to 68221 (117)	B-26G-25-MA
44-68254	B-26G-25-MA
44-67945 to 67954 (10)	TB-26G-15-MA
44-67955 to 67969 (15)	TB-26G-20-MA
44-68222 to 68253 (32)	TB-26G-25-MA

208 AT-32A's were converted from B-26B-MA aircraft, while 350 AT-23B's were converted from B-26C-MO aircraft; AT-23 serials as follows:

AT-23A-MA
42-43358 to 43359 (2)
42-43458 to 43448 (97)
42-95629 to 95737 (109)

AT-23B-MO
41-35371
41-35373
41-35516
41-35539
41-35541 to 35547 (7)
41-35552
41-35561 to 35872 (312)
42-107471 to 107496 (26)

Manufactured for British and French

FK362/380 (19)	Marauder IA (B-26B)
FX109/160 (52)	Marauder I (B-26A)
FB418/517 (100)	Marauder II (B-26C)
HD402/601 (200)	Marauder III (B-26F)
HD602/751 (150)	Marauder III (B-26G)

Chapter 22

Group and Squadron Identification Symbols

Each bomb group was assigned a distinctive mark which was painted on the tail of each aircraft just above the serial number. Within each bomb group, squadron identifying marks were painted on both sides of the fuselage. These marks were letters and numbers about 30 inches high. The squadron symbol was placed just forward of the national insignia and the aircraft identifying number or letter just aft of the national insignia. Thus each Marauder could be identified quickly by referring to the tail mark for the group and the fuselage mark for the squadron and individual aircraft.

Shown below are the bomb group and squadron markings.

322nd Bomb Group	no tail mark
449th Squadron	PN
450th Squadron	ER
451st Squadron	SS
452nd Squadron	DR
323rd Bomb Group	24-inch-wide white horizontal band
453rd Squadron	VT
454th Squadron	RJ
455th Squadron	YU
456th Squadron	WT
344th Bomb Group	white triangle about 30 inches high
494th Squadron	K9
495th Squadron	Y5
496th Squadron	N3
497th Squadron	7I

386th Bomb Group	24-inch horizontal yellow band
552nd Squadron	RG
553rd Squadron	AN
554th Squadron	RU
555th Squadron	YA
387th Bomb Group	alternate black and yellow diagonal bands across upper part of tail
556th Squadron	FW
557th Squadron	KS
558th Squadron	KX
559th Squadron	TQ
391st Bomb Group	yellow triangle about 30 inches high
572nd Squadron	P2
573rd Squadron	T6
574th Squadron	4L
575th Squadron	08
394th Bomb Group	white diagonal band
584th Squadron	K5
585th Squadron	4T
586th Squadron	H9
587th Squadron	5W
397th Bomb Group	yellow diagonal band
596th Squadron	X2
597th Squadron	9F
598th Squadron	U2
599th Squadron	6B

Index